To,

Betsy Moore,
     A great Scholar
with a heart!

ADVANCE PRAISE

"The Accidental Scholar is a fascinating history of ideas tracing the academic and professional journey of a world marketing and management legend, Dr Jagdish Seth. It is an inspiring book for marketing students and a must-read by any academic wishing to make a difference as a successful scholar and university leader."
—Dr Tan Chin Nam, Senior Corporate Advisor and Former Permanent Secretary, Singapore Public Service

"Professor Jagdish Sheth is a brilliant and talented scholar in consumer behavior, strategy, and marketing theory. The most amazing part of the story is Jag's insightful account of how he became what he is, a huge influence in marketing and business, by accident."
—Dr Tan Chin Tiong, Founding Provost of Singapore Management University and Founding President of Singapore Institute of Technology

"Some autobiographies fit in the category of pure storytelling and others in the genre of wisdom literature. Always between the lines of the Jag Sheth's storytelling about his personal and professional life is his confidence that seeking what is good and needed will, not surprisingly in his view, also make for lasting contribution and genuine success. This is wisdom literature."
—James W. Wagner, President, Emory University, USA

"What a great journey! I know it will inspire others. I have enjoyed our friendship of three decades."
—Azim Premji, Chairman, Wipro Limited

"Jag Sheth is a world-renowned scholar and thought leader. All of us have benefited from his wisdom and advice. *The Accidental Scholar* is a very inspiring journey of the making of a scholar. It is full of wisdom."
—Ram Charan, Business Advisor, Author, and Speaker

"Jag Sheth is one of the great minds in marketing. His life journey serves as an inspiration for others to achieve their full

potential. I am honored to call him a friend and know you will enjoy the great insights he provides in business and in life in this wonderful book."
—**Ralph de la Vega, President and CEO, AT&T Mobility**

"Dr Jagdish Sheth is a well-known management scholar and educator. Besides the USA, he has worked across several countries and is widely respected for his extremely sharp analytical mind. He has been particularly active in India and this book will be received with wide acclaim by practitioners across the country."
—**Ashok Ganguly, Member, Rajya Sabha,
Government of India**

"Many readers will find inspiration in this well-told tale of immigration, education, and academic entrepreneurship by the marketing legend Jag Sheth."
—**Alvin E. Roth, Nobel Laureate in Economics, 2012**

"This book takes the reader on a fascinating journey that epitomizes the many dimensions of Dr Sheth. Written with great authenticity, it is the story of a scholar and his contribution to the evolution of consumer behavior, strategic marketing, competitive strategy, and relationship marketing as academic disciplines, together with the sub-text and context that shaped this evolution. What is particularly inspiring is the passion and hard work that have distinguished Dr Sheth as an academic, consultant, coach, and philanthropist. His energy and agility in spotting emerging patterns provides a refreshing perspective right through, as do interspersed nuggets like "markets don't plateau, managers do."
—**Vinita Bali, Business Leader—Cadbury Schweppes,
The Coca-Cola Company, and Britannia India Ltd**

"Jagdish Sheth has truly lived the dream, moving from India to become one of the leading marketing scholars in the world and a successful academic administrator to boot. Sheth's biography offers important lessons for anyone in any field trying to chart their career course."
—**Jeffrey Pfeffer, Thomas D. Dee II Professor of
Organizational Behavior, Graduate School
of Business, Stanford University**

THE ACCIDENTAL
SCHOLAR

THE ACCIDENTAL SCHOLAR

Jagdish N. Sheth
with
John Yow

www.sagepublications.com
Los Angeles • London • New Delhi • Singapore • Washington DC

First published in 2014 by

SAGE Response
B1/I-1 Mohan Cooperative Industrial Area
Mathura Road, New Delhi 110 044, India

SAGE Publications Inc
2455 Teller Road
Thousand Oaks, California 91320, USA

SAGE Publications Ltd
1 Oliver's Yard, 55 City Road
London EC1Y 1SP, United Kingdom

SAGE Publications Asia-Pacific Pte Ltd
3 Church Street
#10-04 Samsung Hub
Singapore 049483

Published by Vivek Mehra for SAGE Publications India Pvt. Ltd, typeset in 11/13pt ITC Galliard BT by Diligent Typesetter, Delhi and printed at Saurabh Printers Pvt Ltd, New Delhi.

Library of Congress Cataloging-in-Publication Data

Sheth, Jagdish N.
  The accidental scholar / Jagdish N. Sheth; with John Yow.
    pages cm
  Includes bibliographical references and index.
    1. Sheth, Jagdish N. 2. Business teachers—United States—Biography. 3. Business teachers—India—Biography. 4. Philanthropists—United States—Biography. 5. Philanthropists—India—Biography. 6. Business education—United States. 7. Business education—India. 8. Emory University—Faculty—Biography. I. Yow, John. II. Title.
HF1131.S495   650.092—dc23   [B]   2014   2014022477

ISBN: 978-93-515-0039-1 (HB)

The SAGE Team: Sachin Sharma, Alekha Chandra Jena, Anju Saxena, and Dally Verghese

This book is dedicated to two of the greatest enablers of my life; my wife, Madhu Sheth and my mentor, Professor John A. Howard.

Thank you for choosing a SAGE product! If you have any comment, observation or feedback, I would like to personally hear from you. Please write to me at contactceo@sagepub.in

—Vivek Mehra, Managing Director and CEO,
SAGE Publications India Pvt Ltd, New Delhi

Bulk Sales

SAGE India offers special discounts for purchase of books in bulk. We also make available special imprints and excerpts from our books on demand.

For orders and enquiries, write to us at

Marketing Department
SAGE Publications India Pvt Ltd
B1/I-1, Mohan Cooperative Industrial Area
Mathura Road, Post Bag 7
New Delhi 110044, India
E-mail us at marketing@sagepub.in

Get to know more about SAGE, be invited to SAGE events, get on our mailing list. Write today to marketing@sagepub.in

This book is also available as an e-book.

CONTENTS

FOREWORD

I feel privileged that Jagdish Sheth invited me to write the fore-word to his autobiography, *The Accidental Scholar*. Jagdish has so many friends and admirers who could have graced these pages describing this outstanding scholar, consultant, administrator, entrepreneur, and philanthropist. Without question, Jagdish Sheth is one of the most original minds in the academic world of marketing and business. His writings, speeches, and research reveal great intellectual breadth and depth along with a great caring about others and about the state of the world.

When I think of the accidental forces that shape our lives, I think of how a youngster named Jagdish Sheth, born in Burma in 1938, moves to different parts of India, is supposed to work in his family's business making jewelry boxes, and somehow ends up with a Ph.D. in Behavioral Economics and teaches at some of the major American universities, writes some of the most influential books and articles in his field, and consults major companies around the world. His is an inspiring story that I hope that young men and women in different countries who have been born with a passion for learning can draw hope that they too can realize their dreams.

Jagdish could have remained in India, worked in his family business, married a wonderful woman, raised children, and have had a happy life. But our loss would have been high. There are so many people in our world who Jagdish has directly or indirectly influenced and mentored that this would have been a great loss.

I met Jag (as we all call him) over 30 years ago at an American Marketing Association conference. I had read the Howard–Sheth *Theory of Buyer Behavior* and I felt that this theory, one of several theories of buyer behavior, was the right one to feature in my next edition of *Marketing Management*. Jag subsequently confided to me that my decision to promote the Howard–Sheth *Theory of Buyer Behavior* had a great influence in establishing his reputation around the world where my *Marketing Management* books were read. I had great respect for Sheth's mentor, Professor John Howard, who played such an important role in Jag's development. John Howard had written his own *Marketing Management* book which set a high standard that I wanted to emulate.

In meeting Jag and wanting to know him better, I invited him to have dinner at our home. My wife, Nancy, prepared a great dinner of steak and mashed potatoes only to hear Jag quietly tell us that he was a vegetarian. We dashed to the refrigerator and finally found something acceptable that he ate while we devoured our steak and quietly admitted our cultural myopia.

Every time that I subsequently met Jag at one of many academic meetings, a feeling of pleasure came over me. I made sure that I had a handy pen and paper ready. When Jag spoke, I made more notes than for almost any other speaker. Jag had a gift for making sense out of the messy events in our social, economic, and political world and what they would mean for all of us and what we could do about it.

In between meeting Jagdish at various events, I would hear about his latest movements through the university world. I saw him as a peripatetic scholar. When he left the University of Pittsburg, he went to Columbia University and to MIT, then he relocated to the University of Illinois, then the University of Southern California, and finally Emory University in Atlanta. Each university wanted to keep him but other factors that he describes vividly in his *The Accidental Scholar* explain the reason for each move. One thing is clear: his travels exposed him to many of the finest minds in marketing and business and helped him formulate many of his own original ideas.

Jagdish did not want to be a pure theorist. He wanted to operate in the real world of companies and movers and shakers. He relished new company and university challenges and engagements and was continually learning new things.

Consider that he started in accounting, planned to learn manufacturing, then he moved into consumer behavior, then social psychology, then into marketing and strategic marketing, then into multivariate statistics, then international marketing, and then into business policy. He is an inveterate learner and every time I heard him speak, I would hear something new about his latest knowledge foray.

Jagdish has written numerous books and articles, all of which are listed at the end of his *The Accidental Scholar*. My personal favorites (in no order) are:

- *Firms of Endearment: How World Class Companies Profit from Passion and Purpose*
- *Chindia Rising: How China and India Will Benefit Your Business*
- *Tectonic Shift: The Geoeconomic Realignment of Globalizing Markets*
- *The Self-Destructive Habits of Good Companies and How to Break Them*
- *The Rule of Three: Surviving and Thriving in Competitive Markets*
- *The 4 A's of Marketing: Creating Value for Customers, Companies and Society*
- *Marketing Theory: Evolution and Evaluation*
- *The Theory of Buyer Behavior*

Marketing managers have also learned much from his *Clients for Life, Winning Back Your Market, Bringing Innovation to Market,* and *The Customer Is Key*.

As a contemporary of Jag's, I relished reading about his experiences with the same people I know in the business and marketing field. Reading their names brought back to me a whole generation that helped create modern business and marketing theory. They include John Howard, Warren Bennis, George Day, William Massy, David Montgomery, Al Kuehn, Frank Bass, Herbert Simon, Raymond Bauer, Martin Fishbein, David Aaker, Ven Venkatesen, Paul Lazarfeld, John D. C. Little, Leonard Lodish, Glen Urban, Julian Simon, Nelson Foote, Donald Lehmann, Warren Keegan, Fred Webster, Donald Morrison, Johan Arndt, Charles Raymond, Henry Claycamp,

Harry Triandis, James Engel, Roger Blackwell, David Kollat, Joel Cohen, David Gardner, William Wells, Robert Ferber, Paul Green, Russel Ackoff, Jeffrey Pfeffer, Johnny Johansson, Bobbie Calder, Kenneth Uhl, Charles King, Peter Wright, Russell Belk, C. W. Park, Tan Chin Tiong, Raj Sisodia, Alan Shocker, Michael Belch, Bruce Newman, Barbara Gross, Lou Stern, Sidney Levy, Stuart Henderson Britt, Gerald Zaltman, Flemming Hansen, Ram Charan, Robert Spekman, Gary Frazier, Alvin Roth, Oliver Williamson, Tom Kinnear, Tom Robertson, Ron Frank, Ajay Kohli, and many other distinguished academics, too numerous to mention.

I also relished reading about Jagdish's challenging work in building or rebuilding the marketing department in the several universities in which he taught. I enjoyed his description of recruiting some of the best top academics to join his department, including how he went to Stanford to hire their best doctoral students. Jag is not just a faculty member. He is a faculty builder, and the best term I can use is that he is an academic entrepreneur. He established new courses (Relationship Marketing) for the first time, new centers (CTM: Center for Telecommunications Management, CRM: Center for Relationship Marketing, etc). All said, he is the dream person sought by any university: a scholar, administrator, change agent, and entrepreneur.

I learned a lot in reading about Jag's experiences on company boards on which he served on compensation and auditing committees and mentoring top management. He learned a lot about how good companies often fail (see his *The Self-Destructive Habits of Good Companies and How to Break Them*).

What is so impressive is Jagdish's wish to give back to his schools, his discipline, his adopted country (the U.S.), and his country of origin (India). It comes from his religion, Jainism, with its triple philosophy of nonviolence, tolerance for the diversity of viewpoints, and rejecting the accumulation of material possessions. He wrote, "The more you accumulate, the more you must give back." Through their Sheth Foundation, Jagdish and Madhu have funded many activities benefitting doctoral students (Doctoral Consortium), the American Marketing

Association (AMA), the Association for Consumer Research (ACR), Academy of Marketing Science (AMS), the Journal of the Academy of Marketing Science and the Journal of Marketing for Best Paper Awards, not to mention their support of various medical and environmental causes. His idea of building a Legends Series of the best marketing writings of the past will be appreciated by many future scholars.

Jagdish Sheth's autobiography is the third recent autobiography to be written by an eminent marketing scholar. David Aaker (*From Fargo to the World of Brands: My Biography So Far*) is highly responsible for developing our interest and knowledge of the key role that branding plays in marketing. He wrote his biography so that his family can remember him and of course, his many friends and fans around the world. My Northwestern Kellogg School colleague, Sidney Levy, who gave us great insights into consumer psychology, published his biography (*One Man in His Time*) about his travels, family, and marketing ideas. And now Jagdish Sheth has rewarded us with a picture of his dazzling life, ideas, and accomplishments.

Jagdish's autobiography tells a fascinating life story in a few hundred pages of what it is to be, in one person, a scholar, change agent, advisor, and entrepreneur, in other words, a Renaissance Man. His *The Accidental Scholar* delivers rich ideas and experiences whose reading would benefit academics and marketing professors, administrators and college department heads, companies wishing to use the talents of academics in their training sessions and on their boards, and consultants and entrepreneurs building their own brands. Jag describes his experiences in a number of industries which he knows well, including telecom, semiconductors, pharmaceuticals, education, manufacturing, and healthcare. As a result of his Board experience, Jagdish has become a "deep generalist" considering all the functions of a business. Ironically, he is now back to where he would have been if he had joined his family's business and took a view of the whole company.

One of the interesting features of his book is that each chapter ends with a Life Lesson that Jagdish learned. Putting these Life

Lessons together would provide a wonderful road map for any new promising scholar to follow.

I found the *The Accidental Scholar* to evoke in the reader wonderful memories of a remarkable generation and the role played by a remarkable scholar and personal friend.

Philip Kotler
Kellogg School of Management
Northwestern University

PREFACE

It was David Aaker's idea that I should write the story of my life. He had just published his own autobiography and strongly felt that others in the academic community will enjoy and benefit from my story.

It took me more than five years since Dave planted the idea. I started to write and found myself putting it aside several times over the years. I am now really glad that it will be published.

The title *The Accidental Scholar* truly summarizes my journey into the academic life. It was the farthest place from my mind. It just happened. And it is the best thing that ever happened.

It has been an incredible journey. I was born in Burma (Myanmar) in 1938 and before World War II. In late 1940, Japan took over Burma and we had to return back to India in a hurry. My father had gone to Burma as a rice trader.

But for a series of accidental events, I would have been a shop-keeper or a trader with less than a high school education in my hometown, earning about $200 per month. Fortunately, my elder sisters, none of whom had high school diplomas, encouraged me to study and focus on education.

Another dislocation was within India from my home state of Gujarat to another state, Tamil Nadu, in the South. Culturally, they are as far apart as Sweden and Sicily in Europe.

I had to learn English from the time I was in middle school and went through college education in English. This proved to be fateful and allowed me to come to the United States with no language barriers.

Culturally, however, America was very different. I encountered interesting experiences, encounters and funny incidents. In fact, I have often thought of writing a screenplay titled "Americanization of Jag," similar to the movie "Coming to America."

This book, however, is not about cultural assimilation and living happily thereafter. It is a story about my academic life and interesting encounters and opportunities provided to me to become an educator. I truly believe that no nation on earth provides the opportunities to achieve your potential as does America. It is for this reason, people from all over the world still prefer to come to the United States and hope to succeed in achieving their dreams as artists, authors, entrepreneurs, corporate leaders, or educators. They are eternally grateful once they survive and thrive, and most of them become great role models to their countrymen and indirectly inspire them to achieve their potential in their respective countries or come to the United States to do the same.

I am grateful for this opportunity and hope to motivate others to also become educators. There is no profession more noble than being an educator and shape other human lives in search of their own potential and personal excellence.

ACKNOWLEDGMENTS

First and foremost, I want to thank David Aaker who strongly encouraged me to write this autobiography.

A great number of friends and colleagues read the earlier drafts of this autobiography and provided their constructive comments. These include David Aaker, Doug Bowman, George Day, Larry Feick, Barbara Gross, Balaji Krishnan, Richard Lutz, Robert Peterson, Arun Sharma, Tassu Shervani, and Ven Venkatesen.

I sincerely thank them for their feedback. I also want to thank Nicole Smith, Lydia Brown, and Beth Robinson for editing the earlier drafts. My special thanks go to Isha Edwards who devoted significant time to rewrite and add to the manuscript.

Of course, the book would not have been written without my writer, John Yow. He is an amazing storyteller.

I also want to thank Vivek Mehra, CEO of SAGE India and his team including R. Chandra Sekhar and Sachin Sharma, for enthusiastically publishing the book.

1

THE JOURNEY BEGINS

It was during a marketing class in my first semester of the University of Pittsburgh's MBA program that I did something I had never done before. My professor was sharing some interesting consumer research data from DuPont (which, at the time, was one of the very few companies that backed up its R&D efforts with outstanding consumer research). This DuPont research yielded the remarkable statistic that 42 percent of American housewives routinely headed out to the store without a shopping list, the implication being that they were buying impulsively. I was sitting in the front row, attentive and respectful when suddenly, I raised my hand. Much like my career, raising my hand was well, accidental.

A few months earlier, the idea of enrolling in a graduate program and relocating to the United States to obtain an MBA seemed farfetched—so did being the only foreign student in the class. Out of respect, the last thing I would do was interrupt a lecture or to speak without having first been called upon. However, before my mind could reconcile my action with cultural courtesies, I posed a question. "Professor," I asked when he nodded in my direction, "does this mean that all illiterate people are impulse buyers?" After what seemed like an eternity, my professor responded, "That's a good question. Let me think about it."

My Family Business

From my family's perspective, the only reason for me to be in school was to gather practical information that could be used in the family business—the production of jewelry boxes. At the time, it was strictly a handicraft industry, a cottage industry in the literal sense. We purchased all the raw materials—velvet, satin, clips, hinges (everything but the wood)—and supplied them to our workers, most of whom worked at home among their own families. This was "contract manufacturing" in the purest form. The husband and head of household would buy the materials from us, and their family members would put the boxes together. We inspected them for quality and, assuming they were up to standard, paid the contract workers, and then turned around and sold the boxes to wholesalers or directly to jewelers. We also had our own staff of eight workers to make three kinds of boxes. One was made to hold silver trophies of various sizes awarded to politicians and government leaders; another was more elegant, with velvet lining designed to hold expensive diamond jewelry; and a third was used for medals or similar awards to business and industry leaders.

During high school, I spent every summer helping out in the family business. My eldest brother ran the business and could not wait for me to graduate from high school so that I could work full-time for him.

When I graduated from high school in 1955, my brother said matter-of-factly, "That's enough education. Come work for me now!" I was a very good student and I wanted to continue my education. I have five siblings: two brothers followed by three sisters. I am the youngest of six so there was little chance that I could convince the head of the family business to change his mind about my working for him. Thankfully, my second eldest brother, who established a career outside of the family business and was a scholar, philosopher, and writer, intervened on my behalf. His logic was that since I graduated as the top student, I *must* go on to college.

A Literal Change in Course

In 1946, we moved to Chennai, a major port city in South India. The move to Chennai made an incredible difference in my life. Had my family stayed in Kutch (Gujarat), there is no doubt that I would have had less than a high school education, become engaged in some form of trade, and would certainly have plateaued. Chennai was a very large and progressive city—one where education was strongly emphasized and, best of all, classes were taught in English. It was in Chennai that my brother worked hard to make a go of his new business. It was also in Chennai that the decision was made to allow me to enroll in a two-year "intermediate" program (akin to a junior college in the United States). While being enrolled in the program, I studied history, statistics, and accounting. Accounting was a good discipline—even a possible vocation with high wage-earning potential. Although history was my passion, it did not offer livelihood.

At the end of the two-year program, I completed a comprehensive, statewide examination. Typically, 30 to 35 percent of the students fail this exam. Those who fail are given a second chance, but not a third. Despite having the highest marks (grades) in the entire state, my brother *still* expected me to work in the business. My performance in the exam qualified me to enroll in a special, accelerated college degree program—a sort of honors program. Only 42 honors students in the entire state were invited to be in the program. The highly concentrated curriculum focused on income tax, insurance, and cooperatives. Since higher education in India is practically free, it was hard to pass up the opportunity. My brother gave in reluctantly.

I attended Jain College, and sharpened my accounting skills. In fact, I was one of 14 of the 42 students who opted to major in income tax. My interest in accounting grew such that I began dreaming of becoming a CPA, known as a Chartered Accountant (CA) in India. The CA exam was very tough. The pass rate was only 5 percent.

In order to become a CA, I would have to work in a chartered accounting firm for two to three years without pay (as an
apprentice or intern). To work for someone else is tantamount
to confessing that you cannot make it as an entrepreneur. My
family would not have supported being a CA.

Garnering Support for College

Frustrated with my interest in pursuing an advanced degree
instead of working for the family business, my brother lamented
with a customer about the dilemma. The well-traveled and
sophisticated customer told my brother that American schools
offered a new business degree program called the MBA. Up
until the late 1950s, Indians went to England for advanced
study—usually in engineering, law, liberal arts, the sciences, or
medicine. The customer, however, advised my brother to let
me go to America.

Since I knew absolutely nothing about America or its universities, I sought the help of a career counselor at Madras
University and he agreed to submit applications to Drake, New
York University (NYU), Cincinnati, and Pittsburgh. Drake did
not have an MBA program at that time. NYU and Cincinnati
had MBA programs, but did not offer fellowships. Cincinnati
and Pittsburgh accepted me. However, I chose Pittsburgh
because I could complete the program in 11 months, which
would reduce my cost of living by a year. Pittsburgh also provided a full fellowship, which paid all of my tuition.

I told my brother that the biggest challenge we faced in
the business was not sales and marketing, but production.
We needed to automate. I wanted to go to America to learn
advanced manufacturing methods. In the name of advancing
the business, my brother approved of my plans.

It cost about $1,000 (roughly 5,000 rupees at the time) to
get to America. I had saved that much from working part-time
for my brother, but I needed 10,000 additional rupees to cover
my living expenses. Fortunately, two families stepped up to
help me. One local family was taken with the idea of a young

man from their community going to study in America and was willing to loan money as an investment in my education. The other was a family of distant relatives in Mumbai who graciously agreed to loan me 5,000 rupees.

Manufacturing or Bust

The Game Plan

Upon completing my MBA, I would get a job for the subsequent 18 months foreign students were allowed to spend in the United States, receiving practical training before returning to India. The brother-in-law of my host family ran a business making plastic cabinets for radios and TVs. He was thrilled by the prospect of shifting his capacity to India and avoiding the looming labor issues in the United States. We agreed that he would give me his machines, I would manufacture his goods, and he would be a guaranteed customer.

A class in behavioral sciences instantly changed all of those plans. Being exposed to people I had never heard of like Freud, Maslow, and David McClelland, and learning about Maslow's theory of motivation fascinated me. I wanted to learn more. Learning more translated to obtaining a doctorate. I applied to the doctoral program at Pittsburgh and was accepted. The additional benefit to being a doctoral student was the small living stipend it provided. Who could turn down such an offer?

Finding My Life Partner

I first saw Madhuri Shah when she was a preteen. Our sisters were good friends and she accompanied her elder sister to my house once. Years later, and before leaving for America, I ran into Madhu who, by then was a stunning, bright, and mesmerizing mature young woman. She was a teacher and was attending a meeting for the young peoples' literary academy I founded as a way to preserve our native language and literature. In India, private dating was not allowed at that time. Couples must meet in a group setting. It was unusual that boys and girls were allowed to meet and mingle.

Madhu was so easy to talk to, and also very beautiful. I told her about my plan to go to America for school and work. We talked about my returning to India afterwards, getting married, and starting a family. Madhu agreed to wait for me. I promised that I would return to India, work in the family business, and she and I would live happily ever after. Instead, after finishing my MBA, in December of 1961, I dropped the bombshell that I wanted to stay for a doctoral degree. Neither of us wanted to wait until I completed my doctorate to marry so I asked Madhu to come to America and marry me. I proposed to Madhu in one of my many lengthy love letters. Going to a foreign land was frightening, but thankfully, Madhu opted to follow her heart, give up her teaching career, be courageous, and come to America. I could not have been more thrilled.

As life would have it, there was just one small problem with my plan. My doctoral stipend was $287 a month, which was just enough for the Immigration Bureau to grant me an F-1 student visa, but not enough for me to have a dependent wife. I needed an income of at least $400 a month. Where was I going to get the extra money?

I approached Professor Bernard Bass about obtaining a research assistantship. Bass was a brilliant scholar in leadership and management and had developed an instrument to measure styles of management (self, interaction, or task oriented). I knew I would enjoy working for him. Unfortunately, Bass had no money to hire me. Through the grapevine, I learned that one of my professors had grant money available. The professor was John Howard, a giant in the field of marketing. He was the same John Howard to whom, six months prior, I had addressed that impertinent question about impulse buyers. Howard was the only professor who could grant me an assistantship. I was scared to death to approach Howard and put off asking for as long as I could.

When I finally summoned enough nerve to go to Howard's office and ask for a research assistantship, I was flabbergasted by his response. He said he remembered me well and told me he really wanted to work with me because I "had a cultural perspective which he lacked." He was delighted to offer me a research assistantship—enough money to bring my bride-to-be to America and get married.

John Howard became my longtime mentor and the man responsible for singlehandedly steering me into the discipline of marketing, in which I have spent my entire career.

Marketing was not my major for my doctorate because it did not exist at the time. Instead, my major was Individual and Group Behavior, with an emphasis in Motivation and a minor in Social Psychology. Marketing was my applied field. I was passionate about behavioral sciences.

LIFE LESSON

I love to theorize and, therefore, have often asked myself about these seemingly accidental sequences of events. "Why did these wonderful things happen to me?" After a while, I had to acknowledge that there is a force out there blessing all of us. Once you recognize that and believe in it, this will reinforce what you do and propel you to do even greater things in life.

In order to find and fulfill your passion, I believe it is important to be resilient and flexible—be willing to go where the winds of fortune take you versus where cultural norms and even your fears retain you. *The bend in the road is not the end of the road, unless you refuse to take the turn.*

2

GRADUATE SCHOOL AND MARRIAGE

As the only foreign student, in my MBA class of 80 students, my adjustment to American culture was not easy.

One day, Dean of Students, Paul Kohlberger pulled me aside and told me that the student dress code for the MBAs consisted of a white shirt with a dark tie and a suit jacket. As opposed to the bright, colorful shirts I wore to accommodate India's tropical weather and dust. Upon hearing of my dress code dilemma, my friend, David Miller, drove me to "upscale" department store, Kaufmann's. He parked his car at a meter. After looking around a bit, I selected a white Arrow brand shirt, which rang up $5.00 at the register. "How about $2.50?" I asked the clerk, who was taken aback by my attempt to negotiate the retail price. "The meter is ticking. My friend here is waiting. Take it or leave it—$3.00," I said. Before the clerk could respond, David interjected, "Jagdish, that's not how we buy things over here." Different from India, I was surprised that in the United States, prices are fixed and sales people have no discretionary power to adjust the asking or retail price.

A benefit of being the only foreign student on campus was having two host families: the Dexters and the Wilsons. Since I could not return to India for holidays and other special occasions, my host families opened their homes to me and ensured my safety, socialization, and my wellbeing. Also, they provided practical tips about shopping, including which brands to purchase.

Discovering My Passion

My experiences in the MBA program increased my thirst for knowledge and ignited my intellectual curiosity. It seemed like each course I took opened a door along a path I knew I needed to keep following. Two of those experiences led to lauded research papers.

In one of my research papers, I generalized Maslow's hierarchy of needs from individuals to institutions and postulated that just as human beings evolve from lower needs to higher, so do institutions. I pointed out that, after all, institutions are collections of individuals and they too, go through evolutionary processes. To prove my point, I focused on three institutions: religion, government, and business. Several conclusions of this paper were: Americans had moved beyond the need for love and affection toward self-esteem and independence. Therefore, a monolithic deity will no longer appeal to them. They will search for the meaning of life within themselves. Based on a nation's evolution toward higher levels of motivation, the needs of its workers will ascend up the hierarchy. The way to motivate workers will no longer be job security or empathy toward workers. It will need more empowerment and the manager must change from the boss to a coach and a mentor. Finally, when a nation is at a safe and secure level, communism has inherent, grassroots appeal. However, as the nation evolves toward self-esteem and independence, communism as a political ideology will collapse.

Despite being purely speculation, logical inference, and maybe a little instinct on my part, the paper drew many accolades. My behavioral sciences professor described my paper as "brilliant." He circulated my paper to colleagues in the department of international affairs. They liked it so much that they encouraged me to change my major from business to political science.

In my finance class, I decided to do a value chain analysis, look-ing at the different stages of the industry, from raw material and paper pulp to milling, paper making, and retailing. As I conducted research, I immediately realized that there were breaks in the value chain. There was a big supply of the raw material, but too little pulp-making capacity. Once a plant was installed and capacity was increased, there was suddenly more production than demand. This resulted in a breakup of vertical integration and sourcing from open and competitive markets. It also resulted in selling excess capacity to others including competitors. My conclusion was that the paper and pulp industry would always be inherently inefficient. However, it is difficult to breakup vertical integration. I advised that it would be best to forecast the inefficiencies and manage in such a way as to minimize them through, for example, careful inventory or just-in-time operations. This seemed to be true across all industries where the value chain has differential fixed versus variable costs at different stages of value-added activities. This paper was more empirical and utilized econometrics.

Whether in mathematical science or behavioral science, I knew I had found something I loved to do—and wanted to keep doing: anticipate future consequences based on deductive logic and empirical inferences.

John Howard Takes Me under His Wing

When John Howard made me his research assistant, it felt like familiar territory. Howard was a well-known rising scholar. He had been asked by the Ford Foundation to help define market-ing as a discipline, and had spent two years as a researcher at Stanford University examining behavioral, economic, and quan-titative aspects of marketing. He also taught at the University of Chicago and at the University of Illinois. Howard was recruited by the University of Pittsburgh to join an increasing number of stellar marketing faculty—one that included Bob Entenberg in retailing, Albert Frye in advertising, and Robert Perloff, Ian Mitroff, and Bernard Bass in organization behavior. By this time, Howard was developing a theory of consumer behavior to probe the great mystery of why consumers become brand loyal.

I soon found myself working on three different projects with Howard. The first was helping him revise his earlier textbook, *Marketing Management*. Howard was a Harvard-trained economist, like Joel Dean and William Baumol, who had developed what came to be known as "managerial economics." Howard's textbook had a similar aim—to get beyond marketing principles and focus on "managerial marketing"—and it became a best-seller in the MBA programs. The first edition was published in 1958 so it was time for a revision. My primary task was helping Howard with the chapter on consumer behavior.

The second project was producing the instructor's guide for Howard's revised textbook. The guide outlines key principles, indicates the punch lines, and so forth. To others, it may be very a tedious assignment, but I thoroughly enjoyed it as I was learning new skills. Of great interest to me was writing cases like Spic and Span (a Procter & Gamble product) for the guide.

The third project moved me from understanding individual consumer behavior to the purchasing behavior of businesses. Inevitably, everyone at Pittsburgh, including Howard and his students, was influenced by Carnegie Mellon's Herbert Simon, the Nobel Prize winner whose wide-ranging intellect probed the fields of economics, organizational theory, decision-making, cognitive psychology, and sociology. Howard was a great admirer of Simon's work and, under Simon's direction, we began looking at buying behavior in a business-to-business situation—specifically, the steel mills. My assignment was to study the purchasing of industrial fasteners (nuts and bolts) and electrical motors, so I had to interview buyers in both categories and map out how they made their decisions.

My questions focused on whether or not "reciprocity" was a factor in the buyers' decisions. The answer from all buyers was an unequivocal, "Yes!" That is, "You buy my steel and I buy your products." The buyers knew that reciprocity is not entirely ethical (and in some cases not legal), but it was the way business was done and they didn't mind admitting it.

"Of course," they told me, "we do business with two or three vendors who buy our steel proportionately. We tell them 'The more steel you buy from us, the more orders you get from us.'"

But here's the interesting thing. If you go to the middle manager (the buyer's supervisor) and use the word "reciprocity," he'll throw you out of the office. Go to the vice president of procurement and what does he say? "Of course, we use reciprocity!" I discovered a theory of management: Middle managers tend to be the most risk averse (cautious and self-protective). This is because they're trying to make it to a vice president level in the company and do not want to jeopardize their future. On the other hand, the vice president has already reached the highest level. Similarly, the lowest level of management does not have much stake in their careers. Therefore, if you plot these three positions—lower, middle, upper management—according to risk-taking, you get a U-shaped curve.

I was learning more about the psychology of buying than the economics of buying. It was less about price and delivery and more about what motivates a person to buy from one vendor instead of another. It was the kind of research I really enjoyed and I knew I had found the right mentor.

I was even more convinced that I was on the right path when Howard invited me to help him develop his theory of buyer behavior. I could hardly believe my good fortune. Howard believed that my unique cultural perspective was invaluable to him, and he also sensed that I was as fascinated by consumer psychology as he was. Eventually, that theory would be published and become known as the Howard–Sheth Theory of Buyer Behavior, which would be the first important step in my journey to becoming a recognized scholar. Howard and I were breaking some unwritten rules. As a young scholar starting out, you are not supposed to write mega theories. You are supposed to write research papers to be published in top journals.

Madhu Comes to America

In between doctorial assigns and discovering my passion, I wrote love letters to Madhu. We were also preparing for our wedding and her relocation to America. To say I was excited about having my bride-to-be with me was an understatement. I bought all the household items including furniture, flatware, and towels. I even found a priest (Professor Kulkarni) to marry us. In keeping with Indian tradition, we needed traditional materials such as candles, coconut, and other wedding essentials, which Madhu brought with her from India. Since our support system was in India, we planned our big day sans our family.

I did not know how to drive and could not afford a car. However, the Dexters were wealthy. They had an estate near the airport with lots of acreage and several vehicles so they picked up Madhu when she arrived in Pittsburgh for our wedding. The day before Madhu arrived it had snowed about nine inches. It was the first time she saw snow so we played in it for hours like two kids.

Madhu and I married on December 22, 1962. She was breathtaking in a white sari with a red border. My best man was David Miller. Since we could not afford to fly in any of our family and friends from India, our surrogate parents were the Dexters and my student advisor, Professor Andrews. Our official honeymoon occurred three months later in March of 1963. Madhu and I took a bus trip to Washington, D.C.

Life could not have been better. I was married to the most beautiful woman in the world, my work was progressing, and I was very happy. Madhu and I lived near the university and walked everywhere. We did not own a car, but that was fine—neither of us had ever learned to drive. In India, only wealthy people drove cars. Everyone else rode bicycles or used public transportation. With my income, I could not even afford bicycle! Our apartment was two doors down from the grocery store. On her first visit to the grocery, Madhu was completely surprised that shoppers selected products from the shelf and pushed their own carts! In those days in India, shoppers were not allowed to pick items from the shelf. Items were placed in a basket by a store clerk.

Speaking of grocery products, there were no Indian grocery stores or restaurants in Pittsburgh then, but Madhu discovered a store in New York City, Kalustan, that sold ingredients for

Indian meals. Mail orders for these items took two to four weeks to arrive and, by then, they would be stale. With a food allowance of $40 per month, we could not afford to waste anything. To help with our transition, my mother-in-law grinded fresh spices and lentil flour for us and sent them by boat. Since even those provisions took several months to arrive, necessity led Madhu to become an exceptional cook. Necessity is the not only the mother of invention, but also entrepreneurship.

An Invitation to the Indian Embassy

In early January of 1963, I received an invitation from the Indian embassy to come to Washington, D.C. The invitation was extended to all Indian graduate students studying management in the United States, and the purpose was to be introduced to two important officials from India: K.T. Chandy and Ravi Mathai.

Chandy was an officer of the government and, as such, he was chosen to head up the new Indian Institute of Management in Kolkata (formerly Calcutta), with Ravi Mathai as his second in command. Little did I know, but many of the people I was meeting via academia would later cross my path.

Chandy's job was to recruit all available management talent to this new institution, which is why he invited all of us to Washington, D.C. He urged us to return to India soon after we graduated, rather than remain in America. He said that to become professors in this new institution would be the opportunity of a lifetime. We would also be aiding in the patriotic effort to reverse the "brain drain" that was depleting India of its most promising scientists and scholars.

I made the trip to D.C. and was persuaded by Chandy's presentation. Graduation, repaid loans, and valuable experience aside, I was inclined to return to India and pursue a career at the new Indian Institute of Management. While Chandy's proposition was important and intriguing, my desire to answer his call would lead me to Massachusetts Institute of Technology (MIT) by way of Columbia, but first I had to complete my doctoral education at the University of Pittsburgh.

Doctoral Exams amid Pitt's Financial Collapse

All was well until the spring of 1963 when the financial collapse of the University of Pittsburgh became inevitable. "Pitt," as it is known, was a private school with Ivy League aspirations. Cornell's Edward Litchfield had been recruited to realize the University's aspirations, and he quickly hired top national talent to bring it to fruition. He also went on a real estate binge. The communities surrounding the university had deteriorated into slums so Litchfield attempted to gentrify by buying up many of the buildings and the land. All of the school's cash reserves were depleted on these capital acquisitions, and suddenly our new chancellor found that he had no money to pay his new high-powered faculty. The dean of the business school, Marshall Robinson, resigned. His job was offered to John Howard, but Howard declined to become captain of a sinking ship. Eventually, Pitt was bailed out by the Mellon Bank and the State of Pennsylvania, and it became a state university.

Amid the financial collapse, Howard decided it was time to leave. However, I still had to take my comprehensive exams. Fear of the outcomes of the collapse led me to rush through my last semester of course work. I still had to pass the comprehensive examinations. Meanwhile, Howard decided that he was going to go to Columbia University. We had to scramble to put together my committee before I sat for seven demanding qualifying exams. My major was Individual and Group Behavior, and that exam was eight hours long. I also had to take three four-hour exams in related areas of specialization, and all four of these exams—in addition to one in my applied field (marketing)—had to be completed in a two-week period. The other two exams were in research methods and social psychology. Finally, there was the foreign language requirement—which is a story unto itself.

Not surprisingly, Pitt preferred that students demonstrate proficiency in a foreign language in which well-known scientific research had been conducted, like Russian, French, or German. But I did not have time to learn another language. So I petitioned the University to either declare English as my second language or accept one of my Indian languages as my second language. It was an unusual request, but once again, fortune intervened on my behalf.

Like Europe, India is a federation and the Indian states have distinctly different languages. All languages are represented on the banknote, because natives of one state cannot read or write the language of the others. My state of origin is Gujarat, and my language is Gujarati. However, I studied Hindi as a second language, and I had a certificate attesting to my proficiency, which I happened to bring with me to America. The University allowed me to declare Hindi as my foreign language, and they found a professor in the School of International and Public Affairs—an Indian who spoke Hindi—to test me. When I showed the professor my certificate, he said, "You are more qualified than I," and he passed me!

I made it through the research methods and social psychology exams, completing the four qualifying exams and the one in my applied field of marketing or five exams in two weeks! As I think back on that experience, I realize that it was a remarkable feat to even attempt let alone accomplish. I started the doctoral program at an even pace in August 1962 and, a year later, Howard was advising me to "hurry up and finish" so that I would not end up "homeless." From July to August 1963, I prepared feverishly to write my exams in September.

I have not been under such pressure, before or since I passed my qualifying exams. Before completing my exams, Howard asked me if I would like to come with him to Columbia University to continue working on the Theory of Buyer Behavior. Since I had no idea how the recruiting process worked between a university and prospective faculty, I told Howard, "You are my mentor. I'll do whatever you say." Also, I had to have a job because Madhu was pregnant.

Howard negotiated a package with Columbia that included me as a full-time research associate (comparable to a post-doc position). He told me to join him in New York as soon as I finished my comprehensives. But there was something else I had to do before I left Pittsburgh, and it turned out to be a major undertaking. I had to find a thesis topic.

My first idea was to expand the paper where I had generalized Maslow's theory to institutions because it had been such a success. Of course, I would do a lot more research and it would be something like a thesis in behavioral sociology or psychology. But when I took the paper to Howard, he tore it apart. "Where is the data?" he asked. "Where is the evidence?" he probed. Howard was an economist and empiricist, and I had simply conceptualized—imagined—things. As far as Howard was concerned, my thesis may as well have been science fiction. I would either have to find another topic or find another professor especially since the original professor, for whom I had written that paper, was no longer at Pitt. (I had sent my paper to Abraham Maslow. He responded that the paper was fascinating and that he hadn't thought of extending it to nations and other institutions, and that I should publish it and continue to do further research in this area. Of course, that did not happen.)

During that hectic summer, I discovered several social psychologists. One was Leon Festinger, who had done important work in cognitive dissonance. Another was George Homans, a Harvard professor who had written a book about individual and group behavior that included fascinating stories about how groups (including gangs) form among young kids. The third was Mujafer Sherif, who studied children at summer camps, looking at how they form their hierarchies and select leaders, and so on.

This work—especially that of Homans—was really interesting to me, so I wrote a full thesis proposal around the idea of testing his propositions back in India—at my second eldest brother's boarding school. It seemed ideal. Behavior there is tightly monitored. Everyone rises at 5:30 a.m. and follows the same strict, daily routine. Plus, there was a new set of kids every year who have to assimilate. What do they do to be accepted? What sorts of power plays go on? How does one survive? I was really excited about exploring all these questions, and a single academic school seemed to offer an opportunity for experiments to test the hypotheses.

I sent the proposal to Homans, who did not provide a great deal of feedback, but did agree that it was an interesting experimental design and that I was validating his theory in a positive way. I presented my proposal to my committee. Doing so led to a debate about whether this was a business thesis. Did I want to become a marketing professor? And if I did, then I had not presented a marketing thesis proposal. If I wanted Howard as my professor, I would have to design a thesis in the marketing discipline. In the end, I had to drop the Homans idea.

Testing the Howard–Sheth Theory

The clock was ticking. It was time to join Howard at Columbia, but I was not finished with my doctorate. Howard stepped in and saved me again. Howard and I agreed—and so did my committee—that my thesis would consist of the actual testing of the Howard–Sheth theory we were constructing. According to the Howard–Sheth theory (1969), consumers go through three stages of learning: Extensive problem solving (EPS), limited problem solving (LPS), and routine responsive behavior (RRB). My position was to determine the following: How do marketers get consumers to that third stage? How do companies engender brand loyalty? The implications for competition and marketing were abundant. I ended up with three published papers in tier-one journals from my dissertation.

LIFE LESSON

A fulfilling life is comprised of a series of hardships altered by a series of good outcomes. Pittsburgh's financial crisis and Howard's departure typify the unpredictable events that positively shaped my life. *How do you know if you have made a good decision? Trust your gut. Listen to your instinct.*

3

COLUMBIA AND MIT

My good friend and fellow MBA student, Bob Voytas offered to drive Madhu and me from Pittsburgh to New York free of charge. We crammed all our possessions and ourselves inside his VW Beetle, hit the road, and arrived at New York City a few hours later on October 1, 1963. Bob had tried relentlessly to teach me how to drive a stick shift. During one of his lessons, I confused the accelerator with the brake and smashed his car into a tree. After paying for repairs, I opted to leave stick shifts alone.

As I mentioned earlier, a full-time research associate is a title that is generally reserved for post-doctoral students. However, opting to allow Howard to negotiate on my behalf was advantageous. The position came with a $9,000 annual salary, which for me, was an astronomical amount. I cannot emphasize how considerate and generous Howard continued to be to me. To make the transition easy, he rented a furnished apartment for Madhu and me so, upon arrival, we had move-in ready residence.

At Columbia, my overarching duty was to help Howard develop the theory of buyer behavior. As my title implied, I was his researcher and co-author. We worked furiously. And, as each chapter was completed, we tested it with students in his doctoral seminar for review and critique.

Mining the Library for Research Gold

Despite the rigor of work, working on the theory with Howard would prove to be the most memorable and rewarding days of my entire academic life. For two glorious years, I had neither teaching responsibilities nor committee assignments, so I was in the library stacks; five floors down, nine or ten hours a day, six days a week. The experience was like going down into a coal mine, with dust, mold, and poor ventilation, but what rich veins of ore I discovered down there! I wandered freely and read everything that looked interesting, learning more and more every day. To this day, I urge students to grant themselves that kind of freedom in their pursuit of learning. I admonish students to check out more than the required reading; to think of the library as a treasure trove; a museum to be explored, or as a bookstore, where we typically take the time to browse from one section to another and often accidentally discover books we were not looking for. For me, those days in "the stacks" at Columbia provided the best opportunity I have had to read extensively and learn things I never expected to learn—or even thought I needed to learn. Once again, a benevolent fate seemed to be guiding my academic journey.

Howard and I had the general idea that all of my research would somehow be integrated into our theory of buyer behavior, but in the process, the theory began to change. All the behavioral scientists we read pushed us in new directions.

One of those scientists was Yale's Clark Hull, one of the era's best known experimental psychologists. Hull was the so-called rat psychologist because he conducted much of his research on rats and dogs while his rival, Harvard's B.F. Skinner, was the "pigeon psychologist." Both contributed to the reinforcement theory of learning, but Howard was particularly drawn to Hull's elegant evolution-based model: Organisms suffer deprivation, deprivation creates needs, needs activate drives, and drives determine behavior. It was not hard to see the relevance of this kind of thinking to our work on consumer behavior.

Hull had a student, Herbert Spence, whose relationship to Hull was something like mine to Howard. Hull, the teacher, had begun to listen to the student, Spence, and together they modified Hull's original thinking. Eventually they would become coauthors and colleagues. I convinced Howard that their new formula was a better fit with what we were looking for than Hull's original theory. More specifically, Hull's original work was based simply on stimulus–response (S-R). It had no cognitive mapping of what goes on in the mind of the consumers when they are exposed to a marketing stimulus such as advertising or new products. We developed a black box between the stimulus and the response or the so-called "S-O-R" theory: Stimulus–Organism (the black box)–Response theory.

Moreover, we theorized that there were two aspects to the function of the mind—first, perception, and then impression or attitude. When somebody communicates something to us, what goes on in our mind? How do we decode it? There is selective exposure, attention and processing, perceptual bias (that is, hearing something different from what was said) and selective retention. So how does the marketing message get translated? Why does one consumer react differently from another when given the same message?

Contributing Howard–Sheth Theory Scholars

In our research, we discovered other thinkers who helped us develop our thinking on perception and attitude. One was David Berlyne, whose work on exploratory search led him to theorize about how and why people pay attention to or choose to explore unrelated things. Since we were interested in how people pay attention to advertising, Berlyne's work was of great interest to me. His theory was that there is an optimal level of ambiguity—that is, a level of ambiguity at which one pays the closest attention. If the message of an advertisement, for example, is not completely transparent, but is something you have to think about, you attend to it with a sharpened focus.

On the other hand, if the message is too ambiguous, the mind shuts off or turns away. Thus, there is a curvilinear relationship between ambiguity and attention: No ambiguity, poor attention; too much ambiguity, poor attention. However, the optimal level produces "vigilance."

Howard and I were theorizing that through experience, we simplify our brand choices over time—moving from extensive problem solving (EPS), to limited problem solving (LPS), and finally to habit, or routinized response behavior (RRB). In other words, consumers go through "psychology of simplification" and become loyal to a brand. But it occurred to me that our simplification resulting in RRB might be trumped by Berlyne's theory of exploratory behavior that might threaten brand loyalty. Specifically, I was looking at the notion that satiation can result in aspiration—the desire for something else, something more or greater achievement.

Still it was Berlyne who pointed out that habit-formation may not be the end of the process. The consumer might still want to move beyond and engage in "exploratory" behavior. To describe this phenomenon, we coined the term "psychology of complication." Our idea was that for often-purchased products, the buyer moves in cycles. That is, even after consumers have found a brand they like and they become brand loyal, they still want to try something else. In fact, when a company introduces a new brand or product, people will often try it just to experience it. And many times, in the process, the old brand loyalty gets destroyed. For our theory, the implications were significant.

Although the Howard–Sheth theory has been sometimes regarded as "rat" psychology, much nonbehaviorist thinking went into the building of the black box in the middle of the S-O-R theory. Ivan Pavlov, Skinner, Hull, and other behavioral psychologists studied stimuli and responses, but for us the mystery was the process—how does it happen in the mind? While I was focused on theory building research, Howard was trying to line up funding to test our theory. He liked to target big corporations and he was good at it.

Columbia's Scholarly Dream Team

Like most great academic scholars, Howard was also an entrepreneur. Scholars like him create their own brand. They know how to get funding, where the resources are, and how to leverage those resources. In science, engineering, and medicine, professors who are lab directors are often world-class entrepreneurs. But even in less dramatic settings genuine scholars have to be entrepreneurs.

Howard enjoyed prestige at Columbia. Courtney Brown, formerly the CEO of an oil company, had been brought in as the dean to add new luster to Columbia's business school and Brown quickly got things moving by raising capital for a new building, Uris Hall. Brown also hired new senior scholars to aid in the school's transformation and Howard was one of the most senior and most renowned of those scholars. So it was not a surprise when, in December of 1963, just two months after my arrival at Columbia, a young man by the name of George Day wandered into our office to introduce himself.

Day had been granted a Ford Foundation Fellowship to get a doctorate degree at any of the top six business schools in America. He visited all of them—Stanford, Northwestern, Harvard, MIT, Carnegie Mellon, and Columbia—to see who was doing what. In the fall of 1964, Day decided to join Howard and me as a Ph.D. candidate.

Another student with whom I worked closely was Prakash Sethi, who had come to Columbia as an MBA candidate after majoring in economics at India's Delhi School of Economics. Columbia had world-class economics faculty led by people like Joel Dean and Arthur Burns. Sethi's mentor was Alfred Oxenfeldt, an economist and a marketing professor in pricing. If it had not been for Howard's arrival at Columbia, Sethi might well have pursued a marketing degree based on pricing. He decided to work with us and, under Howard's direction, I guided his dissertation.

Fundraising efforts led us to General Electric, where we met Nelson Foote. He had done a great deal of household consumer research for GE across all of its businesses—about the ultimate consumer in the household, how the family makes decisions about budgets, who decides where to spend money, and so on. Foote had also recruited a young Ph.D., Robert Pratt, from the University of Michigan, a school famous for Institute of Social Research (ISR) and the Consumer Confidence Index.

At that time, Columbia had a world-class Center for Applied Social Research. Paul Lazarsfeld and a brilliant team of sociologists were creating their own theories about diffusion of information and opinion—and more to the point, about how public opinion is shaped. Columbia had a long tradition of studying public opinion from a sociological perspective. Lazarsfeld was a leader in this field, but he was also an expert in the use of longitudinal panels, a research method that I had been using in my own thesis work. Lazarsfeld's presence on campus gave Howard and me the opportunity to learn everything Lazarsfeld knew about panels—how to recruit and organize, how to test results. Moreover, since our Buyer Behavior Project was panel based, Lazarsfeld became a key advisor to us.

Obtaining My Green Card

Immigration was not easy for a person of Indian origin. Indians had to wait years to become a permanent resident (green card holder) and eventually a naturalized citizen. Had I been familiar with U.S. immigration laws, I would have come to America with my green card in hand because I was born in Burma and very few Burma citizens were allowed to migrate to the United States. In order to obtain a green card, Columbia had to sponsor me as a qualified professional. Moreover, to guarantee that I was not keeping any equally qualified American out of a job, Columbia had to post my position in the local paper for 30 days and consider any application that might come in. I was fortunate that the University was willing to comply. I eventually obtained my green card in December 1964, but there was a one-year waiting period during which time I was not permitted to move between employers. While my immigration status was pending, I interviewed for a tenure-track faculty position at MIT. Hiring officials agreed that I would relocate to Boston, green card in hand, in August 1965.

The invitation to join the faculty at MIT was a direct result of my trip to D.C. and my talk with K.T. Chandy. In fact, the MIT invitation came from John D.C. Little, a senior professor in operations research and also the chair of marketing department. MIT's alignment with the new IIM-Kolkata, India, was a huge draw for me. The arrangement was that I would have a tenure-track position at MIT, but would also be available to teach in Kolkata during certain semesters. I would also be part of the faculty resources that MIT was committing to the successful development of the IIM. All aspects of that deal were attractive to me, so I opted to leave Columbia for MIT.

If it is true that there is no triumph without a trial, then I was not exempt from the process. Save for immigration woes, my time at Columbia was both happy and productive. Our first child, Reshma, was born in New York on March 28, 1964. Her story is integral to mine because she is now a marketing professor at Emory University with me.

Defending My Dissertation at Pitt

When I arrived at MIT in the fall of 1965, I still did not have my Ph.D. I had completed all requirements by commuting between New York and Pittsburgh to meet my panel members and summarizing the results. I submitted the work to my committee in 1965 with the understanding that I would defend the dissertation before I left Columbia for MIT.

My dissertation was abnormally long, largely because it included a comprehensive review of some 400 buyer behavior references, but also because the second part was the testing of the Howard–Sheth theory—how consumers evolve from Extensive Problem Solving to Limited Problem Solving and ultimately, to habit or make Routine Response Behavior.

I returned to Pittsburgh to defend my dissertation before a very unusual group of scholars: Chair John Howard, Dean Albert Frey, Professor Austin Jones, Dean Edward Webber, and Professor Edward Sussna. They all played a role then and later. Ed Webber deserves special mention because he was the only MBA professor who did not give me an A. As a member of my doctoral committee, Sussna, refused to believe that anyone could have read and reviewed that many articles for a dissertation. He did not realize that the final product included my dissertation work as well as two years of full-time research in the stacks at Columbia. Sussna flatly declared that it was presumptuous of anyone to claim to have read and absorbed such a vast body of work. He insisted that the review of the literature be removed.

My thesis contained a significant amount of psychometric work, an area of research with which my Ph.D. committee was not very familiar. To ensure accuracy, the committee recruited a faculty member from the computer science department, Glenn Rodabaush, to review the psychometric aspects of the dissertation. Rodabaush was a student of Paul Horst, who was a giant in the field of matrices and psychometrics at the University of Washington. I had used Horst's work quite a bit in my dissertation.

With only a few minor modifications beyond omitting 400 references, the thesis was ready to be submitted to the graduate school for publishing. I defended my dissertation in August 1965, not long before my departure for MIT. The final work was submitted later that year. As a result, technically, my doctoral degree was granted to me by the University of Pittsburgh in 1966.

Two scholars, who were in the audience during the defense, were professors of marketing at Berkeley, Franco Nicosia (who respected John Howard enormously and introduced himself to me after the defense), and Gerald Albaum. Albaum was also a marketing professor, whom I also met for the first time at the defense. Both men became good friends of mine.

MIT and My First Tenure-track Position

Even though my Ph.D. was not quite in hand, I was hired at MIT as an assistant professor for two reasons. Kolkata was becoming Marxist under the influence of the so-called Naxalites so American professors were uneasy about going there to teach.

I did not have any reservations. I began learning about the IIM program and talking to other professors who had been to Kolkata. It was a significant commitment on the part of MIT and the Ford Foundation, and I looked forward to being part of the initiative.

John Little wanted somebody with a behavioral orientation in the marketing department. Most MIT faculty members were quantitative, and operations-research oriented, and Little was trying to build up the department. When I arrived in 1965, I joined several other new recruits.

Among those already enshrined on campus was Arnold Amstutz, a renowned simulation expert. This was during the days of mainframe computing, and Amstutz designed a simulation game about competitive strategies and strategic planning in the marketing area. Everybody who came through the department—students as well as executives in MIT's Sloan Management Program—had to learn and play Amstutz's game.

Senior professors William Massey, an expert in operations research and stochastic modeling, and Henry Claycamp were already on the team. Eventually, the Ford Foundation recruited Claycamp who did valuable work on a project in India on population control regarding how to use marketing tactics to motivate people to bear fewer children. Later he recruited me to assist with the project.

Several students in the department when I arrived have gone on to become well-known professors. One was Leonard Lodish, who worked with Little to build computer models to determine routing for salespeople, among other things. Lodish went to the Wharton School, where he has enjoyed a distinguished career. Scott Armstrong came to MIT as a doctoral student. I quickly developed a good working relationship with Armstrong. Glenn Urban was a young star from Northwestern and another expert in simulation and quantitative methods. Urban has remained at MIT, where he eventually became the dean of the Sloan School of Management.

Finally, there was David Montgomery; a student of William Massey's who had followed Massey from Stanford. Montgomery arrived the semester after me, in January 1966. We shared a wonderful working and personal relationship. I will never forget the time when Montgomery and his lawyer wife, Toby invited us to their house for dinner. They knew my wife and I were vegetarians so Toby prepared a special vegetarian casserole for dinner, something she had not done before but hoped we would enjoy. Toby brought the casserole into the dining room and, just as she was about to set it on the table, the dish slipped from her hands splattered all over the floor. We all still recall how pizza saved the evening.

It was an intellectually exciting time at MIT. Massey decided to go back to Stanford, and Montgomery soon followed him, but not before they infected us all with their enthusiasm for stochastic processes, such as Bernoulli and Markov chains. Both Massey and Montgomery were experts in this area, as was one of John Howard's old friends from Carnegie Mellon, marketing professor Alfred Kuehn, who used Markov chains to study the evolution of brand loyalty. At a very young age, Kuehn used his simulation expertise to start a consulting company. He did a quantitative study showing that, based on terrain, infrastructure, and other factors, 90 percent of physical space in the United States was inappropriate for locating warehouses. This was a new revelation, which he published to great acclaim in *Management Science*, a leading periodical in the field. Kuehn also collaborated with Massey and Frank Bass, another operations research expert, on a textbook about quantitative methods in marketing. I particularly admired Kuehn's work.

These scholars offered a mathematical and managerial perspective into consumer behavior, just as the Howard–Sheth theory offered a behavioral perspective. They were studying *how* brand loyalty happens. We were studying *why* it happens. It was great synergy.

Publishing, Lifelong Friendships, and My First Car

My days at MIT were busy, productive, and rewarding. I had prepared the final draft of my thesis and sent it off to the University of Pittsburgh, but there on my desk was the review of buyer behavior literature that I had been asked to cut out of my dissertation. I knew that this was a very valuable piece of scholarship, so I began rewriting it as a paper. I showed the rewrite, entitled "A Review of Buyer Behavior," to Martin Starr at Columbia University, editor of *Management Science* and a renowned expert in operations research. Starr quickly saw its value and encouraged me to submit it to *Management Science*, where it was accepted and published in 1967.

It was my first journal publication, and it was a substantial piece of work. With 34 printed pages, its importance has been confirmed by the fact that I received more reprint requests for this paper than others, which have published. It was more than a simple bibliography of the literature because the contents were organized to present a way of looking at the world of buyer behavior. I used the familiar analog to make the point that buyer behavior had been approached from so many diverse perspectives—psychological, sociological, anthropological, economic, and marketing—that it was like the five blind men touching the elephant and making different inferences about its reality. What was needed was a larger view, a grand theory that integrates diverse perspectives into a holistic view of buyer behavior.

My work on "A Review of Buyer Behavior" was essentially completed while I was at MIT. The same can be said about another of my earliest publications. This was a longitudinal study, using data I had access to and analyzing it by means of the psychometric method I had used in my thesis. This paper, "Estimating Parameters Using Factor Analysis," would also appear in a tier one publication, the *Journal of the American Statistical Association*. And because it offered a radically different way of estimating parameters, it also generated a great many reprint requests from a myriad of disciplines including an expert in grasshopper demography and a researcher in sedimentary geology. Both liked the technique and thought it was applicable to their fields of study. Oddly enough, I do not recall any requests from marketing scholars.

While at MIT, I continued my research into consumer behavior with a new information-processing orientation. Howard and

I were using the work of Herbert Simon, James March, and John Reitman, who had created a flow-chart model to assess the question, "Given all the choices one has as a consumer, how does the consumer reduce those choices?" I recruited student researchers to interview consumers and put together the information on the decision-making process. It was a heuristics-based approach. For example, what determines your purchase of gasoline? The heuristic for most people is when the gas tank is three-fourths empty. But some fill up on half-empty, and others let it go almost dry. Our goal was to learn the frequency of each of these heuristics.

My personal and professional lives intersected in some interesting ways while I was at MIT. The research work I was engaged in at MIT was productive, but my day job was teaching. Except perhaps for the MBA students at IIM-Kolkata, I taught some of the smartest undergraduates at MIT I had ever encountered. It seemed like every student was bright and motivated. At the same time, I also taught a class made up of Sloan Fellows in MIT's executive degree program. Companies granted promising executives a nine-month leave of absence to train at MIT to become general managers. The Sloan Fellows was a distinguished program (and still is) so I am not sure what those 40-year-old professionals thought when they realized that their class was being taught by a kid in his twenties. I was privileged to supervise the master's theses of two of Sloan Fellows. One was an executive from Colombia, with whom I became good friends.

While at Boston, Surendra Singhvi, whom I knew as a doctoral student in finance at Columbia, had taken a faculty position at the University of New Hampshire and I visited him there often. Like me, Singhvi is Jain and we would eventually help organize the first Jain center in America.

Madhu and I lived in Winchester, a northern suburb of Boston. This was a change from our life in New York, where we lived in the city and could get around either on foot or by subway. I was a commuter now, so I had to buy a car. I purchased my first car, a used Mercury Comet, from an acquaintance for

$500. The only problem was that the car was a stick shift and I did not know how to drive a stick shift.

Networking Leads to Opportunities

Ven Venkatesan was someone else who I met during my trip to the Indian Embassy in D.C. Venkatesan was a doctoral student at the University of Minnesota. His professor was Robert Holloway who, like John Howard, was in consumer behavior. Holloway had an interest in experimental psychology, so he used experimental methodology to study consumers. He was also a devotee of Leon Festinger, who created the theory of cognitive dissonance. Consequently, Venkatesan approached his work with this experimental mindset.

We failed to keep in touch after the D.C. meeting, but on one of my trips to New Hampshire to visit Singhvi, I ran into Venkatesan. Venkatesan had completed his graduate studies and was on the marketing faculty at the University of New Hampshire. This was a happy coincidence for two reasons. First, Venkatesan needed a car and he was delighted to buy that Mercury Comet, which I barely knew how to drive. I moved on to a used '98 Oldsmobile that leaked oil by the gallon—a total lemon. For someone with such vast consumer behavior expertise, I was not a very savvy car buyer! Second, Venkatesan and I began productive research collaboration at Durham, New Hampshire; a nice little college town that was home to maybe 6,000 students, mostly undergraduates. The town featured one flashing traffic light. If you missed the light, you missed the town. This was my first introduction to small-town American life. There was one general store that doubled as the bus depot, a movie theater, and a few fast-food restaurants. Durham proved to be the perfect setting for a number of consumer behavior experiments.

I had become interested in "perceived risk" theory created by Raymond Bauer, a psychologist in marketing at the Harvard Business School. His idea was that in high-risk situations, consumers will reduce choices and become brand loyal.

Bauer's theory held that when making purchasing decisions in one of three risky categories (Performance, Economic, and Social Risks), the consumer depends more on word-of-mouth testimony and less on advertising and at the same time tends to reduce his range of choices to the most well-known brands. In short, the consumer will be content with what works. There is no attempt to optimize. This was contrary to the standard economic thinking that as a rational being, one should maximize utility.

Bauer's theory offered a simple, but fascinating and powerful new angle on consumer behavior for me and Venkatesan. It was very different from the Howard–Sheth theory, which was complex. I was intrigued by Bauer's theory such that Venkatesan and I deployed it in a number of research experiments using students as consumers. In one experiment, overwhelmingly, the respondents chose the well-known brand, confirming the idea that increased perceived risk produces a less diverse choice. As expected, our group recommended the well-known brand, and their peers, in turn, were increasingly swayed by such word-of-mouth recommendations as perceived risk increased. We also tested Leon Festinger Theory of Cognitive Dissonance that buyers establish consistency between their behavior (their choice) and their belief system. The radical implication from his theory, for advertising and marketing, is that the best advertising really should come after the sale—when consumers are looking for rationalizations. That's when they are really tuned in to read the ads of chosen products and brands. All previous literature in advertising promoted the idea that the job of an advertiser was to convert a person into a prospect, and a prospect into a customer. But this theory suggested just the opposite, which was very nonintuitive.

Venkatesan and I did several experiments along these lines. It was interesting and fun stuff, and Venkatesan and we published several studies in top academic journals, including the *Journal of Marketing Research*.

Eventually, Venkatesan left the University of New Hampshire for the University of Massachusetts at Amherst. Since Amherst was within driving distance of Boston, Venkatesan and I continued to work together and co-authored several papers that were published in the late 1960s and early 1970s. Our working relationship came to an end when I returned to Columbia because the distance between our campuses was too great.

Looking back, running into Venkatesan again was yet another accidental occurrence. Venkatesan eventually settled in at the University of Rhode Island, from which he recently retired. Today, he and his wife, Pam, travel to universities around the world where he is invited as a visiting professor.

Of course, I had wonderful senior colleagues on campus at MIT. One was the renowned Jay Forrester, whom John Howard had urged me to get to know. An engineering professor, Forrester had created a memory device using new technology that MIT eventually sold to IBM. Closer to my field of interest, Forrester had developed a simulation technique called Industrial Dynamics, which expanded the concept of simulation so it applied to entire ecosystems—like a whole industry or an entire economy.

Like so many of the leading lights at MIT, Forrester was an operations research specialist, but there were a few behaviorists there (not in marketing but in organizational behavior) that I enjoyed getting to know. One was Warren Bennis, perhaps the top name in the field of leadership. After many years, Bennis left MIT to go to the University of Southern California (USC) and encouraged me to join him there. Before the end of 1966, I found myself headed back to New York and Columbia.

LIFE LESSON

Entrepreneurship is a prerequisite for being a successful scholar. The two go hand-in-hand. Networking broadly is also a prerequisite. Do not limit connections to just those in your discipline. Even if you do not embrace the work of scholars in other disciplines, at least keep abreast of what they are doing. *Great scholars create their own brand and the door of opportunity swings both ways.*

4

FROM COLUMBIA TO INDIA
AND BACK

The decision to return to Columbia was first and foremost
practical and economic. John Howard's grant-securing
efforts had begun to bear fruit from a number of different
sources. General Electric (GE), perhaps at the urging of Nelson
Foote, came through with money, as did Monsanto. And then
there was a huge bequest (some $350,000) from Chauncey
Williams, who had made a fortune with his famous catalog of
industrial products. Because Howard was so influential and his
work deemed so important, he received this generous gift from
the dean's office. The gift would eventually fund what became
known as the Columbia Buyer Behavior Project, with George
Day managing and Paul Lazarsfeld as advisor.

In all, roughly a half-million dollars were available for the
ongoing work on the Howard–Sheth theory. MIT's overhead
was 42 percent (42 percent of all research grant dollars went
to the university to cover indirect costs), so we would only
net 58 percent of the half-million. Columbia's overhead was
roughly 26 percent, which enabled us to use more operating
cash flow for research. Rather than split the research funds
between the two institutions, it was easier if I would return
to Columbia.

I had enjoyed my first stint at Columbia so I had several good reasons for returning. Columbia wanted me to teach consumer behavior, which was my field of interest. Since the best way to learn is to teach, I really wanted to teach this topic. MIT is obviously a world-class institution, and though my days at MIT were wonderfully productive, ultimately it proved that nothing in my academic journey was going to happen as planned. I was at MIT only for 15 months. Had I stayed one more year, I may never have left.

Columbia was a better fit for a scholar with my interests. I would be reunited with an entourage of people I admired—Paul Lazarsfeld and his Bureau of Applied Social Research, William McGuire and Stanley Schachter in the psychology department—and I had begun to miss all that excitement. My departure was not great news for MIT because, at the same time, David Montgomery was also thinking of returning to Stanford; so of the three young people John Little had hired to build the department (David Montgomery, Glen Urban and me), two of us were leaving about the same time. I remember Little being quite perplexed about this turn of events.

Returning to the Buyer Behavior Project

I really looked forward to getting involved in the Buyer Behavior Project at Columbia—especially since there was an infusion of grant money, which allowed us to do more research. After completing his coursework, George Day put his superior organizational skills to work as project director. Under his leadership, the Columbia Buyer Behavior Project got involved in a fascinating, real-time study for New York–based General Foods, another company Howard had approached for funding.

As a maker of coffee and cereals, General Foods was already very much in the breakfast category through its Post and Maxwell House divisions, but the food category was changing. Women were going to work and, in general, people had less time to cook. Instant coffee was popular, and the traditional bacon-and-eggs breakfast was on its way out. However, as

General Foods was developing concepts for an instant breakfast, Carnation introduced Carnation Instant Breakfast to the marketplace. General Foods quickly responded with Post Instant Breakfast, and the Columbia Buyer Behavior Project began a longitudinal study to test its acceptance. We used our expertise in panel-based research to compare the two products in terms of consumer attitudes and preferences. This was not dry, abstract theorizing. This was a real-world, live-laboratory experiment, where the results were of immediate business consequence.

As a young assistant professor, I had a full teaching load— four classes, two each semester—and I taught in three different areas. First was Consumer Behavior, for which there was no standard textbook at that time. The second course was Marketing Management, which I taught while at MIT. The third subject was International Marketing, which I was teaching for the first time. Since I was from another country, teaching International Marketing appeared to be a natural fit. Eventually, it became an area of special interest for me over the course of my career—the area in which I also published several papers. I also taught in Columbia's Executive Programs, at a place called the Arden House, an estate that had been owned by Averill Harriman about 45 minutes outside the city. The classes met in the fabulous mansion, said to have something like 180 rooms. Unlike MIT's Sloan Fellows program, this was a nondegree program, but the experience at Sloan made me a little less self-conscious about teaching people twice my age.

All of my degree-seeking students at Columbia were in the MBA program. They were required to do the hands-on experiments and field studies I had enjoyed so much in my work with Ven Venkatesan. I encouraged my students to get out into the neighborhood, which in our case was Harlem. All of my students were white, and for the most part had never been to Harlem so it might as well have been a foreign country. I knew that the students would benefit from exposure to otherwise unfamiliar consumers and their behavior.

One of the student projects was in response to a popular and controversial book, *The Poor Pay More*, written by Columbia sociologist David Caplovitz. Using research in Harlem and Bedford–Stuyvesant, Caplovitz found that the African-American consumers in these communities were paying higher prices for furniture, groceries, liquor, and many other products. Why? There were two theories. Probably the most widespread, or the oldest, was the Veblen's theory of conspicuous consumption, i.e. keeping up with the Joneses. Caplovitz rejected that theory, and went in the opposite direction. He saw this behavior as compensatory consumption—compensation for belonging to a discriminated minority. Caplovitz concluded that these consumers wanted to disassociate themselves from their peer group by showing that they were not as poor or deprived as their ethnic identity. It was quite a convincing argument, well documented, and caused a great deal of policy discussion.

I, however, believed that there was a third explanation. I had been working on perceived risk theory, and I felt certain that perceived risk was the explanation for this seemingly odd consumer behavior. I argued that these consumers knew that if they made a wrong choice, there was no recourse. They had no lawyer to help them and the store would refuse to refund their money. They had no power in the marketplace, no consumer rights, and the market, therefore, would not serve these customers as it should. Consequently, they bought brands that they trusted and felt were low risk. They pay a premium for what is, in effect, insurance—ensuring they will not have to go back to the store to wage a losing battle over returns and refunds.

Back inside the classroom, we conducted other types of product research like taste tests. When two products are identical in a blind test, you cannot tell the difference, but people swear otherwise. In fact, researchers knew that in a truly blind test, you cannot tell the difference between Coca-Cola and ginger ale, let alone Pepsi. Of course, most of the students could not tell which was which. It was amusing and instructive to compare perceptions with reality. We did similar kinds of experiments on a wide range of products.

At that time, new physiological measures were beginning to be applied to marketing (something like brain research today) and we started to study the subliminal effects of advertising. The new techniques were not based on asking questions, but on measuring physiological responses. For example, consumer researchers measured pupil dilation as an indication that interest or attention toward the brand or the product. Interestingly, around that time Senator Joe McCarthy, the infamous Communist-hunter, pushed through legislation banning subliminal advertising. Studies were showing the efficacy of these techniques (for instance, in increasing Coke or popcorn sales in theater concession stands), and McCarthy believed the same could be accomplished with political messages—that viewers could be brainwashed.

I was interested in all these new findings and techniques. We were able to demonstrate that there really is some cognition below conscious perception. It was way out there, interesting and nonintuitive stuff, and the students loved it! I loved it too—enough to publish a paper with these and other new findings.

Finalizing the Howard–Sheth Theory

My priority upon returning to Columbia was to finish working on the Howard–Sheth theory. This was especially critical for me, since I was on tenure track and the clock was ticking.

Howard lived in Scarsdale, a suburb north of New York City. We talked regularly on the phone and I went to Scarsdale about once a month to work with him. Howard was always very gracious, as was his wife, Lynn. I was part of their family. Howard's best qualities were that he was a good learner and a good listener. He did not mind opinions that were contrary to his.

For example, I am a believer in logic rather than evidence. The numbers can lie and the evidence can be twisted, so my view is that theory is mightier than evidence. In my belief system, power lies in mathematics and the logic that drives mathematics. But since he was trained as an empirical economist, Howard had his own beliefs. He and I argued endlessly. Our argument about "confidence" as a construct in the Howard–Sheth theory is a good example. Confidence, as in "consumer confidence," is a key concept among economists so naturally, Howard wanted to use it as a construct in the Howard–Sheth theory. I disagreed. Learning produces confidence, especially if it is based on experience. The more experienced I am, the more confident I am about what I am buying. So my position was that "confidence" was a redundant construct. We ended up publishing the book with a footnote saying that the two authors remain in disagreement about the inclusion of "confidence" as a separate construct.

Another disagreement between us had to do with semantics. Howard always preceded the word "theory" with "the." He wanted to call our theory the "theory of buyer behavior." Since it was just one out of many perspectives, I felt we should call it a "theory of buyer behavior." However, Howard's preference prevailed. Later, we occasionally heard comments about the arrogance of authors who would title their theory as if it were the only theory. The one advantage to co-authorship is that you can always put the blame on the other author.

While Howard and I were completing the book, we worked on consumer research at GE. GE had two distinguished people researching buyer behavior: Nelson Foote, an expert on household decision-making, and Robert Pratt, who was recruited from the University of Michigan, where Austrian economist George Katona was founder and director of the Institute of Social Research (ISR). Katona believed in asking people their purchase intentions as a way of forecasting economic trends. If you tell me that you intend to buy an automobile, or a refrigerator, or a washing machine within three or six months, you are giving me a "leading indicator" as to where the economy is headed. This practice was contrary to the thinking of Nobel Prize winner Paul Samuelson, who warned against asking consumers such questions or collecting that kind of consumer information. According to Samuelson, consumer responses to these questions were too subjective. Since consumers are famous for changing their minds, Samuelson felt that the only meaningful measure of economic trends, was "revealed preference" based on what consumers actually do, versus what they intend to do.

Key Columbia Colleagues

In addition to the old friends and colleagues with whom I was reunited upon my return, there were some new colleagues at Columbia who would become part of my journey. One was former Harvard student Warren Keegan, who came to teach international marketing, and with whom I became close friends. Another was Dilip Mehta, a Harvard Ph.D. who had been hired by MIT, but, like me, left MIT to come to Columbia. Mehta eventually left Columbia to go to Georgia State. We would cross paths again in the 1970s. And there was Donald Lehmann, who would become a very well-known marketing scholar and a longtime faculty member at Columbia.

I became good friends with Robert Pratt, who was my age, and I also became well-acquainted with the ideas he brought from Michigan. Foote and Pratt had funded a longitudinal panel of 3,000 households—consumers they surveyed every three months on their buying intentions. GE was in so many businesses—appliances, light bulbs, aircraft engines, medical instruments, plastics and other industrial materials—that its leaders were keenly interested in economic trends. I applied Leo Goldman's "latent class analysis" to GE's data to forecast the sequence and probability of purchasing major appliances, for example. If a consumer buys a washing machine, does she follow up with the purchase of the dryer or does she next buy a refrigerator?

Another key person was Muzafer Sherif, the well-known social psychologist whose work had inspired one of my dissertation ideas. Sherif believed in field studies as a way of understanding how small groups organize and who plays what role. While this was similar to George Homan's work, Sherif's methodology was different. Sherif studied social interactions among children at summer camps. How does a youngster assimilate? Who becomes the leader, and why? He was also very well known for his theory of "assimilation and contrast"—how entities or ideas in the middle end up at one extreme or the other. I had always admired Sherif's work. He shared my office at Columbia for three months one summer.

Fred Webster, who came to Columbia from Stanford, was another young professor who became a good friend. And then there was Abe Schuchman, a specialist in new product marketing, whom I will always associate with a dinner party, which he held at his home. Since I was the only faculty member with an automobile, I agreed to drive my colleagues, Johan Arndt, David Rados, and Donald Morrison to the party. Well, I missed the exit—wrong bridge, wrong suburb. There were no cell phones back in those days to call or search for directions so we were about two hours late for dinner. Schuchman's wife did her best to keep the dinner warm, and of course they were extremely gracious about the mishap. I have seldom been so embarrassed. Like other mishaps however, I gained from the experience. I got to know my colleagues better and formed the beginnings of three exceptional friendships.

Johan Arndt was a Norwegian who came to Columbia after earning his doctorate in marketing from Harvard. He later wrote a fascinating dissertation under Raymond Bauer that focused on the importance of word-of-mouth communication in advertising. He eventually returned to Norway and became an eminent scholar. I would meet him regularly on my travels to Scandinavia. He published several insightful papers and his unfortunate death, at a relatively young age, was a loss to our profession. David Rados also developed an interesting specialty: nonprofit marketing. He eventually wrote a textbook on that subject. Donald Morrison was Bill Massey's student. We attempted to recruit Morrison at MIT. Instead, he decided to join Columbia. After many years, Morrison also returned back to California and we kept in touch mostly at various conferences.

Charles Raymond was a psychologist who joined DuPont's market research laboratory, the best at the time. He eventually came to New York to become president of the Advertising Research Foundation (ARF). At the same time, he was an adjunct professor at Columbia, where we became good friends.

Noteworthy Students

I also had some interesting students at Columbia. Martin Gannon, whose field was organizational behavior, had a special interest in front-line employees, particularly bank tellers, and what happens—in terms of motivation—when they move from the front line into management. He theorized that the tendency is to be initially motivated by financial reward, but that with advancement come the desire for supra-monetary reward—such as recognition, work-life balance, and the like. In this regard, Gannon's work was a further elaboration of McGregor's "Theory Y" and Maslow's need hierarchy. I helped Gannon with his survey research design and served on his thesis committee.

One of our most interesting students was Prakash Sethi. As I mentioned earlier, Sethi was trained at the Delhi School of Economics, the Indian equivalent of the London School of Economics, and had been influenced by its socialist thinking. I believe that Sethi was more passionate about advocacy and activism than traditional marketing, though. He went to Berkeley shortly after graduating (this was in the late 1960s, the heyday of the antiwar protest movement) and soon published a book titled *Up Against the Corporate Wall*. Needless to say, it had little to do with marketing, but was rather about how Kodak was engaged in breaking up unions in Rochester, N.Y. It was actually a piece of investigative reporting, and it generated quite a stir.

Thanks to Howard's entrepreneurship and myriad connections, Sethi's dissertation was unique. Sethi's thesis project had to do with Excedrin, a new analgesic that was going up against the already established Tylenol and Bayer aspirin. We studied the introduction of Excedrin into the Milwaukee market using two kinds of advertising. One group was exposed to the product through "pulse" advertising, where the product is advertised during a set period and then advertising ceases for several weeks; and the other group was exposed via the same dollar amount allocation to continuous advertising every day for the same number of minutes. Which kind of advertising yields better results? That was the subject of Sethi's dissertation, and I was asked to help him analyze the data.

There was also Brian Campbell, who deserves mention for having done a dissertation which tested some of the propositions of the Howard–Sheth theory. Specifically, he studied "evoked sets," i.e., the relatively few brands that a consumer will actually consider in product categories where multiple brands are available. Our theory held that in such huge categories as detergent and toothpaste, the individual consumer will actually consider only a few brands; she will probably have one she usually buys, along with a couple of others as suitable substitutes. Brian's dissertation was one of the first scientific proofs of our theory of evoked sets. Unfortunately, I do not think he published an academic paper from his thesis.

I also had a few noteworthy foreign students. One was Paul Pellemans from Belgium, who came to Columbia to do his dissertation on how attitudes predict behavior and used our Buyer Behavior Project as his database. He returned to Antwerp and will later factor into my story. Also, Columbia was the place for top Israeli doctoral students, and I had the privilege of working with a few: Michael Perry, his brother Arnon Perry, and Schlomo Lampert.

My workload at Columbia matched my workload at MIT: I was working on the Buyer Behavior Project, pursuing my scholarship, and teaching my classes. Not long after I returned to New York, the IIM in Kolkata contacted me. There was a new Director of the Institute recruited from the industry rather than from the government; his name was Krishna Mohan and he was the chief marketing officer at Hindustan Unilever. He came to New York to lure me to Kolkata as a visiting professor—and it worked. I was not in a position to ask for a sabbatical, but at Columbia, it was possible to earn a leave of absence by teaching extra classes in advance. So I taught three classes per semester for two semesters and earned a semester off. I planned to go Kolkata in January 1968, which would also give me the summer off before returning to Columbia.

Returning to India

When we returned to New York, Madhu and I decided to live outside the city. Our first move was to the other side of the George Washington Bridge to a small town called Leonia, next to the better-known suburb of Fort Lee. Here, our little family would expand to include our son Rajen, who was born in Englewood Hospital on February 22, 1967.

Leonia was a well-established suburb with tradition. There were no movie theaters and bars were not allowed. It was a conservative Italian community, well-protected against all the vices of the modern world, and not particularly well-informed about that world either. We rented from an Italian family, and when my wife mentioned to our landlord's wife that we were Indian, the woman thought we were Native Americans—like the Indians she had seen on television. She wondered why I was not wearing a feather in my hair and war paint on my face. Madhu told her about the country of India and also cleared up the misconception that I was a doctor because I had Ph.D. versus an MD.

Returning to India at the end of December 1967 was welcomed because it offered an escape from the harsh New York winter and the opportunity to reconnect with both our culture and our family.

Neither of us had been back to India since coming to the United States seven years earlier so we were looking forward to the homecoming. If all went well, we might remain in India for good. After all, it was clear that the IIM would like to have me as a permanent faculty member.

Financially and otherwise, the trip was a huge undertaking. Even though I had some money set aside for the trip, there were other constraints. My second eldest sister's husband died unexpectedly, leaving her widowed at a young age with two small children to support. As a relatively forward-thinking family, we wanted her to become self-supporting, rather than simply count on the generosity of her in-laws. My eldest sister's husband, who ran an import business in Mumbai, suggested opening a retail store in the suburbs where she could be the store owner or manager. That made sense, and I was asked to provide funding for the store.

I was still paying off my debts and, with a growing family, we had more financial needs. Fortunately, credit cards had begun to appear on the scene and were being heavily promoted. I had one, so I borrowed money against it and sent it to my sister. This enabled me to spend the money I had set aside specifically for the trip to India: travel, gifts for everyone back home (an inviolable tradition), and several cases of the baby food for Rajen, which would not be available in India.

With what seemed like all our worldly possessions, we departed for India in December 1967. As soon as we arrived, I was asked to teach a one-week seminar to a class of senior executives in the beautiful resort town of Simla, in the foothills of the Himalaya Mountains. The family went with me, and we were in a beautiful lodge for nine days. The class, it consisted of some 20 senior executives, all of whom thought I reminded them of their son. I counteracted their perception of me by learning everything about their companies beforehand, and then counterbalance the age difference with knowledge of where their businesses were headed and strategies they needed to implement.

Teaching in Kolkata

Because of the Naxalite influence, IIM was a campus teeming with social activism. Even though it was not a particularly pro-business environment, the exchange was still intellectually stimulating. One of the people who used to visit the campus was Amartya Sen, who eventually won the Nobel Prize in economics. Because of the politics that prevailed on campus, Krishna Mohan had to take some precautions about my appointment. He was afraid (perhaps rightly so) that I might be the target of some resentment if my Indian colleagues realized I was paid in U.S. dollars funded by the Ford Foundation. He asked me not to stay in the downtown area where American visiting faculty lived and installed me in Barrackpur, a military compound. I was the sole resident of a large palace-like bungalow that had been given to the Institute; it was a huge house where I lived alone (since Madhu and the children had gone to our hometown, Chennai, to live with her parents). My "cover" was that of visiting faculty member, being paid in Indian salary, and that I had been given this bungalow as part of my housing allowance.

I did not have a car so I was picked up each day by another faculty member and taken to the campus. Since I was helpless when it came to domestic chores like cooking, cleaning, and laundry, I employed a personal assistant, Subhan, who took excellent care of me. Looking back, I suppose I was quite spoiled by it all. This pampered life was epitomized by the fact that when it was time for a haircut, the barber would come to me in the bungalow!

On the other hand, I had not worked harder than I did during those six months. I have always worked hard, but the Institute stretched me to do more. In addition to my teaching load of more than 70 students in each class (compared to 30 students at Columbia University), I faced the formidable task of completely redesigning the marketing curriculum, an assignment for which my experiences at MIT and Columbia helped. We added the most up-to-date courses from the American curriculum, courses like market research and product management, and brought the program up to a high standard. This overhaul was badly needed, so the redesign was well received.

Major Research Projects

Historically, Kolkata had been India's most popular city for corporate headquarters. It had been the Eastern capital of the British Empire, and consequently all the biggest and best British companies were there, including Imperial Tobacco Company (now ITC), which wanted to conduct a research study on cigarettes and brand positioning. This was the first of three projects I completed. We used perceptual mapping derived from multidimensional scaling to study how consumers perceive different brands of cigarettes. For example, one dimension was image, or price–quality relationship and the second dimension was mild versus harsh cigarettes. We plotted all the brands based on how similar or different they were perceived by consumers. This told us where too many brands were already clustered with consumers, presuming no difference and where the gaps were, representing an opportunity to introduce a new brand.

A second project, a joint study conducted by IIM along with the engineering consulting company Dastur & Co., was even more far-reaching. India had invested heavily in developing a domestic machine tool industry, led by Hindustan Machine Tools (HMT), a government enterprise. There was also a major export initiative and the big producers (HMT, Kirloskar) wanted to know how Indian machine tools were perceived abroad, especially in Europe. Could a nation known primarily for snake charmers and spicy food compete globally in the machine tool industry? What kind of image would machine tools from India have, and, if it was negative, how could the image be changed? My task was to interview all of the Indian machine tool manufacturers about their product lines, and then, on my way back to the United States in June 1968, I stopped in several European cities to talk to prospective customers and distributors. Ultimately, we published a report for the government that presented our recommendations on how to promote heavy engineering products made in India.

I recall being in Stockholm, where my work on the project had gone well and where I had been generously hosted by the Indian Embassy. I also met Professor Folke Olander through Robert Pratt at the University of Michigan. He had returned to Scandinavia as a professor of economic psychology. I was supposed to fly from Stockholm to Paris, but this was 1968 and a huge anti-Charles De Gaulle student protest was raging. My flight was diverted and landed in Brussels. It was a madhouse anyway, but my problem was compounded by the fact that I had an Indian passport—which meant that I also needed a visa to get into and out of every country in Europe except England (or the British Commonwealth).

Since Belgium had not been on my itinerary, I had no visa to get out. "What do I do now?" I wondered. I was told that I could go to England, and the airline immediately rerouted my baggage. But the Belgian authorities would not let me out of the airport without a visa. It was by chance that I was able to get a room in the airport Ramada Inn while the mess got sorted out. I was there for two days—which was all right, except that, without my luggage, I had no clean underwear. Indians are very fussy about these things.

When I arrived in London, I visited the Alfred Herbert Co., one of the largest machine tool distributors in the world. It was in Coventry, an industrial town with an automotive and aerospace focus. I got the royal treatment with a luxurious room in a guest house that had oak beams rumored to be more than a thousand years old. The food and accommodations were first-class, but of course my hosts had no idea I was a vegetarian. Their world-class chef served up extraordinary salmon dish—a specialty, for VIPs only—and, of course, I had to eat it. It was a fascinating experience as I had never tasted fish before.

The third big project, which was really under the auspices of MIT and the Ford Foundation, involved population control. India, like China, had come to view population growth as a liability, and the government wanted to initiate a large-scale birth control campaign. MIT, with funding from the Ford Foundation, was researching the problem, and I worked with MIT professor Henry Claycamp. The data were fascinating. In 1914, India's birth rate was 4.1 children per woman—both in metro and in rural areas. Fifty years later, the statistics had changed dramatically: While the birth rate had dropped dramatically in urban areas, it had remained the same in rural India. This meant that population control was not a metropolitan problem. No doubt factors like education, lack of housing space, and high cost of living were already making metro residents conscious of birth control, so we needed to assess what was going on in the countryside.

We found two prevailing ideas. First was the belief on the part of the Indian farmer that the birth of a child was God's blessings, an act of God. How could we change this belief? How could we convince these farmers, that, in fact, whether or not to have children was a decision that lay entirely in their hands? I should mention that, at that time, birth control techniques were male targeted. The pill was not allowed, nor was tubal ligation, as a matter of government policy and cultural beliefs. That meant that our job was, first, to disseminate on transistor radio (since there was no electricity) the message that the farmers could take control of this issue; and, second, assist them by distributing condoms.

Distribution was an interesting marketing challenge. At that time, the government was still "nonaligned" and very much anticolonial in sentiment. The cold war was going strong, and multinationals were disinvesting. There was a handful though, like Hindustan Lever, ITC, and Brookbond Tea, that had managed to penetrate into the most remote parts of the country. Coca-Cola had entered the Indian market and was successful in rural distribution. Brookbond Tea had half a million agents in the country, walking or on bicycles, going door-to-door selling loose tea. ITC also had a good distribution system, since tea and cigarettes were ubiquitous products. Our solution was to encourage the multinationals to carry condoms along with their products as part of their corporate social responsibility and deliver the supply to neighborhood clinics or government depots in the rural villages.

Trying to change the mindset of these farmers was quite a challenge especially given cultural norms about being blessed by God if you produce eight or nine children.

In advanced economies with more educated women, the tendency to have a large family declines. The prevailing belief system was that the more women got educated, the less their desire to have large families, and the fewer children they produce. In India, of course, the situation was still very different, so I worked on a marketing plan and a distribution strategy to bring birth control to the Indian countryside.

The population control project was not limited to rural areas. The work went on in the cities too, but rather than condoms, the favored technique was the vasectomy. In Kolkata, for example, which had been the jute capital under British rule and which remained an industrial hub, medical vans pulled up to jute mills and factories, and the doctors and their assistants performed up to 100 vasectomies daily! Workers were offered some sort of incentive (often a transistor radio, which was hugely popular since it required no electricity); then, once they had undergone the procedure, they were given a few hours rest and returned to work the same day.

Returning to Columbia

It was a busy six-month period. When I had a minute to spare, I visited Chennai where Madhu and the children were staying. The days flew by. Before I knew it, it was time to return to America. After the detour through Europe, I arrived back in New York in time for the fall semester of 1968. I was greeted by the massive student uprising erupting on campuses across the country to protest the Vietnam War. Columbia was a hotbed of this antiwar fervor; in fact, the Students for a Democratic Society (the infamous SDS) took over Uris Hall. They proclaimed—with calculated irony—that the best place from which to manage their protest was the business school. This was where I worked, so I got an up-close look at this great "happening." I was *not* thrilled. I came from a generation where students were taught to revere their teachers and the academic institution.

Eventually, my attention turned to more mundane matters—like finding a parking place. When I returned to Columbia, I was making about $13,000 a year—pretty good money in those days. A car cost about $2,500 dollars, which I could afford, but I could not afford to park it in the city. A permit in a city garage would have cost something like $50 a month, and Columbia did not provide parking. We were all at the mercy of street parking, which entailed being mindful of the city's street-cleaning schedule, which, near the university, was something like 11:00 a.m. to 1:00 p.m. every day on alternate sides of the streets. I had afternoon classes so by 1:00 p.m. many of us would be circling like buzzards, waiting for the street cleaners to be gone.

Finding street parking was some very interesting sociology. We did not know each other personally, but recognized each other's cars, and did not try to compete for each other's spaces. It was like classroom seating, where you take a seat the first day and then stick to it. I would get there a little before 1:00, begin circling and waiting for my space to open up, then park and dash into my building. I would be in my office by 1:15 and in class by 1:30.

Since I arrived to school in the afternoon, I would stay late, and my reverse commute would be relatively traffic-free. My commute was to and from Oakland, N.J., a small lakeside community of some 80 families to which Madhu and I had decided to move when we came back to Columbia from India. It was a pretty long drive but when we visited Howard at his lake home in New Hampshire, we found the environment very appealing. Plus, Madhu loves water. Because of that, we moved into a duplex on the New Jersey lake. It was a wonderful place for the children, and it provided us the opportunity to acquire our first pet—a cat, which lived with us for 18 years. As we strolled around the neighborhood, the cat would walk beside us like a dog. I even bought a rowboat, and during long summer evenings I took the children (and the cat) out on the lake to paddle around saying hello to our neighbors on the shore.

Though I recall those evenings with pleasure, I must say that my situation at Columbia was not perfect for a variety of reasons. For one thing, despite the fact that by now I had begun to publish quite a lot and was definitely on the radar a rising young scholar, many continued to perceive me as John Howard's assistant. I had gone to MIT, in part, to break away from that perception, but when I returned to Columbia, I realized that the perception was still in effect alive. At the same time, other universities were trying to recruit me (Harvard had tried while I was at MIT), and now, back at Columbia, I was considering other possibilities.

A New Beginning

One of the first things I did after returning to Columbia from MIT was to organize a national conference on consumer behavior, or "buyer behavior" as we were calling it then. All the "young Turks" in the field came to present their papers, which I subsequently collected into an edited book called *Models of Buyer Behavior*. James Engel at Ohio State had heard about the conference and he visited Columbia to meet with John Howard and learn more about the Columbia Buyer Behavior Project.

Engel was a rising star, building a strong department in consumer behavior at Ohio State, and he hoped I would join his team. I declined this invitation, but the story ends with an ironic twist. Engel and his two young colleagues (David Kollat and Roger Blackwell) went on to write a textbook on consumer behavior which became the standard work. The fact is that Howard and I were supposed to write a textbook to accompany our theory book, but we never got around to it—a missed opportunity.

At any rate, though I did not accept Engel's invitation, I was beginning to wonder if my future lay at Columbia. I was chafing under this persistent misapprehension that I worked for Howard, and I was also getting frustrated in my attempt to be promoted to associate professor. True, I was hurrying the system. I was supposed to be in rank for six years before being promoted, but I only had four (including the one at MIT). Nevertheless, as I was preparing to leave for my visit to India, I let it be known that I wanted to be promoted. When I returned, Columbia said no to going up for early promotion and tenure ("We love you, but this is premature," was the response). I had some support from senior faculty like Howard and Martin Starr, the editor of *Management Science*, and my teaching evaluations were superior, but the school would not bend the rules and allow an early promotion.

In addition to this disappointment, other factors began to weigh on me—like the cost of living in and around New York, the long commute, and most important, the environment in which my children were growing up in. Madhu had also begun to have misgivings. We were immigrants, and the neighborhood had no other Indians. Reshma was almost 6 years old, and we were beginning to worry about the experience our children, as minorities, would have in a suburban public school system. The school she would have gone to in Oakland seemed to be deteriorating and of poor quality, but at the same time, both Madhu and I were advocates of public education. We believed our children needed to go to public schools, where they could learn to coexist with all types of people from various cultures, so we were open to the possibility of moving.

In the end, I decided to accept an offer from the University of Illinois. Going there turned out to be the best thing that ever happened to me.

Farewell to Important Colleagues and Friends

Before departing for the "cornfields," I looked back at—and gave thanks for—the very solid foundation that was developed for my journey. A few of the superb doctoral students I had the privilege of working with, and learning from, at Columbia were a part of that foundation. Mentoring these doctoral students was an important part of my own career. I have already mentioned several of them—Brian Campbell, Martin Gannon, Paul Pellemans, Michael Perry, and Prakash Sethi—so I need only to acknowledge my good fortune in having been able to work with them. The situation was the same with several young scholars (Johan Arndt, Fred Webster, David Rados, Dilip Mehta, and Warren Keegan) who had also joined Columbia in the 1960s.

The senior-most among all the students I worked with was George Day. I was not on George Day's thesis committee but we worked very closely on the Buyer Behavior Project (BBP). George became the Director of the BBP, and his dissertation came out of the BBP—again focusing on attitude-behavior discrepancy or congruence. George used the data collected on Post Instant Breakfast as a new product competing against

Carnation Instant Breakfast, and his thesis was later published as a book in its own right.

Another major component of my experience at Columbia was teaching in consumer behavior, international marketing, and marketing management. My teaching experience at Columbia was enormously valuable.

Being able to organize conferences was a skill that would be important throughout the rest of my career. As I mentioned earlier, I organized a conference right after my return from MIT—on buyer behavior, with the book, *Models of Buyer Behavior*, that grew out of it. The conference was a success.

My years at Columbia proved extremely fertile for my career as a publishing scholar. My first publication, "A Review of Buyer Behavior," came about when I returned to Columbia from MIT. Also, by the time I was preparing to leave Columbia, much of the work I had done with Ven Venkatesan had made its way into print. A couple of our research papers also appeared in a book edited by Johan Arndt; others were included in the proceedings of the AMA's Educator Conferences. But most were published in academic journals like the *Journal of Marketing Research* or the *Journal of Advertising Research*.

At the end of my tenure at Columbia, I had more than 10 publications to my credit and *The Theory of Buyer Behavior* was in print. In this, as in so much else that has shaped my career, I have been incredibly lucky. I had worked hard and was fortunate to be so blessed. I was grateful for my time at Columbia. I give credit to that wonderful institution for nurturing me, for stimulating my intellectual growth, and for fully preparing me for the next step in my journey. Columbia helped me tremendously in my research efforts, and also in my efforts to engage students in research. All these, then, were the building blocks I brought with me to Illinois.

Lure of Illinois

Shortly after my return from India, I had contacted Ledyard Tucker at the University of Illinois. Tucker was an expert in factor analysis. In fact, he had developed a technique called three-mode factor analysis, which allows management of not only a matrix, but of three-dimensional data. I loved his work and I had used his approach both in my dissertation and in the paper published in *JASA*. Indeed, one of the things I found most attractive about Illinois was that a number of brilliant psychometricians—Tucker among them—were on the faculty there. The others included Lloyd Humphreys, Maurice Tatsuoka, and Raymond Cattell—men who were extraordinary in their field, pioneers in psychometrics.

Similarly, since my minor was social psychology and my major was individual and group behavior, I was happy to find that there were several well-known social psychologists at Illinois as well: Charles Osgood, Donald Dulaney, Harry Triandis, Martin Fishbein, and William McGuire. In short, there were a lot of great people in areas I was interested in, especially attitudes and the attitude–behavior relationship. Just as important, these psychologists and psychometricians were receptive to working with business school faculty. They did not frown upon the idea of working with someone, like me, who was in the business school. I met some of them when I interviewed, and they warmly embraced me and my research interests.

The environment in my own field, marketing, was also quite attractive. The business administration department was new—a merger of several smaller departments—and it was actively recruiting young scholars. One scholar they recruited just before my arrival was Joel Cohen, who received his Ph.D. at the University of California, Los Angeles (UCLA) under Harold Kassarjian. Cohen was interested in the behavioral aspects of marketing—as opposed to the managerial aspects—which fit well with what I was interested in. He was steering the Illinois marketing faculty—which had been shaped by such old lions as P.D. Converse, Hicks Huegy, and Fred Jones—away from its traditional economics orientation and into the new behavioral orientation, and he wanted me to join him. Cohen's enthusiasm was infectious, his work was exciting, and he played an important role in luring me to Illinois.

Another important factor that bore on the decision to go to Illinois: Champaign-Urbana was a wonderful college town.

It was exactly what Madhu and I were looking for. It was full of other professors who, like me, believed in public education, and we felt it would be a perfect place for our children. It would be more intellectually liberal, full of people who traveled widely. There would be foreign students and faculty, people of all nationalities, and the educational environment would be stimulating. To cap it all off, living in a college town would mean the end of my long commute.

So everything came together—personally and professionally. And my experience at Illinois, supported by the foundations laid at Columbia and MIT, propelled me forward more than I could have imagined.

LIFE LESSON

Regardless of how many scholarly papers you write, your reputation—in whatever discipline—often rests on having produced thought-provoking books. Some examples are: *The Wealth of Nations* (Adam Smith), *Gone with the Wind* (Margaret Mitchell), *Motivation and Personality* (Abraham Maslow), *Unsafe at Any Speed* (Ralph Nader), and *The Practice of Management: A Study of the Most Important Function in American Society* (Peter Drucker). *Write with fervor, depth, purpose; concepts that will not just impact, but change commerce and culture for the greater good.*

5

ILLINOIS: MY ACADEMIC LIFE

I felt really good about Illinois. I liked the people and felt that they genuinely wanted me to become a part of their community. That is what I told Joe McGuire, dean of the College of Commerce, when I visited the campus for an interview in the fall of 1968. McGuire took me to dinner at the end of the day and asked me what I thought of Illinois.

"I love it," I told him, but then added, "of course, I can't make a decision until Madhu has a chance to come see it." I told him Madhu would have to visit the campus and get a feel for the community. Well, because of my accent, McGuire thought I was saying, "Mother." He didn't say anything, but he must have thought I was single and a "mama's boy." A few weeks later, I returned with Madhu and we had dinner with McGuire. After I introduced Madhu, he asked, "Where is your mother?" Much to McGuire's relieve, I'm sure, I said, "My mother is in India. Why would she be here?"

Once the decision for Illinois was made, Madhu and I opted to build our first home. I was offered the position of associate professor with tenure, and my salary jumped to $18,000. Still, our financial situation was precarious, in part because I was still helping my sister in India. What was I going to do for a down payment for the house? To my surprise, the university wielded such economic clout in Champaign-Urbana that the local bank told me they would loan me the money for the down payment as well as for the mortgage. In April of 1969, we met with a builder, signed a contract, arranged financing, and returned to Columbia. When we moved to Illinois at the end of the summer, our new house was completed, on time, and according to our specifications. I found this to be true about the Midwest culture: What they promise, they deliver.

We built our house near a good public grade school, Yankee Ridge School, to which our children could walk to in just a few minutes. The university campus was also close by, so it was easy for me to come home for lunch, which I preferred because of my vegetarian diet. So the family had breakfast together and then when the children walked home from school for lunch, I would be there also. One day Reshma's curiosity finally got the best of her. She said, "Dad, you are always home. Why aren't you working?"

In virtually every way, University of Illinois was quite different from Columbia. While Columbia is private, Illinois is among the top 10 state universities in the nation. In graduate education, Illinois' academic departmental structure was also different. Before my arrival, Illinois had a traditional Germanic academic structure. Each discipline had its own department, and the head of the department would typically be an iconic professor, whose students followed in his footsteps after earning their degrees. Illinois had recently restructured the College of Commerce and several of the business-related disciplines—marketing, organizational management, business law, etc.—were consolidated into the business administration department, which was my department.

Illinois was in transition—you might say, rising from the ashes—but I had wonderful colleagues. I already mentioned Joel Cohen. Cohen was really the one spearheading my recruitment along with a couple of UCLA students he had lured to Illinois for their doctorates (Ray Suh and Terry Vavra). The department also had a distinguished seasoned faculty like P.D. Converse, in whose name a major AMA award was endowed, Fred Jones and Hicks Huegy. I had enormous respect for these scholars, though their work in agricultural marketing reflected both their era and Illinois' location in the "cornfields." They were retiring. The senior faculty were represented by the economist Robert Ferber, who was also head of Survey Research Laboratory, an opinion research center anchored to surveys; Seymour Sudman, an expert on sampling and questionnaire design; Richard Hill in industrial marketing; and David Gardner in marketing theory. At Columbia, my attempts to bridge the chasm between psychology and marketing were problematic so it was good to know that would not be the case at Illinois. The psychometricians and social psychologists welcomed me warmly and I felt comfortable being at Illinois.

The Accidental Administrator

It was never my intention to be an academic administrator, but the circumstances warranted it.

At Illinois, a department head could not be replaced by the dean. Deans ran the undergraduate programs, whereas departments reported directly to the dean of the Graduate College, under the direction of the vice chancellor for research. When I arrived at Illinois, the department was led by an acting department head, Richard Evans. I did not know anything about Evans, but I was about to find out.

As it happened, a few months after my arrival at Illinois, William Wells and I organized a conference on multivariate statistics at the University of Chicago. This was a fast-growing area in the marketing discipline, and was a special interest of mine. I took two of my senior colleagues with me: Robert Ferber and Seymour Sudman. I knew that a top Ph.D. student from Wharton, Vithala Rao, was planning to attend and was interested in a faculty position at Illinois, so I made arrangements for the three of us to interview him. Rao's professor was Paul Green, one of Wharton's finest, and it seemed quite likely that Rao would earn a reputation in multivariate statistics and especially in multidimensional scaling and conjoint analysis. The interview was a success. Both Ferber and Sudman liked Rao, and I was excited about pitching this bright young prospect to Dick Evans.

Evans, by the way, was a top operations research scholar who had come from Case Western Reserve the year earlier. I told Evans about Rao and suggested that Rao be brought here for an interview. Evans glanced at the résumé and said, "I see he has worked for Russ Ackoff." It turned out that Russ Ackoff had taken the entire department of operations research from Case Western to Wharton—the entire department, that is, except for Dick Evans. Evans, instead, came to Illinois. He had not forgotten or forgiven. The fact that this young man had worked for Ackoff was all Evans needed to know. Hiring him was out of the question. Evans would not listen to anything I had to say. So we lost Rao to Cornell, where he became a world renowned marketing scholar.

It turned out that everybody was unhappy with Evans anyway and not hiring Rao was the last straw. Soon after, the department faculty decided to replace Evans, and three names emerged as candidates for interim department head. One was Robert Ferber, who had been instrumental in the restructuring of the college a few years earlier. He would have been the best choice, but he declined. As director of Survey Research Laboratory (SRL), he commuted to another SRL office in Chicago weekly. Then there was Norton Bedford, a well-respected accounting professor. Although Bedford taught courses in the MBA program housed in our department, accounting itself was a separate department, not part of business administration. Because our faculty did not want a head from another department, Bedford was not offered the job. I was the third candidate, and I said yes primarily to get Dick Evans out.

My first task as an administrator was to straighten out the mess that remained from the departmental consolidation of multiple disciplines and degrees into one business administration department. The other task was to streamline the workings of the five disciplines and make them function as one. In all, something like 18 graduate degrees—master's and doctorate—were now being offered by the department, and I had to rationalize them. I spent an enormous amount of time looking through old file boxes, reading through hundreds of documents, trying to understand the histories of all these departments and degrees. Mind you, this was in the days before computers so the latter was no easy task. Fortunately, the department had an outstanding administrative assistant, Connie Shaw, who had as many as 10 assistants working under her. This capable team was a tremendous help.

Though perhaps unspoken, the larger goal was to make the business administration department respected within the College of Commerce. It was widely accepted that the accounting and finance departments were the leaders, with strong research reputations and lots of clout, while the business administration department was chaotic. We had some good faculty members, especially in marketing, and I took those positives and went to work on our internal reputation. It required internal marketing, and providing thought leadership at the College of Commerce level.

Shaping a new long-term strategy, the faculty collectively decided to focus on marketing and organizational behavior with an emphasis on behavioral sciences. Rather than a number-based economic perspective, we shifted to a more behavioral, psychological perspective. That is, we wanted to make the psychology of consumers the focus of marketing, and everybody rallied behind this new direction. It helped that we had a great psychology department ready to support us.

We did the same thing in management. The traditional approach had been manufacturing oriented, with a heavy emphasis on production and personnel management, still under the influence of Frederick Taylor's theory of scientific management (Theory X). We moved beyond that paradigm to focus on the psychology of organizations, and of the individuals working in them. What are their motivations? Why do they join an organization? Why do they leave? How should they be rewarded, motivated or kept from leaving? Again, we were watching and abetting the emergence of Theory Y. Basically, we decided to change the notion of management into organizational behavior.

Recruiting for Our "Field of Dreams"

In addition to the new directives, my second job—and really the most important one—was to recruit new young faculty. It was a challenge, but an enormously satisfying task. I believe my most meaningful accomplishment during that short administrative career was to motivate many wonderful young people to come to Illinois. Illinois was famous for engineering and agriculture sciences, respected in some branches of the social and physical sciences, and had once been strong in economics, but its reputation in marketing and management had weakened over time. We all hoped that new directions, ideas, and people would change that. It was a "field of dreams"—if you build it, they will come.

To attract young talent especially from the East and West Coasts, I flew out to Berkeley, Stanford, and UCLA, and just walked in and said, "I'm here to recruit your doctoral students for faculty positions." They would give me a room to set up shop, and the Ph.D. students came to talk and listen to our behavioral focus and alignment with the psychology department. "Come to create the excitement," I would tell them, and proceed to rave about the university and Champaign-Urbana. Since I was genuinely passionate about the strong new department we were building and the new directions we were heading, I was successful. I was able to recruit more than a dozen bright young minds of which (at least) 10 are now world-class scholars in quantitative sciences, organizational behavior, and marketing.

For example, there was Alvin Roth from Stanford, a game theorist and now a professor at Harvard. At a very young age, he discovered a flaw in the mathematical formulas used in the "Theory of Games and Economic Behavior" by Jon von Neumann and Oskar Morgenstern. He was so impressive that Kenneth Arrow, a Nobel Prize winner in economics, wrote letters on his behalf. I persuaded him to come to Illinois and we rewarded him appropriately. I have always believed that if somebody is talented, they should be promoted when relevant versus when they are up for tenure. We promoted Roth in less than four years to associate professor with tenure, then less than three years after to full rank. So by the age of 29 or 30, he was a full professor. I was immensely pleased that Roth was awarded the Nobel Prize in Economics in 2013.

In organizational behavior, I encouraged Jeffrey Pfeffer from Stanford to come to Illinois. He's now back at Stanford and a giant in the field. At the time, Pfeffer was married and his wife wanted to get a law degree. I explained the situation to our law school dean. While I did not beg for favors, I did ask him to consider her record. "If she meets your admission standards," I said, "and you're able to take her, it will help me out." She was admitted and Pfeffer joined us.

Then there was Gerald Salancik, a Lithuanian-American with a Ph.D. from Yale, where he was a research assistant for Charlie Raymond, a colleague with whom I was doing some consulting work in New York. I liked Salancik and encouraged him to come to Illinois. It helped that he was originally from Chicago, where there is a strong Lithuanian community, so for him it was basically a homecoming.

Joining us in marketing was Peter Wright, a brilliant young scholar we recruited from Penn State. We also recruited Russell Belk from Minnesota where I had met him as a doctoral student. He was working on three-mode factor analysis, which I was interested in. I called him up and was able to convince him to join our expanding team in Illinois.

We also recruited Johnny Johansson, a Swede, from Berkeley, where he had studied under a Nobel Prize winner in economics. I made an offer to him even before the AMA interviews and he accepted the offer. We also recruited Frederick Winter from Purdue, who eventually took the administrative route and ended up department head. He subsequently became the dean at the University of Buffalo and then at the University of Pittsburgh.

That is how it went, and all these great people simply turned the place around. Illinois was on fire; full of energy and an extremely exciting place to be. Most of all, Illinois is truly an academic community. There is no class distinction—either by discipline or by rank. Professors in other disciplines are not just your colleagues but also your neighbors. They go to the same church; their kids sleep over with yours. So the typical discipline-based bias (which often works against business and marketing faculty) was nonexistent.

Also, the top administrative officers—president, chancellor, vice chancellor—all lived in the same neighborhood as the faculty. Each fall, I threw a big party at my house to welcome new faculty and invite department heads from other disciplines, deans of other colleges, and the vice chancellor. Everybody would attend. Imagine a brand new recruit sitting at a party talking to the vice chancellor. At most institutes, that just does not happen.

Because we were not constrained by rank, we could avail ourselves of a myriad of wonderful learning experiences. If one of our young faculty members was teaching a doctoral seminar in his field, the rest of us would sit in his class to learn.

The Unconventional Approach Pays Off

The environment at Illinois was unconventional in other ways. For example, some of the faculty we were trying to hire were psychologists whom we wanted to bring into our disciplines— marketing and organizational behavior. Bobby Calder, from the University of North Carolina, was a specialist in small group theory. I wanted to recruit him, but I also believed in maintaining high academic standards, so I went to the head of our psychology department, Morton Weir, to get his faculty's assessment and also to motivate Calder to come to Illinois. Needless to say, this was unheard of—for a business professor, in particular, to go to an academic department head and say, in effect, "I want my faculty member to be judged by your faculty. Would you hire this person in your discipline?"

That turned out to be an important event in my administrative career. Weir liked that I had asked psychology department faculty to interview and assess prospective faculty members in business administration. So, when he became the vice chancellor, he pulled me up into university policy by appointing me to the Graduate College Executive Committee. This was important not so much for me, but for the business faculty in general, which previously had little voice in university policy matters. Illinois' College of Commerce continued to be represented at the university level by economists, but Weir helped change that by getting me into university policy-making on a number of different committees, which focused on cross-disciplinary courses and research programs.

I also served for nine years on the Promotion and Tenure Committee at the university level. Now that was a job. The applicant's dossier could be no more than 50 pages, but there would often be well over 100 of them—all of which would arrive during two weeks in December. I remember receiving stacks of paper, three to four feet high, and all would have to be reviewed by the end of December.

But this work was particularly important, and while on the Promotion and Tenure Committee, I suggested a couple of much-needed innovations. We used to get cases from two areas which, in my opinion, were operating without regard to strict academic standards. One was the College of Agriculture's extension service. These faculty typically had master's degrees, and their work was in the field, advising the farmers. They had no research publications, and my view was that you should not advance up the tenure-track academic ladder without producing strong publications. The other was library science. Again, the terminal degree was the master's, and graduates would become librarians. But with that position, at Illinois, would also come the rank of assistant professor and the possibility of being promoted on up without publications.

This concern led us to create a new category of long-term employment—without tenure—and we called it "academic professional." These faculty were given three-year contracts, at the end of which they would be evaluated on performance, but not on research. So faculty in these two fields (there were others, but these were the largest) decided which track they wanted to advance on—the "academic professional" track or the traditional tenure track. The academic professionals could be promoted up the ranks—even up to full professor (in other schools they are sometimes called "professors of practice" or "clinical professors"), but they could not be tenured. The new system worked well.

On the other side of the "academic standards" coin, I also became an advocate of the position that scholarship alone should not be the arbiter of a faculty member's ultimate fate. It was my opinion that no tenured faculty member should retire as an associate professor, so in my work on the Promotion and Tenure Committee, I championed another new track—based on length of service. My thinking was that we had a group of people—presumably good people, who have always loved the campus, always served and mentored the students, and always stood ready to do more. They were not publishing after getting tenure. We came up with the idea that 25 years after tenure, these people should be eligible to apply for full professor on the length of service criterion. Promotion was not guaranteed, but neither would it be based on publications. Tenured associate professors had an opportunity to show what else they had contributed toward the university's excellence (e.g., exceptional service, foreign assignments, fundraising, administrative leadership), and to be rewarded for it. It proved to be hugely popular and graceful way to honor those who had given their lives to the university. Often the promotion would take place shortly before retirement, so the retiree could carry the title of full professor into emeritus status.

Sensitivity to such an issue was a result of my having come from a tradition of respect for the experience and wisdom of the elders. I was very green, still in my early thirties, and my heritage served me well in this respect. Remember, we are talking about the late 1960s and early 1970s, the era when the "older generation" was treated with suspicion and contempt. I saw this absurd attitude affecting even the academic community where the young hotshots ridiculed "old geezers." I saw iconic scholars: Fred Jones, P.D. Converse, Hicks Huegy, and Paul Dauten being disregarded. Many of these older luminaries came to the ends of their careers embittered by this turn of events. They had spent their lives at Illinois, and were now being alienated and discarded. I blamed the "publish or perish" culture for failing to pay these faculty the respect they deserved.

Dauten, for example, was not only a full professor, but cofounder of the Academy of Management, yet he was kept at a salary of $18,000 indefinitely, even when our starting salaries for assistant professors had reached that level. I wanted him to retire gracefully. He knew that I respected him. Respect is shown with your eyes and body language, not just your words. Dauten saw that—as did the others of his generation. We made sure to honor them for their service, legacy, and their contributions. Dauten's wife, Gloria, had made a lot of money as a landlord of student apartments, so money was not what mattered to him. It was the respect and I remember him breaking down in a meeting because he was so moved by what we were trying to do for him.

Yet another interesting problem required sorting out at the university level. Illinois was one of the leaders in the emerging science of mainframe computing, and our computer science department was ranked first in the nation. The money poured in from military contracts and the National Science Foundation (NSF) grants, and with special nurturing from the vice chancellor for research, the discipline grew. The problem was that it emerged as a separate academic unit and while it offered undergraduate and master's degrees, it never reported to any college. For example, the computer science faculty came before our Promotion and Tenure Committee without having gone through any departmental review. Clearly, the process was unfair. The baby had become a big boy—now what to do?

David Lazarus, a physics professor, and I were given the task of figuring out what to do with the computer science department. It had to be housed somewhere—the question was where. The math department was one possibility, which made sense since much of computer science is math-based. The other possibility, electrical engineering, also made sense because that is where the hardware exists. The head of computer science was my neighbor, and I knew he would be willing to listen. He also knew that the handwriting was on the wall. He was just looking for what would be best for computer science. He wanted to preserve his legacy.

So Lazarus and I made what I believe was an historic call: We decided to have the hardware and software come together. The hardware scholars in electrical engineering knew very little about software, and the software scholars knew very little about the hardware. Yet, as Lazarus and I saw it, the world was all about convergence, about coming together, and we thought it best to have the two disciplines learning from each other. The only way to accomplish this was to house computer science in the electrical engineering department and to rename it. It was truly a defining moment, one that led to innovation. The World Wide Web, the first search engine, chipsets (that is, the embedding of software into chips)—all these things came from the integration of software and hardware. Three campuses had been vying for the top position in electronic engineering: MIT, Stanford, and Illinois. We took some pride in the fact that our solution to the "computer science department" problem was quickly embraced by MIT.

Weir, who was a terrific change agent, put me on yet another mold-breaking committee, one whose task was to create a system through which *every* administrator would be evaluated every five years. Heretofore, in the traditional Germanic system, the department heads could theoretically serve for life. To remove a department head required a faculty revolt, in writing, signed by a super majority, which went not to the dean but directly to the vice chancellor. So we created a committee, SCOPE (Study Committee on Peer Evaluation) and a process, Committee on Peer Evaluation (COPE) to formally evaluate all administrators, from department heads to the vice chancellor. This was a key transformation, and the process is still in place today.

Meanwhile, an interesting development was taking place at the student level. During the early seventies, the U.S. economy was in a recession. There were no jobs for the university's liberal arts graduates, so students who otherwise might have majored in history or English began applying to business schools. We had limited seats, so our admissions standards for the undergraduate programs suddenly skyrocketed. In fact, we became the toughest college to get into based on SAT or ACT scores and high school GPA. Only the chemical engineering department from which such luminaries as Jack Welch (General Electric) and George Fisher (Motorola and Kodak) had graduated was up there with us. Suddenly, we were setting the standard, a radical shock within the university. It was a fun part of my job to watch those standards rise and then maintain them. Today, the College of Commerce continues to receive very good undergraduate students, which makes teaching a joy!

Having performed admirably as vice chancellor (or chief academic officer), Weir had hoped to move up to chancellor. When that did not happen, he left Illinois to take the helm of Boys' Town, a major nongovernment organization. John Cribbett, a law professor, was asked to be the acting chancellor. That meant Weir's position was vacant, and four "young Turks" were finalists to become the new vice chancellor. I was one of them; Rita Simon in sociology was another, and there were two others. That was the only job in administration to which I would have said, "Yes, I will do it." I did not want to be a dean, nor did I want to be permanent head of my own department. But in this position, I believed I could make a difference. The position had impact campus wide, and I was already so involved across disciplines. It would have meant personal sacrifice—less research, less publishing, less teaching—but I thought it would be worth it.

It turned out that none of us was chosen. When John Cribbett became chancellor, he called each of us individually into his office and explained his decision. "I have only two or three years left," he said, "and I want somebody who I have worked with before." He hired Ned Goldwasser, a physics professor, who had been running Fermi Nuclear Laboratory in Chicago which was affiliated with the University of Illinois. Goldwasser, once he settled into his new position, called me up to say, "I need you here." In truth, he knew who had been contending for the job, and he was very smart about co-opting us.

It turned out, though, that my career in administration was not quite over. I became the Acting Head of business administration in 1970 and served for two years, during which time I was also quite active at the university level. After completing the job of consolidating five separate disciplines into one cohesive department, and since I had no desire to become permanent department head, Kenneth Uhl stepped in. He was at the University of Iowa and had previously turned down the job, but he was now willing to come back and take over. He did a great job and was accomplished at the politics and the bureaucratic wrangling—the stuff I never enjoyed. In 1978, Uhl died suddenly of a heart attack. I was in the Grand Canyon at the time, on vacation, and got a call notifying me—and asking me to return to the role of acting head.

A New Challenge: Creating an Executive MBA Program

One of the key accomplishments of my second term as department head was the creation of the Executive MBA Program. It was a two-year program, with classes offered to senior executives on weekends. The weekend MBA program effectively accommodated those who were too busy rising through the professional ranks to get a valued graduate degree in business. Instituting this program stirred up a number of interesting debates. One concerned the weight given to in-classroom hours. I had to battle against the typical liberal arts mindset and get the university to agree that even though these students were in the classroom only half the normal time, they still should earn the full credit due to peer group meetings for learning and research projects. We pushed the analogy to engineering, with its emphasis on lab work, and finally prevailed with the argument that we were assigning sufficient work outside the classroom.

Another accomplishment had to do with program fees. Since we were providing extras like books and meals, we were charging an extra fee on top of the normal MBA tuition, and the university was uncomfortable with this idea. We came up with two-tier pricing: the standard MBA cost, plus $5,000 for all the expenses we were incurring. Another major battle ensued, but we managed to obtain approval. The program is still going strong today. In fact, in addition to the executives who enroll, there are now many administrators—from the university, nearby hospitals, and other nonprofit institutions—who come to study management. In 2012, the EMBA Program relocated to Chicago, where there is greater market demand.

There was something like 55 faculty members in the economics department, which translated into great political clout. Members of the economics department had no academic respect for the other disciplines in the College of Commerce where it was housed. Its faculty were intellectually arrogant. They looked down on the other business disciplines, including accounting, which ranked number one nationally in undergraduate and graduate ratings, and they especially looked down on faculty in marketing and organizational behavior, with its Rodney Dangerfield-like reputation.

I had endless, good-natured arguments with economics faculty, often involving Julian Simon, who had insisted on a dual appointment. Half of Simon's salary came from the economics department where he taught one class, and half from the business administration department. When Simon's annual salary was increased by $750, I told him, "Okay, I'm good for half, but I have to go to the economics department to get the other $375." Well, they said, "No way!" They would not absorb the other half of Simon's raise. "As far as we're concerned," they said, "(Business administration is) just not a science, so Simon doesn't meet our standards."

We were all friends and neighbors, but this was a debate between two ideologies. Their intellectual arrogance just killed me. For perspective, I suggested that the economics department move to the College of Liberal Arts and Sciences, because that is where their value and belief system would be appreciated. "But if you go there," I reminded them. "Your average compensation will drop by $2,000 per faculty member! You are making more money here and at the same time looking down on the rest of us. So make up your mind about what you prefer." Several years later, the dean changed the College of Commerce into the College of Business and moved the Economics department in the College of Liberal Arts and Sciences. A balance of power was established in the business school as a result.

Illinois proved to be a fertile ground, and my career blossomed, evolving and expanding along several parallel paths. Administration was one. Research was another. My research interests shifted over time. I remained interested in consumer behavior, the field where I had begun as a doctoral student and in which I had directed several doctoral dissertations, and I found myself drawn to the particular area of attitude/behavior discrepancy. Does a positive attitude toward a brand or product or category lead to positive behavior? If not, why not? What are the inhibitors that come into play? In the Howard–Sheth theory we posited attitude as a major construct, so I began gathering data from consumers about their attitudes. In a college town, it was easy to interview homemakers and family members, so information was readily available. Also, because the psychology department was so large, Illinois also had a behavioral lab for research testing; then we, too, built a lab in the College of Commerce. The huge student population provided subjects for research, and doctoral students were available in large numbers to assist. This new research direction was generating a lot of excitement.

At the same time, I was becoming increasingly interested in multivariate statistics. I had begun teaching a doctoral seminar in that area, which meant that I also learned a lot. Besides, Illinois was so strong at the university level—in statistics, mathematics, and methodologies—that it had its own mainframe computer-based software. While most universities borrowed software from UCLA, Illinois created its own, called SOUPAC. What made this software unique was that it engaged the students and researchers to actually write instructions for the manipulation of matrices and therefore tell the computer what to do. It wasn't just a black box. So we actually learned how the technique worked, which was exciting, and it pushed me further into multivariate techniques.

Corporate Collaborations Proved Key

For me, Illinois was the right place and I was there at the right time. Chicago, just a couple of hours north, was the home of a major market research company, Market Research Corporation of American (MRCA), which proved to be a goldmine of consumer data. John Howard opened yet another door for me. Howard and the founder of MRCA were good friends, and Howard suggested that I be granted access to the data base. The company gathered information from 10,000 households, all of which reported weekly on purchases from grocery and drug stores. So, here was this treasure trove of data—who bought what product at what price and with or without coupons or other "deals," and where. These data were used by countless industries as a way of managing consumer loyalty, and I had permission to use it. Since I had expertise in panel-based research, I knew how to get full value out of this material.

Over time, several doctoral students did their dissertations utilizing the panel data. Two that I remember distinctly focused on measuring the "deal-proneness" of the consumer. They were Paul Winn and Edwin Hackelman. In addition to routine questions—What brand did you buy? What size container? How much did you pay?—panel members were also asked if any special deal or promotion had been involved in the purchase. We tracked close to 100 different deals, looking to create a profile of the deal-prone consumer. The findings were surprising. Lower income consumers, presumed to be most deal-prone, never took advantage of such promotions, while college-educated consumers did. Both dissertations confirmed this thesis—that the lower socioeconomic population did not take advantage of deals. This finding had significant policy implications, because if the deal is patronized by only 15 percent of consumers, the other 85 percent are subsidizing the deals by paying full price. In other words, the poor were subsidizing the affluent. Fascinating stuff—and just one example of the kind of research insights we were able to generate from access to this huge database.

Consumerism was on the rise during the early seventies, and I was interested in this movement. President Kennedy had advocated a "consumer bill of rights," Ralph Nader's *Unsafe at Any Speed* had been published in 1965, and, now, in the late 1960s and early 1970s, consumerism was becoming a very interesting area for research. The Federal Trade Commission began to aggressively play its role in overseeing advertising and marketing practices, and antitrust issues made big headlines on the newspaper business pages. Inevitably, scholars were getting more and more interested in consumerist issues. For example, one very concrete result of "consumer rights" was the implementation of unit pricing. As a researcher, I was interested in finding out who was using this new, never-before-available information. What we found would have been surprising—had we not already been studying deal-proneness: Less affluent consumers paid no attention to unit pricing, but college-educated consumers loved it.

Through John Howard, I met Colston Warne, a socially aware economist in New York who had a great idea for a nonprofit enterprise. Warne wanted to publish an inexpensive newspaper, tabloid-style, targeted to disadvantaged consumers in Harlem and Bedford-Stuyvesant to provide them with product ratings and information on automobiles and other consumer goods. It turned out his target audience had no interest in the publication, but Warne figured that *somebody* had to see its value, so he put it into a glossy monthly magazine, *Consumer Reports*. He quickly discovered that more than 40 percent of his readers were college-educated, at a time when less than 20 percent of people were going to college. So again, people who would seem to need consumer information the least were the ones using it the most.

It was an interesting and exciting time to be writing papers and supervising dissertations designed to give information and data to government policy makers. My own interest in these issues eventually led me to write a paper called "Surpluses and

Shortages in Consumer Behavior," an assessment of the whole field. It concluded that, so far, we knew very little about how consumers behave. But I did formulate two laws: First, those who do not need information use information; and second, those who should not consume, do consume.

As my research interests were shifting, so were my methods: from relatively small surveys to large-scale samples derived from databases. This shift was abetted by my friendship with Charles Raymond. He was director of the world-class DuPont market research laboratory. From there, Raymond became president of the New York–based Advertising Research Foundation (ARF) and at the same time developed a consulting practice. I asked him to present a paper at a conference that I had organized at Columbia University before coming to Illinois. We became good friends thereafter. Raymond asked me to join him in building a large database from a consortium of a dozen or so packaged goods and pharmaceutical companies. We gathered data on a global basis and began to develop market insights from it. We called the database World Data Monitor and it, in turn, led to a variety of interesting projects. We found ourselves collecting huge amounts of data from secondary sources such as *Reader's Digest* and the United Nations, added company sales data, and built some very sophisticated analytics.

This era marked the emergence of another interesting perspective into consumer behavior —psychographics. The notion was that we needed to understand not only the psychology of customers at the product or brand level (attitudes toward the brand and attributes of the brand), but also at the product category level, and at the level of the consumer's "lifestyle." This new tradition began at Purdue University under Charles King and others who emphasized the psychographics of consumers rather than their demographics. Demographics were thought to be less relevant because both poor and rich were buying the same things, and psychographics became the new alternative.

One of the proponents of the discipline was William Wells, with whom I had crossed paths when we organized the conference on multivariate statistics at the University of Chicago. Wells had joined an advertising agency in Chicago where he collected large-scale data on what are called AIOs (activities, interests, and opinions)—in other words, lifestyle. He had an inventory of some 350 or 400 questions that asked these lifestyle questions—a holistic approach—and the data were used to break the market into psychographic rather than demographic segments. It was a hot area, and Wells' database provided another source of data that two of my doctoral students used for their thesis work.

New Opportunities via APA and ACR

My research efforts were underpinned by my involvement in two academic organizations that kept me focused on the psychology of consumers. One was the American Psychological Association (APA). Since I had done quite a bit of work using psychometric techniques, Ledyard Tucker recommended that I be inducted into the APA's Division 5. I was not a psychologist, but I minored in social psychology, I had studied psychometrics, and I had Tucker's recommendation, so I was invited to join. Once I had become a member of the organization, I discovered Division 23. This group had a strong focus on consumer psychology, and most of its members were psychologists, like Charles Raymond, who were interested in advertising—and therefore marketing. I soon became more active in that division and eventually organized the program of Division 23 at the APA's national convention. My involvement in APA culminated in my serving as president of Division 23 and ultimately becoming an APA Fellow.

My association with the other organization began with James Engel, who organized a workshop on consumer behavior at Ohio State in 1970. Because I had organized the conference on buyer behavior at Columbia right before leaving for Illinois, I was invited to the conference at Ohio State. Approximately 40 scholars were invited, and it was an intense workshop. It was funded by the American Marketing Association, but at that time, the AMA was not interested in the psychology of consumer behavior. Its focus continued to be on industrial marketing, agricultural marketing, market research and other older disciplines. Consequently, at the end of the conference, a handful of us, under the leadership of Engel, decided to start our own organization, the Association for Consumer Research (ACR). Our intent was not to be a branch of AMA but a stand-alone organization, and from the outset it was nurtured at Illinois. Joel Cohen was very active, along with David Gardner, economist Robert Ferber, and opinion researcher Seymour Sudman. We all got involved in the evolution of ACR by organizing annual conferences at different universities. Ven Venkatesan was also very instrumental in the formative nurturing of ACR. Several younger faculty members we had recruited at Illinois including Peter Wright, Russell Belk, and Bobby Calder became active participants in ACR along with our doctoral students, including Richard Lutz and C.W. Park. I was elected president of ACR in 1984–85 and encouraged the organization to start an international conference. The first was in Singapore in 1985 and chaired by Tan Chin Tiong and me.

My research interests broadened further when I began teaching a doctoral seminar on marketing theory. It meant a thorough study of the field, the whole history of marketing, which eventually led to an academic book for doctoral education in marketing theory. Like the Howard–Sheth book on buyer behavior, *Marketing Theory: Evolution and Evaluation* (with David Gardner and Dennis Garrett), was a comprehensive journey on the evolution of marketing thought as a discipline since the early 1900s. Through research, I discovered that from the early 20th century to the late 1970s, there had been 12 different schools of marketing thought. But nobody had organized them into a framework; and nobody had evaluated them from a scientific perspective. So it became a standard textbook for doctoral students in marketing theory.

The late 1970s and early 1980s also saw the discipline shift in the direction of strategic marketing. MBA programs were becoming more dominant, and managers were increasingly looking toward marketing to help them develop strategies for growth. Thanks partly to Philip Kotler's work, strategic marketing was becoming a hands-on tool, using the SWOT analysis and resource allocation frameworks developed by BCG (Boston Consulting Group), Shell Oil and General Electric. At the same time, Michael Porter's book, *Competitive Strategy*, became essential to marketing strategy. While the concept of the "four Ps" of marketing was introduced in the textbook by Jerome McCarthy, Kotler's introduction of strategic marketing became very popular in the teaching of MBA classes. My interests also began to shift toward strategy and the future. This was more macro and managerial in perspective. The *Marketing Theory* book also nudged me in this direction. In short, the micro behavioral perspective in consumer behavior became less exciting.

Then another stroke of my accidental journey manifested. The seminars I taught on multivariate statistics got the attention of AT&T. It had a large panel of 30,000 consumer customers and 30,000 business customers. I was invited to help analyze these data, much as we had done with MRCA data, but in this case, we got to send our own questionnaire to the consumers, asking about demographics, psychographics, equipment purchases, what type and the number of phones in the households and so forth.

At a corporate level, AT&T had an internal budget of $11 million for market research—MRIS, or Market Research Information Systems. Billing information of sample customers from each of the revenue accounting offices—about 100 of them—was passed along to our database, and we converted it into a market research tool using what I had learned doing longitudinal panels. Marvin Roscoe ran MRIS, and he and I really bonded. In those days, AT&T was like a public enterprise, where research and publication were strongly encouraged. Roscoe and I published a number of papers together in ACR proceedings and in academic journals like the *Journal of Marketing* and the *Journal of Applied Psychology*. Roscoe was a fulltime AT&T employee but became very interested in consumer research and an active member in ACR.

Even though AT&T brought me in because of the seminar on multivariate methods, I also taught seminars on market segmentation, consumer behavior, and marketing strategy.

The most challenging and rewarding were workshops for Bell Labs Scientists and for Western Electric. I was also invited by the General Motors Tech Center that housed GM's R&D organization. I worked primarily with the division that researched consumers and society—trend-spotting really —and we got involved in some fantastic futuristic projects. Just about everybody I worked with had a Ph.D. degree, but in a variety of disciplines: economists, experimental psychologists, cultural anthropologists, you name it. Their entire objective was to publish, publish, and publish! So we published in transportation research journals and tried to win grants from government agencies like the Department of Transportation and the National Highway Safety Administration.

One of our most memorable projects investigated the so-called metro-guideway system, or the "dual-mode" car. The idea behind the project was that public transit wasn't taking off, so how can one create a hybrid system, where the private auto and public transportation come together? The answer (maybe) was a moving highway on which cars would be transported from their suburban neighborhoods to the in-town business district. Inside the city limits, there might be driverless taxis, where the rider uses an ID card for entry, punches in the destination, and the taxi transports him or her there. No pollution, no noise. It was a vision of the future that fit perfectly with the impact of the first energy crisis of the seventies along with the consumerism movement and the rising tide of environmentalism.

We did simulations of two cities: Denver and Detroit. Neither had a metro system and, therefore, less debate and opposition. Of course, engineering was the major focus of the project, but our team studied the sociological impact, which was really interesting. For example, a key issue we uncovered was concern over what people would do for the half-hour they were sitting in their cars on the moving highway. If their workday has been stressful, will they start drinking? And if so, what happens when they exit the highway? People also worried about what would happen when the whole system shut down due to massive power or computer failure and people were stranded in their cars. Would they be attacked or vandalized? This stuff was so futuristic and interesting, but real world at the same time. Recent experiments with driverless and automated cars are a reminder of the futuristic research we did in the late seventies and early eighties.

During those days working with the Tech Center at GM, I would go to Warren, Michigan near Detroit maybe 10 times a year. Quite a few of us were born outside the United States but were naturalized American citizens. Since I was a vegetarian, we all went across the river and over the bridge into Windsor, Canada, to one of the best Indian restaurants in North America. Going was easy, but coming back entailed going through American customs and immigration. Usually we would be asked a bunch of questions and released to go, but every now and then, the U.S. immigration officers would want to look the car over. The problem was that we would usually be in a Cadillac or Olds 98 that had been designed for testing of various kinds, and the trunk was full of strange-looking testing equipment. There is no telling what those customs officials thought we were smuggling across the border. Sometimes, they would get intensely curious about the exotic Indian desserts we were bringing back to the secretaries in the office. It was always an interesting experience.

Looking to the Future

Because of the growing interest in strategic marketing, I increasingly became engaged in projects geared toward the future. Strategic marketing is all about anticipating the future and that led me back to demographics. The two psychographics-based dissertations I had directed both demonstrated that while psychographics are useful in special product categories (e.g., taboo products or products associated with conspicuous consumption), the method is not very effective for ordinary grocery products. For most of life's daily necessities, psychographics offered little insight. So I returned to a place where I was very comfortable—analyzing the trends, which, in this case, were the changing demographics of America. Much of this has become received wisdom by now, but in the 1970s, what was happening to the nation's demographics was a relatively new field of inquiry. I soon realized that much was going on and that the changes were multidimensional.

First, the population was aging rapidly—obvious now, but, again, few were thinking about the implications three decades ago. The huge population of baby boomers was approaching middle age; in another generation they would be approaching retirement as it is happening now. What were the consequences for marketers? The trend would not be reversed, and I realized that the issue would only grow in significance.

Virtually all marketing since World War II had been targeted to a family, a household, of 18- to 34-year olds. Age 34 was regarded as the peak of the "fully nested" family. But this target was clearly going to shift: to 30–45, then 40–55, and now it is 45–60. What would our new need be as this trend continued? I foresaw that four needs would be arising: Health and wealth preservation as well as security, and changing interests in both active and passive recreation.

There has also been a huge shift in the passive recreation that TV and other media offer. When boomers were young, Disney, Ed Sullivan, Carol Burnett, et al., were considered family entertainment. It was clear that such programming would lose its popularity once the kids left home, and we have witnessed the predictable shift to real-world drama like "ER," "Law and Order," "CSI," and "60 Minutes." In retrospect, this seems like old news, but marketers who foresaw these changes 30 years ago placed themselves way ahead of the curve.

A second major demographic change I monitored had to do with changing lifestyles. The traditional definition of family—the breadwinner husband, the homemaker wife—was obviously shifting. What happens to family life when both spouses are working? First: an empty house Monday through Friday, from 8:00 a.m. to 5:00 p.m. When we first asked who would be at home, the answer was the family dog. But I maintain that even the dog is gone now because we are increasingly becoming a cat society. Moreover, 20 years from now we will not even have cats. We will have electronic interactive pets that provide companionship and caring affection. People think I am kidding, but think about the love and affection we give to inanimate toys like a doll or a teddy bear.

The second big change to family life is that the homemaker will no longer be doing homemaking. The fact is that most outsourcing does not come from corporate America but from the American home. Working women have no time for cooking, cleaning, and childcare. They hire all these jobs out. At the same time, what society gives up as a daily activity always comes back as a hobby: hunting, fishing, baking breads, gardening, and now cooking. It is amazing to see the popularity of the Food Channel and Celebrity Chefs!

A third major demographic shift is a significant change in the ethnic mix. What happens to our society when minorities become majorities? Society becomes truly multicultural. We will have a segment we call Anglo, just like we have segments of Hispanics, Asians, and Africans. This has not only implications for marketing, but also for the political parties in the United States.

We were doing a great deal of this kind of thinking at AT&T, where we created a whole new area called "customer insights." With all these data to mine, we were able to see patterns, future scenarios, and long-term implications—including some that were counter-intuitive. For example, it was always assumed that one of the key factors contributing to long-distance calling is how often a family has moved across local phone boundaries. When you move, you call friends and family back in the old neighborhood. So when we plotted the number of moves against long-distance calls, we expected to see a positive correlation. But we did not. Why? The Census Bureau's claim that Americans were becoming mobile actually was deceptive. Our research in the early 1980s showed that 70 percent of people never moved out of their county of birth—never moved out of the *county*, to say nothing of their state. So mobility proved to be all local and had no correlation to long-distance calling.

Yes, the Census Bureau was right that 25 percent of Americans moved every year or 18 months but it turned out to be the same 25 percent who were doing all the moving. This revelation generated a very interesting hypothesis: The real umbilical cord is broken not when the child moves out of his parents' house, but when the high school student leaves the local community for college or a job. It is this college-bound person who joins the 25 percent of mobile Americans, because once a person goes away to college, the anchor to hometown is diminished.

From strategic marketing, my research interests made the transition to competitive strategy. I began to look at the world of competition, as opposed to the world of customers, a shift that would eventually lead me to write a book called *The Rule of Three* (with Raj Sisodia). By the mid-1970s, a large database had been collected at GE—called PIMS—to which many other large companies had contributed as well. GE allowed the database to be housed at Harvard, and many scholars began doing research there on the correlation between market share and profitability. It was the economies of scale concept: the larger the market share, the greater the profitability. I became very interested in that idea, but my view was that market share was only half the story (or just one of the five blind men touching the elephant).

Another part of the story was revealed in small niche or specialty companies and this became apparent in shopping centers. You have the anchor stores such as Sears and JC Penny, who are volume-driven retailers but in between, there are all the specialty retailers, who are margin driven and command 20 to 30 percent higher prices in the same location. Marketing competition consists of part oligopoly and part monopolistic competition: those who are niche players (margin driven), and those who are full line players (scale driven). Economies of scale are in play on one side, and on the other is a uniqueness for which consumers are willing to pay a higher price. Both can succeed; where you do not make money is in the middle, or "the ditch" where you have neither volume nor margin advantage.

During my years at Illinois, my research interests, like my academic experiences, continually evolved and expanded. As the next two chapters illustrate, Illinois would allow me to grow in other ways as well—by traveling to other campuses (in the United States and abroad), by developing a rich and productive "professional" life, and by writing books and papers for an ever-larger audience.

LIFE LESSON

Do not make major decisions in life based on cognitive debate; with the endless weighing of pros and cons. Act out of your emotions, impressions, and feelings; you can always analyze later. If you have positive expectations and then you feel even better after you have first-hand experience, you know something special is happening. *If you follow your dreams, your dreams will unfold.*

6

ILLINOIS: TRAVELS AT HOME AND ABROAD

The Howard–Sheth theory had generated considerable attention, and with a number of articles about it appearing in respected journals, I found myself traveling frequently to other universities to give lectures, and, increasingly, receiving overtures from universities interested in having me join their faculty. Thus, in the fall of 1973, I found myself traveling to the University of Pittsburgh to spend a year as a visiting chaired professor.

It was an interesting situation. I left Pittsburgh in 1963. In the decade following, the school's financial situation had deteriorated, leaving the business school to languish for most of that time. A number of the faculty members I admired were gone, including Bernard Bass and John Howard. When I returned to Pitt, the business school was just trying to rebuild. Fortunately, a great dean, Gerald Zoffer, had taken the helm. In fact, Zoffer would enjoy one of the longest tenures for a business school dean on record. He had been an assistant dean when I was there and was promoted during the turmoil. Eventually, Zoffer became an icon. When I returned to Pitt, Zoffer was working diligently to revitalize the school. Under him was Alan Shocker, who came to Pittsburgh as a marketing professor.

Prior to leaving Pitt, each discipline in marketing had a very distinguished senior professor. For example, John Howard filled that role in managerial marketing while in advertising, it was Albert Frey. When Frey retired, the Albert Frey Chair of Marketing was created in his honor, and Shocker asked me to accept that chair on a permanent basis. I could not commit to a permanent position, primarily because it would mean relocating my family, but I was able to commit to being a visiting professor.

Why did I agree to go to Pitt, even for a year? Loyalty and gratitude. When your *alma mater* asks you to return as a chair professor, you are being offered the highest honor they can bestow. Accepting was the appropriate response. Besides, I liked the fact that Pittsburgh was revitalizing, and I believed I could contribute to that effort—especially by mentoring students and junior faculty members. Also, Frey had been on my thesis committee, so accepting the visiting professor position was my way of honoring him and thanking him for what he had done for me. Yet another reason was that I felt the need to take some time off from Illinois. I was doing too much administrative work, and I saw this offer as a sabbatical of sorts where I would be able to focus on my research and writing.

Madhu did not want to come with me to Pitt. Unlike the home we built when we first moved to Illinois, we lived in a custom-made abode that met Madhu's specifications. Now that she was settling in and really enjoying it, she did not want to move. Also, the children were comfortable in their school, and we did not want to disrupt their education. The compromise was that I went alone and commuted between the two cities. It was only five hours or so by car—convenient enough for me to return to Illinois once or twice a month.

I rented a two-bedroom apartment half-way between the airport and the campus, in a suburban community called Green Tree-Mt. Lebanon. I wanted proximity to the airport because I was doing a significant amount of research for Bell Canada and the Canadian long-distance consortium TCTS, now called TelCom Canada. The work I had started with the Bell System

(AT&T) had been successful, and the Canadian companies wanted to duplicate it.

I felt very good about returning to my alma mater. It was good to get reacquainted with former colleagues and professors and to rekindle pleasant memories. Also, Alan Shocker was unique. He and I bonded immediately. He was single, and so was I "temporarily," so I went to his home practically every week. Shocker had a passion for wine and, because alcohol sales in Pittsburgh were government controlled, he would drive to Washington, D.C. and bring back cases of his favorites. He also loved pistachios, though where he got those from I do not know. Anyway, we would have wine and the pistachios and do nothing, but talk about academic life.

Among my many colleagues and friends at Pitt, one with whom I became very close was a student named Michael Belch, who enrolled in my doctoral seminars. He lived "on the other side of the tunnel" like I did, so we commuted together. Belch went on to become a well-known professor in advertising, and, along with his brother, George Belch, the author of a best-selling textbook in advertising. At Pitt, he helped me with research on a project I spent a good deal of time during my stay.

Measuring the Howard–Sheth Theory Takes Priority

While quite useful, the Howard–Sheth theory was also quite complicated, and there remained the issue of how to measure it and how to test it scientifically. If you cannot test a theory, it may not be valid. Howard and I had originally intended to write a textbook, as well as a case book—projects we never got around to. At Illinois, where I became so close to the social psychology department and interested in psychometrics, I noted that one of the best social psychology theories in attitudes had come from Daniel Katz at the University of Michigan. This work was on the functional values of attitude—that is, you form attitudes and opinions to serve a function. I used his theory a lot, but it was not used by everybody because he never tested it. By contrast, the psychology department at Illinois had a very good young scholar, Martin Fishbein, who had adopted the theories of experimental psychologist Donald Dulaney *and* had created a measurement tool by which to test them. Now, I could see Fishbein's work taking off. The point, for me, was easy to see: If I do not have a measurable theory, it will not be widely used.

Consequently, while at Illinois I became preoccupied with designing an instrument to test the Howard–Sheth theory, and I brought this project with me to Pittsburgh. My intent was to go back to my dissertation, as well as to the Howard–Sheth theory, and come up with testable hypotheses as to why people buy what they buy. Through this research, and also through directing dissertations and working with students, I posited five fundamental values (needs or wants), by which we are driven when we make a choice. Then I developed an inventory of questions with which I could measure the power of each particular value. In that way it becomes a measurable, testable theory. The five needs are: Functional Value, Social Value, Emotional Value, Situational or Conditional Value, and Epistemic Value.

At Illinois, Bruce Newman was the student who did much of this work with me and who eventually became my doctoral student. As my research assistant, he did many studies of students and their choice behavior. When I went to Pittsburgh, I wanted to continue this work, and Michael Belch became my student and colleague. However, rather than confine the theory to consumer choices, I felt the theory was universal and could be applied to any kind of choice. Why get married? Why smoke marijuana? Why play computer games? Surprisingly, the model was able to predict behavior with more than 90 percent accuracy. The eventual result of this work was published in a book called *Consumption Values and Market Choice Behavior* (with Bruce Newman and Barbara Gross).

One of the most interesting arenas into which we took this five-value model was electoral politics. Could we predict election results? Why not? Elections are a choice. So Belch and I did several studies using a small number of focus group interviews where we would ask what kinds of campaign promises were likely to appeal to voters. Historical analysis had discovered before some important shifts in how people are motivated to align themselves politically. There was a time when people were born into a party very much like we are born into a religion. If you were born into a Republican family, you stayed Republican. But this began to change after World War II, especially with the rise of the labor unions. The notion emerged that if you were working class, you were likely to be a Democrat, whereas if you were an educated business professional, you were likely to be Republican. That is, we had begun to select our political affiliation by our social and economic status.

I believed that theory was also becoming obsolete. I saw that people, increasingly, were making their choices based on candidates—not the party or the economic class of the voter. In such a scenario, candidates' views really mattered. And if I could classify those views into five values, then I would have an instrument by which to predict which candidate you are likely to vote for. Think about it: abortion rights, for example, might be classified as an emotional issue; the problem of poverty could be a social issue; what to do about the economy could be a functional issue; or maybe it was just time for a change (epistemic). This was the end of the Nixon-Ford era, a time when people were really fed up with the Republicans and were looking for a new direction. Belch and I applied the theory to the mayoral race in Pittsburgh, the governor's race in Pennsylvania, and eventually to the national election (though by then I had left Pittsburgh).

We also worked together in one more area, which became Belch's main interest. He was fascinated by advertising. I had done some research in that area, and my view was that the typical consumer is probably exposed to 3,000 advertisements every day, but remembers only a few. Why? Howard and I had addressed that question in our book, and I wanted Belch to study it in depth. The design was simple: you count the number of times an ad comes on TV, then ask people whether or not they remember it. Belch moved on to do great things and we remain great friends.

Corporate Consulting Study Yields Real Results

I was involved in one more memorable project while at Pittsburgh. Just before leaving Illinois, I started working with TelCom Canada on a study of the long-distance network it owned along with a consortium of other phone companies. With on-site manager Tony Schellinck, I embarked on research using a 5,000-household panel created from the company's billing records.

Does advertising work? This was of interest not only to the company's management, but also to the regulatory commission overseeing the industry. The commission's position was that spending money on advertising was wasteful, and the ratepayer should not have to shoulder the burden. So we were asked to conduct scientific research to determine whether a dollar spent on advertising generated at least a dollar of revenue. I had been involved in a similar project for AT&T Long Lines, where we had found that, in fact, advertising does pay. We found the same kind of "elasticity" you see in pricing—that is, if you reduce the price, people buy more or more people buy.

We conducted a scientific study meant to answer for the regulators whether advertising works—and the extent to which it works. It was quite powerful. We did everything right. We showed the advertising to one sample of people based on the database, and withheld the advertising from another sample, to get a clear picture of the before-and-after effect.

It turned out that one dollar of advertising produced seven dollars of revenue! It was a significant result. The findings were persuasive. As a result, the regulators bought the model and agreed that advertising was an expenditure they would allow—that is, as a tax-deductible expenditure for the company. Thus, it was more than just a business issue; it was a public policy issue, with wide ramifications. The surprise was that Schellinck decided to quit his job and come to Illinois as my doctoral student.

It was a short nine months, especially with much of the time spent traveling. In addition to my work in Canada, I traveled to

With my two brothers, circa 1958

Graduation portrait, B.Com. (hons), Loyola College, Madras

Class of Loyola College, Madras (1957–60)

Literary club meeting in Madras, India where I met Madhu (to the far right)

With my siblings upon my departure from Bombay

University of Pittsburgh, MBA graduation class, 1962

Wedding at Heinz Chapel (University of Pittsburgh)
with Professor Kulkarani and David Miller, 1962

My host family Mr and Mrs Charles Dexter at our wedding

My first car (a used Lincoln Mercury)

Madhu, the love of my life

Home in New Jersey on the lake

Young family portrait

At the Taj Mahal with my family

With Ven Venkatesan and Nalin Parekh

With family at Gary Frazier's wedding in Champaign, Illinois

30th anniversary and vow renewal in Chennai, India

Celebrating our 50th wedding anniversary in 2012

other campuses to give a faculty seminar. But I was also going to European universities—namely, to Tilberg University in the Netherlands, to Bergen, to Gothenburg, and to Copenhagen Business School in Scandinavia. And I was traveling back and forth to Illinois, largely because of all the doctoral students I worked with plus my administrative responsibilities.

Being a visiting professor was a memorable experience and, like my stint at IIM-Kolkata in India, a source of great professional growth. Pittsburgh would have preferred that I accept a permanent position. It was a nice situation, the chemistry was good, and I believe I could have contributed to the leadership of the doctoral program, but Madhu did not want to move. We were both very happy in Illinois. While I declined the opportunity to stay, the Pittsburgh chapter of my life had a happy ending. I had been asked by Northwestern University near Chicago if I would be interested in being the first chair holder in its marketing department. It was an excellent department, which included scholars such as Lou Stern, Philip Kotler, Sidney Levy, Gerald Zaltman, and Stuart Henderson Britt, a giant in psychology who had come into marketing. The problem was that if the chair went to any one of these giants, the others would be alienated.

I was invited by the rising star in the department, Phil Kotler, to visit the Northwestern campus. He had written the famous textbook in marketing management, and the book's inclusion of the Howard–Sheth theory had led to great exposure. I agreed to come for an informal visit. Kotler and his wife, Nancy, graciously allowed me to stay at their house, and Nancy prepared a delicious chicken-based entrée. I had forgotten to let them know that I was vegetarian—something Phil and I still laugh about that to this day.

Kotler has extraordinary organizational skills. He collected all the marketing-related clippings from business journals and kept them carefully organized in file drawers, all for the purpose of biannual revisions of his textbook. It was quite impressive. I must say that Kotler is a brilliant writer. He has the unique ability to make a textbook a joy to read.

Ultimately, I decided I would not formally interview for the Montgomery Ward Chair in Marketing. It was a quality-of-life decision. I did not see anywhere in Evanston that we could buy a contemporary home. Phil suggested we look further north, in the suburban communities around the lake shore, but I was not interested in returning to the life of a commuter. So I declined to return to the campus for a full interview. The chair did eventually go to Kotler.

Interestingly enough, it was a young scholar named Gerald Zaltman, a sociologist who had come into marketing and made a great name for himself, who had been leading the charge to get me to come to Northwestern. Ironically, I had been thinking about trying to get Zaltman to come to Illinois! After I declined to join him at Northwestern, he let me know that he was looking for other opportunities. I suggested that he go to Pittsburgh. I really believed it would be a great place for him. As it turned out, Zaltman took the job and he completely turned the department around. Shortly after his arrival, a stream of bright young marketing doctoral students poured in, and Zaltman proved to be a fabulous mentor. Under his tutelage, at least a dozen top scholars came out of the program. So there was a nice symmetry. I left, and Pittsburgh continued to flourish all thanks to Zaltman. My daughter, Reshma was admitted in the doctoral program at Pitt and she was keen to have Zaltman as her advisor. Unfortunately, Zaltman decided to leave Pitt to go to Harvard.

Zaltman's position was filled by a Korean student from Illinois, C.W. Park who was also my former student. After a stint at Kansas, Park joined the University of Pittsburgh where he enjoyed a stellar career and became Reshma's advisor. In terms of professional lineage, my biological daughter became my "academic" granddaughter via Park—creating three generations of scholars.

Back at Illinois, I found myself increasingly involved in university administration. When I was not involved in university issues, I was traveling, or so it seemed. My seminars on multivariate statistics had become extremely popular in Europe, especially in Scandinavia, so I found myself in Europe virtually every quarter. If I was not giving a lecture on a university campus, I was attending the annual conference of European Society of Marketing and Advertising Research (ESOMAR), a market research professional society in Europe. Tilberg University was very much into economic psychology, or the psychological approach to understanding the economic behavior of consumers, which is now referred to as behavioral economics. In London, there was Unilever's market research company, Research Bureau Limited (RBL), which did a lot of research on Unilever products using the Howard–Sheth theory as a new way of looking at the world of consumers. So was the case with Philips in Netherlands. I also consulted with Testologen in Stockholm frequently.

An old friend, Flemming Hansen, who had been a visiting professor at the University of New Hampshire in the late 1960s and who I knew from the early days of the Association of Consumer Research, invited me to come to Copenhagen as a visiting professor at the Copenhagen Business School (or Handelshojskolen). Given that I was traveling there so often anyway, I thought an extended stay in Europe might be a good thing.

As is so often the case, the reason I said "Yes" to Flemming had less to do with my profession and more to do with my family. Madhu has always been wiser than me. She is curious about the world and wants to explore it. She also felt very strongly that our children had grown up caught between two cultural extremes: The extended family of traditional Indian culture and the nucleus family of modern American culture—really two very different definitions of what family means. She thought it would be a fine thing to immerse the children in cultures that lay between these two extremes.

Diversion to Copenhagen

Once I accepted Fleming's invitation, Madhu and I decided that the children would not go to the American school. We enrolled them in Copenhagen's excellent international school, where most of the children were sons or daughters of diplomats or international corporate executives. Reshma was 12 and Rajen was 9, and it was a wonderful experience for them. Reshma learned French and Rajen learned German.

Copenhagen was yet another example of unanticipated good fortune that ensured that our ideas found a home in Scandinavia—as well as in England. Unlike in Germany and in southern Europe, scholars in Scandinavia read English academic literature. Scandinavian students are taught in their local language, but their scholarship is English-language oriented. This connects them to American thought, especially in business and marketing. I was also fortunate that there was a growing interest in multivariate statistics in Scandinavia.

Of course, my personal connections to Scandinavia were numerous, beginning with Folke Olander at the University of Michigan. It was Olander who met me in Sweden when I was working on that machine tool industry project in route to the United States from India. Also in Sweden, at the University of Gothenburg, was a professor named Bo Wickstrom. Wickstrom was a keen student of social and economic development in Africa, and since I came from a non-American culture and had published papers on international marketing, he and his colleagues were interested in my perspective. Volvo was headquartered in Gothenburg. A fellow named Bo Arpi, its director of market research, was doing his dissertation in marketing. We connected when he invited me to lecture to Volvo's marketing managers. I later reciprocated by inviting him to come to Illinois as a visiting scholar. There was also Otto Ottesen, who developed a research framework to measure advertising effectiveness. We became good friends and I convinced him to visit Illinois for a semester. Finally, there was Johan Arndt, who I knew since our days at Columbia. From Columbia he returned to the University of Oslo, where we reconnected.

Most important of all—particularly in terms of my visiting professorship—was Flemming Hansen at Copenhagen Business

School. That institution has become one of the largest and most prestigious business schools in Europe. I was privileged to be invited back in 2007 when it celebrated its 75th anniversary. In 1977, Hansen had two reasons for urging me to spend a year there. The first, of course, was to teach at the business school, but Hansen also had a private practice as a marketing consultant, and he invited me to be an advisor to his firm. So I split my time in Copenhagen, working at the university as well as helping Hansen with his private-practice clients.

Several of Hansen's clients were quite interesting. Among my most memorable experiences was working with the Lego Corporation. The company's founder had designed Legos with a social and educational agenda. These toys were not just playthings; they were meant to improve motor skills, perceptual skills, and cognitive skills. The target age range for the toys extended from early infancy, when motor skills are first developing, all the way to high school, and the products were designed with ever-increasing complexity. I was told that people who administer Intelligence Quotient (IQ) tests wanted to use Legos as a measurement tool, but the owner—still in charge after 40 years—refused. He did not want the product to be politicized. Our project used multidimensional scaling to identify opportunities for new product introductions and for positioning existing product lines.

A second great project had to do with two brands of beer— Carlsburg and Tuborg—both made by the same company, which was a major client of Hansen's. Even more interesting, the parent company was a charitable foundation that funneled all profits from both brands into social and community causes, such as the opera house or downtown revitalization. It was my first experience with a for-profit company owned by a charitable foundation. In any case, the two brands competed at the consumer level, with Tuborg perceived to be primarily for intellectuals while Carlsburg was for the working class. We used psychographics to analyze the imagery associated with each brand by interviewing consumers of each. I enjoyed this work because I had done beer studies in America and had watched with interest as Miller resurrected itself by targeting blue-collar drinkers who head to the bar after a hard day at the steel mill or on the assembly line.

Yet another of Hansen's fascinating clients was a publishing company that owned two dailies. One was *Politiken*, a high-brow, liberal newspaper like the *New York Times*. All the educated people read it. The other, *Ekstra Bladet*, was the opposite—incredibly sensational, full of classified ads offering every imaginable sexual service, and featuring in every issue, a full-frontal-nude photo of a beautiful Scandinavian woman. The two editors hated each other. *Ekstra Bladet* was selling maybe half a million papers of its Sunday edition, and its editor was reaping the rewards, while *Politiken* might sell 100,000 copies. My project was to see if the two papers should be sharing content and columnists, and I remember well the heat of those debates. Our recommendation was that the union would not work. Readers of both papers would cancel their subscriptions. And in Europe much more than in America, subscriptions are a large source of revenue for newspapers.

On the academic side, I was continuing my research on the five values of consumption (functional, social, emotional, situational, and epistemic) model, which led to a stream of research on which I focused while in Scandinavia. These Scandinavian scholars were very much into business-to-business marketing, or industrial buying behavior, which had been the subject of my paper, "A Model of Industrial Buying Behavior" in the *Journal of Marketing* some years earlier. Just as the American focus had changed from industrial marketing to consumer behavior, that shift in focus was about to come to Scandinavia. What I could bring to Scandinavia now, however, was my interest in buyer–seller interaction. Rather than considering only consumers from their viewpoint (as in the Howard–Sheth theory), or marketers from their viewpoint (as in managerial marketing), I was looking at how the two interact in the marketplace. I proposed that it is the gap between the two that we need to understand, and to this analysis I brought the five values model.

That work produced another good paper, "A Theory of Buyer Seller Interaction," part of the growing literature on buyer–seller interaction. We were all heavily influenced by behavioral sciences at that time.

Before my family and I knew it, it was time to go back to Illinois, but we returned with wonderful memories. Scandinavia was an unforgettable, life-altering experience. Not only were the kids exposed to children from all over the world, but our whole family spent a great deal of the time traveling around Europe. Out of the 10 months we were in Scandinavia, Madhu and the children spent four of them traveling by Eurail pass from one European city to another. Often, it was possible for me to arrange to give a lecture or seminar at the university in the city they were visiting so that I could join them.

One of our best trips was shortly after we arrived in Copenhagen to attend the annual conference of ESOMAR in Venice. This was our first visit to that incredible city. From there we traveled to Aix-en-Provence in southern France, where the local university was hosting a conference in the nearby Gregorian monastery. The conference participants were to stay in the monastery, and there was a rule prohibiting children on the premises, but I explained that my family was traveling with me, and they made an exception. How fortunate for my children. There is nothing like a monastery: the peace and quiet, the self-sustaining lifestyle and, in this particular monastery, the beautiful Gregorian chanting.

My family owes a deep debt of gratitude to Flemming Hansen for making our year in Scandinavia memorable. It came as a great shock when I learned that Flemming had suddenly passed away on July 23, 2010, just a few months after his dear wife's death.

Both of these lengthy trips—to Pittsburgh and to Copenhagen—allowed me to continue and expand what I call my "professional life," or my career outside the walls of the academia. Illinois helped me grow in yet another important way.

LIFE LESSON

A change of perspective and a change of pace are tremendously re-energizing. Make time for rest, but also time for innovation. Inspiration usually stems from diversity so be sure to mix it up a little. You will have to push past obstacles to find your plateau. However, it is from this plateau that you will be able to see clearly. *Instead of seeing the glass half empty, see it half full and then invite others to have a drink.*

7

ILLINOIS: PROFESSIONAL WORK AND DEPARTURE

Thanks solely to the stubbornness of Dick Evans, it is safe to say that my foray into academic administration had come about purely by accident. I do not suppose I would call my research accidental, yet the areas into which my research led me, and the variety of projects I found myself working on, could not have been predicted. And now I turn to another development in my life at Illinois—my work in executive education and, more generally, my professional life—which was similarly fortuitous.

Because we lived modestly, my salary of $18,000 was sufficient to keep our heads above water. However, with two children I knew I would need a second income. Due to its location in the cornfields versus the city, Illinois did not have a strong executive education program—a program where, in addition to their regular classes, faculty could teach continuing education to managers. There was one summer program, but it was small and already fully staffed by faculty who were not going to let go of this extra income.

When I arrived at Illinois, our field was shifting from operations research to psychometrics or multivariate statistics. As this new area became more prominent, practitioners were very interested in learning newer techniques for market research, especially clustering and multidimensional scaling. It was quite specialized—having much to do with mainframe computing, data mining, and statistical analysis. At the time we were using statistical packages of the day, including BioMED, SPSS, and, eventually, SAS.

The Institute for Advanced Technology Comes Calling

I started teaching a seminar for managers through the Institute for Advanced Technology based in Washington D.C., which was funded by Control Data Corp. Control Data Corp. was a mainframe computing company in competition with IBM but which held a dominant share of the education market. It was in Control Data's best interest to propagate the use of these computers for running complicated statistical software programs capable of massive data analysis. I was already teaching a doctoral seminar in the field, so I wrote to the Institute and offered to teach a course in multivariate statistics. They said yes, sent a contract, and my parallel career was off and running.

The largest markets for such courses were always New York, Chicago, and Washington. I would prepare a two-day workshop, get all the materials ready, and fly out the night prior to the workshop. The Institute handled all the logistics, including registration. I was paid $500 a day, or $1,000 for the two-day seminar. I asked my friend Paul Green to teach with me cluster analysis and multidimensional scaling because some of the techniques he mastered were not my forte. I hired Paul to cover those parts of the workshop. He would teach for half a day out of the two days. This program was such a success that Paul and I taught all over Europe together.

Another lucky break followed. At one of the programs in New York, a couple of people from the Bell System (old AT&T) were in the audience. After it was over, they called the Institute to ask if the program could be offered in-house at AT&T, at their own training center rather than in a hotel. The Institute declined, saying it did not offer in-house training, and suggested that they contact me directly. I was more than interested, to say the least, and we set up a meeting at O'Hare Airport in Chicago. Over time, I developed and delivered a dozen in-company programs on all kinds of topics: applied regression, forecasting, market segmentation, consumer behavior, etc.

The Bell system and executive education, supplied the second income stream that I needed. But I should note that the multivariate techniques we were exploring had more applications across the business world. For example, credit card companies had begun using "discriminant analysis" to figure out to whom they should issue credit cards. This method could "discriminate" between those who were creditworthy and those who were not because computer analysis determined which indicators in the credit application were most relevant. For instance, data showed that the most important factor was length of residence. Homeowners, especially those who have lived in the same house for longer lengths of time, are perceived as more stable—and better credit risks—than apartment-dwelling transients who are probably moving around frequently. The second most important indicator was marital status (though this may have changed in the past three decades). The point is that data analytics and modeling through multivariate statistics determined who got the card.

The U.S. Internal Revenue Service had a similar challenge. With the resources to audit only 5 percent of returns, the agency used to randomly pick one out of 20. But cheating on your taxes is not random. A more effective method is to use these statistical methods—applied to past audit records—to identify the likely cheaters from the noncheaters. What is the most important indicator of cheating? It is occupation. Self-employed people cheat more than salaried people. The second most important indicator is adjusted gross income, while the third is charitable contributions. The computer crunches data on these three variables and comes up with a score. If you are self-employed with a high income, and giving lots of money to charity, you will be flagged by the Internal Revenue Service. A great side-benefit of this approach is that it takes the power away from the local agent, who otherwise has the potential to discriminate on a racial or political basis.

The Start of My Publishing Career

So my "executive education" work was well underway. I was seeing the world—from Europe to Japan, learning an enormous amount and, of course, enjoying significant supplemental income. And it was all so serendipitous. I needed the money; I had the expertise; and the workshop opportunities continued to increase. The timing could not have been better. And the Institute for Advanced Technology could not have been more helpful. The Institute was run by a retired General, to whom I owe a huge debt of gratitude. He liked me, nurtured me, and opened a promising door for me. That door led to others, including the one into the Bell System, which, years later, would lead me to Atlanta.

Over the years, my professional career continued to expand and along with it, I developed an interest in writing books for a professional audience, as opposed to strictly scholarly books and articles. From teaching seminars in multivariate techniques, market segmentation, and marketing strategy, I came to realize that there was an audience for the kind of material I was presenting to managers or MBA students who would become managers. I began to cultivate this audience, to write my so-called professional books while still at Illinois, and though the work has continued, this is an appropriate moment to mention a few of the early fruits of this labor.

From my reading and teaching in strategic marketing, I discovered a framework created by the Boston Consulting Group (BCG) that addressed growth patterns among the businesses of a given conglomerate—very useful for big companies like GE. The framework went something like this: If you have a dominant market share in a fast-growing industry, it is a "star" business. If you have a dominant position in an industry that has matured and is likely to decline, that is your "cash cow." If you have a small share in an industry that's declining, you have a "dog." If there's a rapidly growing industry out there in which you have small market share that is your "question mark." Of course, all these designations are for resource allocation in your long-term strategy. The notion was that you take the cash cow businesses, in which you invested in the last generation, harvest them now, and pump the money into newer businesses. In other words, you constantly deliver growth by investing in young industries and plateauing mature industries.

I never really liked this framework because I do not believe that markets plateau. Similarly, products do not plateau. It is managers who plateau. The so-called mature products actually have a long life, especially well-known consumer brands. The best brands of today are those that were created 50 years ago, or even 100, like Coca-Cola, Colgate, or Tide. Of course, this is the kind of contrarian thinking I have always enjoyed. And I also believe that the successful academicians are those who are willing to question the prevailing wisdom and look for alternate explanations: The best scholarship is about seeing things from a different perspective.

We took case study after case study, examining products or brands that were successful over time and noting, in many cases, how they had been reinvented to suit new needs or meet new times. Nylon and Dacron—these were products that lived on. That became the theme of my first book for professionals, *Winning Back Your Market*. Each chapter took a mature brand or product category and explained how to create new growth. It was well received, and invigorated my new endeavor in writing books for the professional market.

Immediately, I wrote a second book for professionals, though this one grew out of my academic research. Toward the end of my tenure at Illinois, a research area in which we were all involved was the "diffusion of innovation." Behind it was the idea that people embrace change—through opinion leaders, for example. Again, I took the opposite view; I argued that just as consumers do not make choices, but rather reduce choices, so consumers do not embrace change but rather resist change. I began to study the reasons for that resistance, and, for the marketers to overcome them. As it happened, I had two very good doctoral dissertations come out of that inquiry, and one of those students, S. Ram, became my coauthor on *Bringing Innovation to Market*.

A third book was inspired by a somewhat different motive. The early 1980s saw a boom in the popularity of so-called business books. After the incredible success of *In Search of Excellence*, publishers like The Free Press, John Wiley, McGraw-Hill, Harper & Row (now HarperCollins), and many others began clamoring for the next big title in the business genre. My idea was to write a book along the lines of *In Search of Excellence*, but focus on customer service—best practices, that kind of thing.

I had a friend and colleague, Milind Lele, a Harvard Ph.D. in economics and strategy, who worked in Chicago for a consulting firm called the MAC Group—Management Analysis Center—and who subsequently became part of Gemini Consulting. Lele wanted to start his own consulting company and asked me to work with him on a book that would give his new company an edge. My view is that you cannot succeed as a consultant unless you have a unique framework or research process with which to win your clients. So we decided to do an exploration of customer satisfaction, customer service excellence, by examining best-in-class companies in different industries based on rankings published by *Fortune* magazine. I wrote to all these top companies—Delta Airlines, Boeing, John Deere, Caterpillar, Jaguar; the top one or two in each category—introducing myself and my coauthor and describing the research project. It was quite exciting. Lele would spend a day at each company, where he was hosted by an external relations representative, and set up interviews. Lele did all the interviewing, as a way to pave the way for future consulting work, and the book that grew out of this project was *The Customer Is Key*, which did quite well.

So I had three books come out very quickly—all professional writing. And I made a commitment at that time that I would continue to write for both audiences—academic and professional.

Leaving Illinois

Indeed, commitment to the professional arc of my career was one of the factors that ultimately convinced me to leave the University of Illinois. To that wonderful institution I will always owe more than I can repay, but as the decade of the 1970s came to a close, I began to feel that the time had come to move on. While what was happening in my professional life shaped this feeling, other changes were in the wind as well.

In the first place, problems were arising in my own discipline. We had created a distinct identity at Illinois by focusing on consumer behavior. We took a behavioral perspective, and were the dominant voice in the Association for Consumer Research (ACR). But all this began to change as we entered an era of turbulence. The exciting research we had pioneered in attitude–behavior relationship had plateaued, and the paradigms we had created began to be questioned. I recognized this myself and even wrote an article which helped incite the turmoil. In "Surpluses and Shortages in Consumer Behavior Theory and Research," I wrote that our approach anchored to multi-attribute rational preference had played itself out and that we needed to broaden our inquiry; we needed to consider different, wider areas of consumption such as excessive and deviant consumption. We also needed to research the emotional and irrational behaviors. Some of our ACR member-scholars began generating research on consumer phenomena that were on the fringe of normal consumption.

This caused considerable debate, in-fighting, and ill feelings in the discipline and especially in ACR leadership. I wrote a second article, "Acrimony in the Ivory Tower," to try to calm the troubled waters. Its point was that we needed to get over the turmoil and get on with our scholarship. My greatest concern was for the doctoral students, who were becoming confused about what they should be focusing on.

Secondly, I, myself, was changing, personally and professionally. Living abroad in Denmark had a profound effect on me. It broadened my horizons, which was reflected in my professional and academic interests. I was shifting from a micro approach, on individual customers, to a more aggregate-market approach; from a strictly behavioral perspective to a nonbehavioral perspective. The book I was working on at the time (marketing theory) also encouraged this broadening of my interests. I even began to appreciate the larger economic perspectives to which, as a behavioral scientist, I had given little consideration until now.

At the same time, my department was going through a period of change. Immediately upon my return from Denmark in the fall of 1977, Uhl, left for a visiting professorship in Australia and asked me to manage the department during his absence. My first challenge came from the Association to Advance Collegiate Schools of Business (AACSB), the body in charge of the accreditation of business schools. It mandated that we teach two new areas as core subjects in the MBA program: international business and strategy. To start up the international business position, I quickly went after Anant Negandhi, from Kent State. He had married a German woman and had taken a two-year sabbatical to live in Germany. When he returned to Kent State, the political winds on his campus had shifted and the research center in international business he had created was gone. It was time for him to leave, so I brought him to Illinois.

As for the other position, Uhl called me from Australia to say he had found a professor there we should recruit—a Welshman by the name of Howard Thomas. I recruited him and Thomas eventually became the dean of the business school at Illinois. From there he went on to deanships at other universities, including at prestigious Warwick University in the United Kingdom and now the School of Business at Singapore Management University.

Our department had been dominated for some time by marketing, an area staffed with very senior people (Robert Ferber, Seymor Sudman, David Gardner), and the view was that the organizational behavior (OB) area needed to be revitalized. Louis Pondy took on that job and eventually became the department head. Tragically, Uhl soon died of a heart attack and I was asked to temporarily take over the department. I tried to maintain the fragile balance between marketing and OB until the department leadership went to Pondy. Unfortunately, soon thereafter he was diagnosed with terminal cancer and relinquished his leadership role. With that, a void was created.

In addition to Negandhi and Thomas, we recruited Gary Frazier and Roy Howell in marketing—two young people with bright futures. On the OB side, we recruited Greg Oldham and Joe Porac. We did our best to spur the vitality of the department, but things were just not happening. I was getting impatient. Despite the number of bright people we had, there was no cohesiveness or excitement in the department.

If all this were not enough, there was also radical change at the university level. The Office of the Chancellor seemed to be a revolving door. When Weir left the university, John Cribbett became the acting chancellor. Then he retired and Weir came back as chancellor of the university. When Weir returned, I asked him, "What do you think about the College of Commerce? Does it have a future? Will the university invest in it?" After all, thanks to the upheaval in the job market caused by the energy crisis of the seventies, we had the highest undergraduate admissions standards of any school in the university. But Weir's response was clear: "Jag, we will never invest in the College of Commerce. It is strictly a vocational school. It is practice oriented. It is where we train people to become accountants." He was painfully frank, but if the business school was not going to be a center of excellence for the university, there was little incentive to stay at Illinois.

A Mid-life Crisis

It was 1979 and Ram Charan and I were asked to design a leadership program for the Bell System called the Bell Advanced Management Program (BAMP), much like Harvard's Advanced Management Program (AMP). It lasted one month and was targeted strictly for high-potential senior executives to understand strategic thinking and competitive markets.

The timing could not have been better. This was the end of the 1970s and the beginning of the 1980s, and then . . . boom! In 1982, came the big announcement that the Bell System would be broken up into the seven Baby Bells and AT&T. In 1984 the Baby Bells would start operating as stand-alone companies. What a massive shift!

With deregulation and the coming divestiture of the Baby Bells, the world was changing. The CEOs of AT&T, John DeButts, followed by Charlie Brown, were serious about getting people to understand the new reality. So the company asked Charan (who had left academic life to become a fulltime consultant to large corporations like GE, Alcoa, and Bell) and I to design this mandatory program for high-potential executives.

But there was a big problem. Illinois didn't understand—and didn't seem to want to understand—where the industry was going. It was a historic opportunity, with profound change coming to some of the biggest enterprises in the nation—Western Electric would become Lucent; AT&T would become a long-distance company; and all these large phone companies would be independent. Charan and I were involved in the company, and thought it was so exciting. It was no longer about regulation and technology. It was all about competition and customers. But, I found no real enthusiasm at Illinois. What we were doing was relegated to a peripheral activity. The university did not realize what a powerful forum the BAMP program created and how huge the industry really was. The vision was not there, and that was frustrating to me.

I felt I was coming to the end of my tenure at Illinois, the institution that made me who I am—in every respect. No institution stretched me or allowed me to fulfill my potential like Illinois did. Illinois provided both the right values and right opportunities. It taught me what true scholarship is all about, especially in terms of mentoring the next generation of scholars. It gave me important leadership opportunities, especially roles and responsibilities at the university level. Illinois even allowed me to gain experience in executive education, on the professional side, which was a whole new area of personal and career growth for me.

In addition, Champaign-Urbana had proved to be the perfect place to raise children. Because it was a college town, there was a prevailing belief in academic excellence. Our kids enjoyed the broadening experience of growing up with other professors' children, and they got a great education. Not only did they get a fine education in public schools, but both ended up going to Illinois as undergraduates. They could have gone elsewhere because they were good students, but they really felt good about Illinois. As well they should.

While the University of Illinois' business administration department seemed to be in a mid-life crisis, the whole university was in transition. The traditional disciplines no longer attracted students as they had in the past. Formerly, great departments, like math, English, psychology, and fine arts were losing students to programs that led directly to job opportunities. Confusion blurred the university's vision. There was turmoil everywhere, and I felt it too. Jokingly, I called it my midlife crisis. And what do you do when you are in a midlife crisis? You go to California!

LIFE LESSON

If I could do it all over again, I would not try to write so much so fast. A better model would be to write one book, based on one big research idea or project, and then write several spin-offs in the same area. Timing is important. Pace your publication schedule better than me and know when it is time to change. *The role of an institution—whether a university, a family, a religion, or a government—is to make ordinary people extraordinary and Illinois did exactly that for me. Find the institution that will make you extraordinary.*

8

FROM CORNFIELDS TO
PALM TREES

While considering where I might relocate, my essential requirement was that I be able to pursue both my academic and professional interests. I wanted to go to a place that would nurture both. Initially, it looked like that place might be the University of Southern California (USC). Donald Vinson, who had won the doctoral dissertation award for which I had served as judge, had gone to USC after developing an executive education program in banking at Louisiana State University (LSU). It was Vinson who prompted the idea of going to USC.

The dean at USC was Jack Steele, and the associate dean was Roy Herberger, whom I knew because of my interest in international marketing. Herberger had designed an international MBA program at USC called International Business Education and Research or IBEAR. Similar to the Sloan Fellows program at MIT, IBEAR was an 11-month program, designed for foreign managers.

Herberger and Steele were a dynamic team, and Herberger, at the urging of Vinson and with Steele's blessing, invited me to California. I went there for the first time in 1979 and was blown away. I had no experience with the lengths to which private universities can go to recruit senior faculty, but I can say now that they go all the way. They took me to the top restaurants in Hollywood, where even in those days it would cost several hundred dollars per person for dinner. Money was no object. They put Madhu and me up at the best hotels, right on the beach. I had never experienced such luxury in recruiting. They encouraged me to look around at my leisure and I returned, I believe, twice more. On one trip, I brought the children along, and I can remember the dean playing pool with my son. This was serious recruiting.

I liked one area for us to live and so did Madhu. We looked at the same house in Palos Verdes three times. There was stagflation following the energy crisis; interest rates were sky-high, but prices were way down, so the opportunity was there to buy a very fine house. All the signals were positive and when USC made me an offer, around March or April, they were so sure that I would accept for the next fall that they printed my name on the brochure announcing my appointment.

We returned to Illinois and agonized over whether to go or stay. Ultimately, we opted to stay put, primarily for the children's sake. Both of our children were still in high school. After my year in Denmark, we had sent Reshma to study in India for two years, at a school (Rishi Valley) based on humanistic values run by a well-known Indian philosopher and educator. It was not easy to get in. In most cases—believe it or not—the parents applied for admission as soon as a child was born. The students grow their own food, with the help of staffers, and the teachers live on campus. We heard about the school from a young man who had come to Illinois to do his Ph.D. in electrical engineering. He had studied there and convinced us that it was the most unique school imaginable. Reshma went there for ninth and tenth grades, which meant that she still had two years to go when she returned to Illinois.

It was 1981 and I found myself on the campus of the National University of Singapore (NUS), which was a very interesting coincidence. A student from Singapore, Tan Chin Tiong, had come to Penn State to get his Ph.D. in marketing and I became acquainted with him through my frequent visits to the campus, which was a hotbed of consumer behavior research. Like the IIT and IIM schools in India, NUS is a highly respected institution. Only the top 10 percent of high school students are admitted and graduates are likely to become government leaders and powerful bureaucrats.

After completing his Ph.D., Chin Tiong returned to Singapore and became a faculty member in the school of management at NUS. At these top schools (as in Europe), there is only one professor per discipline, and in management the one professor was an economist on the verge of retirement. Very quickly then, Chin Tiong became the head of management and invited me to come in as what the British system calls an "external examiner."

Under this system, an external eminent scholar becomes a sort of quality assurance officer—to ensure the exams are demanding and that the grading upholds high standards, as well as to review the honors theses across all management disciplines. Because my background was so eclectic—both behavioral and quantitative, including marketing and psychology as well as accounting and finance—I could review the 20 to 25 theses, each about 100 pages long. I accepted a two-year appointment, and my responsibility was to spend at least one week per year on the campus. They paid my travel, hotel, and other expenses, but there was no honorarium.

Basically, it was a kind of service. But what I got out of it was a new view of Singapore—as an incredibly vibrant nation, utterly transformed from the sleepy little peninsula I had visited in 1968. It was the most modern city you could imagine, and I was delighted when they extended my contract for two additional years. Eventually, Chin Tiong introduced me to the leaders of various government agencies, including Dr Tan Chin Nam, permanent secretary, who got me involved in many of his strategic planning meetings as he transformed, repositioned, and created organizations throughout his public sector career. The effect was to increase my macro and international perspectives. I saw a lot of excitement in Asia, and this encouraged me to think that maybe moving to Los Angeles would not be a bad thing.

As it so happened, USC had searched, but had not found the right person to fill the faculty opening, so they approached me again. Was I still interested? Well, I had more flexibility now, especially in terms of family. Reshma had completed high school in Champaign-Urbana and was now ready to enroll at the university. Our son, Rajen, was younger and would have to finish his last year of high school in California, but still the move would be less disruptive than it would have been a few years earlier. I was becoming increasingly Asia-centric, so I was now more willing to revisit the idea.

The Bell system announcement came in 1982, and my frustration with the BAMP program at Illinois also influenced my decision. In short, I decided to accept USC's offer. Again they had done a fantastic job of wining and dining me. They offered me a very generous package—including a 12-month contract as tenured faculty, which increased my salary by one third. And with an additional increase over my salary at Illinois to cover the cost of living in Los Angeles, I was told I was the highest paid professor in the School of Business. Because I had generated quite a few doctoral students at Illinois who were becoming well-known scholars in their own right, USC wanted me to focus primarily on doctoral education. The result was that I was assigned two doctoral seminars per year, a relatively light teaching load. In addition, I was given two half-time research assistants and a full-time administrative assistant, as well as a generous travel budget. I could not have asked for a better offer.

Yet USC managed to sweeten it a bit more. At that time, the hiring process required that any incoming professor, even a chaired professor, could not join the faculty with tenure. Steele had brought in some big names: Warren Bennis, a top scholar in leadership; Edward Lawler, whom I had tried to hire at Illinois; James O'Toole, a great name in management; and Arthur Laffer, an economist from the University of Chicago, famous for the Laffer curve. Our negotiations went on so long that there was not really time for the whole complicated approval process, so they waived it and I joined USC with tenure.

Herberger, the associate dean, then stepped in to help seal the deal. He told me, "Jag, there is one thing you absolutely must get in writing before you sign the contract—a parking space close to the School of Business. Get it now. After you arrive it will be too late." So, to top everything off, I got a reserved parking space close to my office.

Joining USC's faculty in the fall of 1983 presented a problem for me. At Illinois, the 1983–1984 academic year would have been my hard-earned sabbatical—a year-long leave of absence. If I started at USC in the fall, I would lose it. I explained the situation and USC came through for me again. They offered to pay my salary for the coming year so I would officially be on their payroll, but that I could stay at Illinois for the year to continue supervision of doctoral students.

Requesting a Leave of Absence

Leaving Illinois was a critical decision for me because not only would my son be graduating from high school that year, but several of my Illinois doctoral students were approaching graduation. Their thesis work was in the pipeline, and I wanted to be there to see them across the finish line. For example, there was Sigurd Troye, who had come from Norway to study under me and who is now a well-known professor there. Another was Bruce Kossar, whose work in multivariate statistics was of special interest to me.

Then there were two students—S. Ram from India and Adam Finn from Australia—with whom I conducted experiments on innovation resistance. (It was Ram with whom I wrote the book, *Bringing Innovation to Market*.) Another whose work I wanted to see through to completion was Mujafir Shaikh, an Indian student in mechanical engineering. Somehow he had become interested in the work we were doing, so I was very involved in his research as a part of his committee. And finally, there was Bruce Newman, with whom I had become quite close and with whom I would also become a co-author.

Again, I have to say how grateful I am to Illinois. The university agreed to the arrangement and allowed me to keep my office and all the related amenities. Eventually the one-year leave of absence was extended to two. I remained at Illinois through 1983–1984 and from 1984 began commuting back and forth between Los Angeles and Champaign-Urbana.

Illinois hoped I would stay on after the two-year leave of absence. Why was I leaving? Was I unhappy? These were good questions. But there was a simple answer. As soon as I got to USC, I started a center for the telephone industry, which meant that there was no way I could come back to Illinois even if I wanted to.

Keeping hope alive, Illinois continued to extend my leave of absence. Moreover, during the third year, 1985–1986, they asked me if I would come back as dean of the college. Vernon Zimmerman, who had been dean during my second stint as department chair, had stepped down, leaving the position open. He was an accounting professor with a passion for international accounting, and my keen interest in international business had bonded us. When he left the dean's office, there was faculty interest that I should be considered for the deanship. For one thing, I had experience at the university level and would therefore be able to represent the interests of the College of Commerce. For another, I was an accomplished scholar and administrator and had many good friends among the business school faculty. My industry contacts meant that I would also be an effective fund-raiser.

I had no desire to be dean. The only administrative job I had ever aspired to at Illinois was the vice chancellorship. However, I felt obligated to my friends and colleagues so I spoke with the new chancellor, William Gerberding. By that time, we had established a very successful executive MBA program, which drew executives from the big companies in the area—Caterpillar, Illinois Power, Archer Daniel Midland (ADM), and Kraft.

I had invited the chancellor to the opening reception of the Executive MBA Program, but he dismissed the program as a "degree-granting mill." So it wasn't surprising that when I went to talk to him about the deanship, there was no chemistry between us. I knew that meant the deanship would not work for me. I declined to be considered as a formal candidate.

At the same time, USC was becoming increasingly attractive to my new "Asia-centricity." Herberger, especially, appreciated my interest in Asia and knew I would be able to help in the IBEAR Program. Also, by now my Singapore friend, Chin Tiong, had introduced me to his brother, Chin Nam, who was the second in command at the Economic Development Board (EDB), the agency that drives the future of Singapore's economic development, much like the role MITI played in Japan. This was more macro, geopolitical stuff, very exciting to my expanding interests in these areas, and more reason for me to be enthusiastic about settling in California.

Lucky breaks and good timing were my constant companions, and each institution that employed me found ways to add new dimensions to my professional experience and to enrich my life. I had a knowing feeling that someone, somewhere was continuing to bless me. Looking back, I appreciate more and more that "the force was with me."

Upon arrival, I wasted no time immersing myself in my new life at USC. Any university that hires you at the level I was hired will have high expectations, and so very soon I found myself working the equivalent of three full-time jobs.

My first responsibility was to provide leadership for the dramatic changes taking place not only in the department but throughout the university. This meant contributing my experiences to a steady stream of committees, meetings and discussions whose purpose was to steer the university into the future.

The very large marketing department was in the middle of an overhaul. Right after me, a number of good faculty was brought on. There was Ben Enis, from the University of Missouri; Ed Tauber, who had his own market research company until Jack Steele recruited him; and Gary Frazier, whom I had recruited at Illinois in 1979. Wesley Johnston and Robert Spekman were bright young associate professors focused on business to business marketing. So there were lots of good new people. The question was what do we do now?

At the same time, the moment had come to ask some faculty to retire, a job the dean specifically asked me to head. Four faculty members, in particular, had been in the department for some time but were no longer doing any research; we had to figure out what to do with them. Two of the four were good citizens; they were not scholars, but they were teaching well and participating in service to the school. So we kept them. We decided that the other two needed to be nudged to retire. Basically, instead of contributing to the academic life of the department, they were using USC as a base for their own consulting businesses.

The retirement package offered them was very generous— much more carrot than stick—beginning with one year off with full pay, then 40 percent of salary (averaged over the last five years) for rest of the retiree's life. These faculty members were only in their late forties to early fifties, so it really was quite an offer. In fact, when I saw what USC was offering, I jokingly told Steele, "I'm ready to retire now."

Still, the larger problem remained. Our department had three subdisciplines: mathematical modeling (including operations research and multivariate statistics), the behavioral sciences (including consumer behavior and the psychological aspects of marketing), and managerial marketing. Each had enough faculty members to wield some power, and each wanted its own perspective to prevail. My job was to bring them together, to persuade them to coalesce under a common vision, as we had done at Illinois with the emergence of the behavioral perspective. But here the task proved impossible.

We tried to figure out some focus area to agree on like entertainment marketing. Hollywood was in our backyard and the studios put a lot of money into marketing new movies. Maybe we could unite our expertise in that area. On the other hand, we also had plenty of faculty members who had worked in industrial marketing, business-to-business. They all understood industrial buyers as opposed to consumers, and we thought that might provide a nexus. We kept trying but, unfortunately, never came to a resolution.

Committee Work Expansion

We were also trying to overhaul the Ph.D. program, and I was asked to be the coordinator for the doctoral students in marketing. I was teaching two doctoral seminars, so it made sense for me to be active in that program, but at the same time we were doing curriculum review and basically retooling every aspect of the program. Consequently, from 1984 onward, I served on the school-wide Ph.D. program committee.

In fact, Steele was keeping me quite busy at the school level, over and above my work in the department. Of special importance was the school's Personnel Committee, which advised not only on promotion and tenure decisions but on the whole range of faculty issues that came before the dean's office. I was named to that committee in 1983, even before my actual move to Los Angeles. In 1987, I became committee chair and served in that capacity until my tenure at USC ended.

We also had two executive education programs I was asked to help with. One was a nondegree, in-company program that USC wanted to expand. Because of my work on AT&T's BAMP program at Illinois they thought it was appropriate that I help guide that expansion. So I served on that program's steering committee for four years. The other was our EMBA (Executive MBA) program. This was a degree program for managers, with courses meeting on the weekends. Herberger had designed the IBEAR program, but another group was working on this EMBA program and recruited me to help them try to come up with something unique. Instead of the standard MBA program, where we would teach the functional disciplines of marketing, finance, accounting, and operations, we were looking for something that would bring all of these disciplines together. In the end, I was asked to be part of the EMBA core faculty from 1985 to 1989.

My most critical appointment came when the dean asked me to serve on the university promotion and tenure (P&T) committee. Weir had asked me to do the same thing at Illinois, and given that background, Steele thought I could make a valuable contribution at USC. However, this was a different experience. The P&T committee at USC was so large that it was divided into various disciplines and I was part of the social science committee. At Illinois it was a two-week process. All committee members received the huge stack of portfolios in

December and reviewed them simultaneously. At USC, it was a year-round process. Individual faculty members went into a room where the binders were waiting, reviewed them alone, and confidentially made their comments. So while there were eight or nine of us on this committee, the only times we met together were to receive our initial charge from the provost and to resolve disagreements on specific promotion and tenure cases.

During my last two years at USC, I served on yet another committee at the university level: Special Committee on Appointments, Promotion and Tenure. As its name implies, the task of this committee was to resolve the increasing number of "special cases" in this important area. The medical school was huge, with its own separate campus, and most of the exceptional cases seemed to come from there. Their faculty just could not conform to the typical liberal arts arrangement of six years in rank before promotion. They felt they deserved special consideration. Other schools, too, were constantly trying to bend the rules. After six years if you still have not established proper scholarly credentials, you are supposed to be out. But "up-or-out" was not strictly enforced. Loopholes were created. Department heads might put their at-risk faculty member on leave of absence, so the clock stops, or a research grant might suddenly come through to stop the clock. There was no firm policy, and all these "special" cases came before our committee.

The numbers were mind-boggling. If memory serves me right, we would get more than 100 of these cases each year. And, obviously, because each was special, you could not just read the portfolio and say yes or no. Forget anonymity: you had to get involved, to get to know these people and listen to their stories. Our job was to create an acceptable policy, to close the loopholes, but at the same time to be fair and understanding. It was very difficult, and it was a lot of work.

Back inside the department, my teaching began to shift. The doctoral seminars were supposed to be confined to the same three areas I had taught at Illinois—marketing theory, consumer behavior, and multivariate statistics, but then I was prevailed upon to teach in our flagship EMBA program, where senior executives from all over came to the campus on weekends. The idea was extra load, extra compensation. However, while I enjoyed the executive education program and wanted to keep teaching in it, I soon got tired of the extra load and did not really need the extra compensation. At the same time, it became clear that we had plenty of faculty who could teach multivariate statistics, so I dropped that from my repertoire. As my passion for consumer behavior was waning, my interest in marketing theory was growing. The result was that, for most of my years at USC, I taught the marketing theory class and, on weekends, the EMBA class.

The marketing theory class absorbed me, at least in part, because of the book on the subject that I was working on (which surveys the 12 distinct schools of marketing theory that have evolved since 1906). At Illinois, with the help of my student, Dennis Garrett, I was putting together a complementary volume: a compendium of readings from the authors whose works I had referenced in the book. The book was a synthesis of the discipline, from my own perspective, and I felt strongly that it needed to be backed up by readings from the original authors. Many of these writings were in books and textbooks, which meant obtaining reprint permissions from publishers. It was a huge job, with which, thankfully, Garrett provided tremendous help. The finished volume ran to some 800 pages. It was one of the great projects of my marketing theory classes.

The marketing theory class at USC was different from the one I taught at Illinois. At Illinois, we did not allow MBA or MS students to join our doctoral seminars. At USC, though, there were not enough marketing Ph.D. students, and we had a rule that all elective classes had to have a minimum of 12 students. So I taught the class in the evening and opened it to MBA students, and the classes promptly filled up. Surprisingly, I found the MBA students to be as intellectually curious as the doctoral students.

Those were great classes—and memorable evenings. Even though the class ended at 9:30 p.m., no one wanted to leave. My colleague Gary Frazier, whom I had recruited to Illinois, became an even close friend at USC. Frazier married a young woman named Kyoung who was a successful fashion designer. He honored me by asking me to be one of his groomsmen, which I had thoroughly enjoyed. When he came to USC, he and Kyoung moved into Palos Verdes, the same neighborhood where my family lived. Kyoung got a job with a casual wear company, where she prospered. Frazier taught an evening class the same time I did, and since the young couple had no children, the three of us would have dinner together at a nearby Mexican restaurant. We did this every week, and it was a wonderful bonding experience. Our friendship endures to this day.

Of the students who chose to work under me in the doctoral program at USC, four stand out.

First was Tasadduq Shervani, who had been studying at Oklahoma State before coming to work with me at USC. He was an extraordinary student and we became very close. I was getting increasingly interested in strategy at this point, and had begun formulating a new framework, which came to be called "The Rule of Three." I wanted Shervani to work with me on this new endeavor, to help me write a book on the subject. Also, I was doing independent consulting work as in-house advisor in several companies, as I had done at Illinois. One of my clients was Tektronix in Portland, which had asked me to design a marketing curriculum for about 100 managers and executives. I designed nine separate classes, two days each, to be taught over a period of one year. Shervani became my key assistant on that project as well. He went on to become a professor at Southern Methodist University and has his own very successful consulting and training practice.

Shervani's own work involved a new economic theory influencing the marketing discipline in a big way—"transaction cost economics," advocated by Oliver Williamson. The traditional theory, which held that all that matters in the marketplace is the price, was originally challenged by Nobel Prize winner Ronald Coase. He had grown up working in New York City's garment district and had observed the importance of relationships. Coase theorized that company behavior is often predicated on relationships between suppliers and customers. He saw that suppliers actually dedicate assets (people assets, factory assets, or whatever) to a given customer, so the customer is not motivated purely by the market transaction. Williamson added that the cost of doing transactions again and again is so high that it becomes preferable to find an alternative to transaction pricing—that's the essence of transaction cost economics.

Coase's theory was getting a lot of attention, and I was moving in the same direction from a different perspective. After reviewing the 12 theories, in the marketing theory book, I looked into the future of marketing and came to two conclusions. First, in marketing we do not have a comprehensive theory, only various subsets and we need a single synthesizing theory to move our discipline to the next level. Second, in its infancy, the task of marketing had been to capture first-time customers, but now as a mature economy what matters most is customer retention and loyalty of existing customers.

Our society had moved from the agricultural to an industrial age, where for the first time, people were buying branded, ready-to-eat products: cereals, rice, milk, breakfast foods, and so on, all the way up to appliances and automobiles. Marketing was originally organized around customer acquisition. But by the 1980s, the consumer market had matured, and repeat buyers were now a much larger segment than first-time buyers, by as much as a 90 to 10 ratio.

Marketing's task needed to shift to customer retention from customer acquisition. For that reason, I had begun thinking about relationships, about how to retain loyalty. I also concluded that we should no longer focus on prospective customers but, rather, on existing customers. In fact, this was the genesis of the Howard–Sheth theory, with a focus on how customers become loyal to a brand despite increasing choices.

Shervani's thesis sought to test Williamson's theory in a marketing context. He wanted to test his hypotheses in the real world, (in a business-to-business context) and he was able to get cooperation from several companies—Motorola, IBM, Xerox, 3M, NCR, HP, and others—to understand how long-term relationships are formed and maintained between a customer and a supplier.

My second student of note was Robert Windsor. Windsor was, well, different. He really did not enjoy being a traditional student, and he was quite independent and intellectually ahead of others. I was doing work in the strategy area, and he was interested in one of the theories in that field called population ecology, which brought a Darwinian perspective to competition—survival of the fittest—and it was producing an interesting new body of strategy literature. I like students who do what they want to do as long as they do it in a scholarly way. My job is to nurture the idea but challenge it at the same time. Windsor was developing his own sub-theory, called "island ecology," which examines what happens when a new competitor, like an alien species, is introduced into an eco-environment where harmonious coexistence has prevailed. He used it to analyze two industries—cigarettes and automobiles—and he did some very effective computer simulation work to make his argument. I thought it was brilliant and enthusiastically became his thesis advisor.

Third was Prem Shamdasani, who came from the same school in Singapore (NUS) where I was invited to be the external examiner. Shamdasani was one of those bright students sent abroad to earn the Ph.D., fully funded by the government for five years, in exchange for returning to Singapore. Shamdasani's thesis was on alliances between suppliers and customers, and, like Shervani's dissertation, it helped with the important work of bringing Williamson's theory into the marketing context.

The last of these Ph.D. students I want to mention is Barbara Gross, a bright and determined student. She came to the doctoral program in marketing because she had been working for a market-research company, had an opportunity to teach part-time, and decided that she wanted to go into research and teaching. What she did not realize was that doctoral students at places like USC are expected to emphasize research over teaching. Like Windsor, she was not sure that USC was a good fit. I became her mentor and we became lifelong friends. In addition to her academic predicament, Gross also had personal problems to deal with. Her mother died and then her father, both within one year. Also, she wanted to have children but was discouraged from doing so by her other professors, who insisted she do her thesis first. My view was that you cannot stop the biological clock, but you can stop the doctoral one.

I brought Gross in as the third author, along with Bruce Newman, who had done most of the research at Illinois, on *Consumption Values and Market Choices*. This was the book that grew out of the "five values" theory, the measurement instrument we had created and that Mickey Belch had tested on political campaigns. Newman continued to use the theory in the classes he taught at the University of Wisconsin at Milwaukee (he is now at DePaul University in Chicago). We decided to write a book, and Gross became our third author.

Gross also co-authored a paper in *Journal of Marketing*, a time-oriented historical analysis of advertising that covered 100 years in one of the oldest women's magazines, *Ladies Home Journal* still in print. She actually managed to get her hands on 100 years of back issues. Our hypothesis was that the emphasis of advertising had shifted over time. When women primarily were homemakers, it was all about how to do that job better—how to use the right ingredients in a recipe, what cleaning products worked best. But as women went to work outside the home, it became more about convenience—how to save time and effort at home, how to free the woman from housekeeping work. Content analysis of advertising aggregated over time demonstrated quite clearly this shift in the message of advertising.

Gross left the program shortly after her parents died and she became pregnant with her first child. She began doing real estate work and was not sure she ever wanted to complete her doctorate. But I told her she had already done so much—she was a top student—that she was too close to the end to walk away. I told her I would do whatever it took on my end, and after three years away and being pregnant with her second child, she completed her thesis. Gross subsequently joined the marketing faculty at California State University, Northridge, which offered a balanced emphasis on both teaching and scholarship that she appreciated and nurtured her research interest in marketing education, as well as consumer behavior. She eventually went into administration as the Chief of Staff for the University President.

During this time, innovation continued to be one of my research interests. I was intrigued by why innovation is sometimes accepted and other times resisted. Everett Rogers, a scholar in USC's Annenberg School of Communication, had written a classic book on diffusion of innovation. An expert in rural sociology, he examined how farmers adopt innovations—like tractors, hybrid seeds, new fertilizers, and the like. What he came up with was a theory of opinion leadership. His argument was that there is a group of opinion leaders in the farming community who serve as gatekeepers. If a company wants its innovation adopted, it must work with those people. If the opinion leaders stamp it with their approval, everybody else comes along.

I had developed a different perspective, namely innovation resistance. My view was that opinion leaders were but a small group, just 10–15 percent—market elites. While they might indeed be "market makers," we still needed to understand why the masses resist change. Obviously, some innovations succeed, but most fail—in spite of the endorsement of opinion leaders. This was a fascinating area of study to me, especially since we in the western world are very pro-change. But this may not be true in traditional societies.

One more endeavor consumed me at USC, and I was deeply involved in it almost from the moment I arrived. In fact, the most intense year I have ever had in my life was 1984. The 1983–1984 academic year was intense because I was going back and forth from Illinois to California. It was a hectic time, and an experience with Newman was typical of that year. From his early undergraduate days at Illinois, Bruce Newman had become a family member to Madhu and me. When Madhu wanted a hedge planted at the edge of our backyard, he and one of his classmates dug every hole for the fast-growing, short-lived poplars, as well as for the slow-growing, long-lived evergreens that would eventually replace them. I persuaded him to join the doctoral program at Illinois, and, after graduating, he went to Baruch School of Management in New York. When he found that the big city was not to his liking, he moved on to the University of Wisconsin at Milwaukee, and then back to his hometown of Chicago at DePaul University.

As I was frantically trying to physically move from Illinois to USC, Bruce sent word that he was getting married. The wedding was scheduled to take place in Milwaukee. Our flight out of Illinois was scheduled for the day after the wedding, and we were in the middle of packing up our whole household. Commercial flights did not fly to Milwaukee from Champaign-Urbana but the University of Illinois had a school of aviation to train pilots, mostly for agricultural work like crop dusting. In terms of arrivals and departures (even though they may have been just training flights), it constituted the second-largest airport in Illinois, next to O'Hare. In other words, there were plenty of planes there, so Madhu and I chartered one and flew to Milwaukee. It was essential that we be there to be at Newman's wedding. A car picked us up and took us to the wedding, and then, maybe three hours later in all, the car took us back to our plane and we flew back home. It was a mind-boggling experience.

In my early days at USC, as I mentioned earlier, I had what amounted to three full-time jobs: One was teaching and research, another was all of the administrative leadership work, and the third was executive education (my own professional work). But what I really wanted to do was to start a center for the telephone industry. The idea came out of the BAMP program, and eventually I started the Center for Telecommunications Management (CTM) at USC in early 1985.

My journey has been filled with fortunate encounters with eminent scholars—Abraham Maslow at Brandeis University, George Homans at Harvard, Muzafer Sherif at Penn State,

Stanley Schacter and William McGuire at Columbia, Harry Triandis, Marty Fishbein, and Ledyard Tucker at Illinois, and of course, Warren Bennis, Everett Rogers, and Jack Steele at USC. So many great scholars in fields, different from my own, were so helpful to me. They were all helpful in supporting my research even if it provided an alternate perspective.

LIFE LESSON

One of the great lessons of an unpredictable journey is to be flexible. Like for-profit entrepreneurs, academic entrepreneurs must be flexible. What you think will work may not and many things may not work out the way you expect. *When opportunity knocks, answer the door.*

9

USC CTM AND ATLANTA

When the Bell system break-up was announced in 1982, I was doing some work for one of the already-deregulated consumer electronics division of AT&T—a maker of handsets. The head of the division at that time was Randall Tobias, a vice chairman of AT&T who was about to become chairman. There were already about 1,800 retail phone centers, and I was teaching a three-day program to Tobias's managers about consumers who come to shopping centers to buy phones. As soon as the announcement came, I went to Tobias's office and said, "Randy, we need a separate center for understanding the competitive future of the telecom industry. Having already been on the deregulated side of the business, he fully understood that the focus was going to need to shift to customers and competition. He gave me his blessing: "Go and start your center and I will help you."

Since my move to California was already set in stone, I could not launch the project at Illinois. However, as soon as I arrived at USC in the fall of 1984, I went to Jack Steele and began to explain to him that we had a great opportunity. I would create a Center for Telecommunications Marketing, housed in our Marketing Department. Tobias and I agreed that the teaching and learning of marketing was the key, because the regulated industry had never had to market. I told Steele I would get the telephone companies to fund it, especially AT&T.

The break-up took place in 1984 and suddenly we had seven Baby Bells not talking to each other—each playing its own game. Worse yet, separation from AT&T ended like a bitter divorce. Each Bell was looking for an outside perspective on customers and competition. In 1983, right after I accepted the USC job, I got a call from one of the Baby Bells in the Midwest, now called Ameritech, asking me to take a two-year leave of absence to come to Chicago and become an in-house, full-time advisor on how to organize the new company. A precedent had already been set. In 1982, when the announcement came and all the Baby Bells were staring into an uncertain future, one of them—U.S. West, which became Qwest—hired a professor from the Wharton School to come full-time to guide their reorganization. The Baby Bells were all looking for help and I was tempted. Ameritech said that I could stay in Champaign-Urbana and commute to Chicago. But I was already on USC's payroll. Besides, I worried that if I shifted to industry, I might not ever return to the academic world.

The Telecom Center Venture

The offer to be an advisor in industry was flattering. Once word got out that I was leaving Illinois, I received other offers. One was from AT&T, who offered me a position as an officer in the company. It was a lucrative and influential opportunity, but I declined. I knew that if I became a company employee, I would no longer be able to see things objectively or say things honestly. I told them that I would be more helpful as an advisor, and they agreed to employ me in that capacity.

Another offer came from the University of Texas in Austin. William Cunningham, whom I knew from Michigan State, had become dean there, and he tried to recruit me. Again it was tempting. He was a good friend and a great leader. He offered the same package as USC, but pointed out that in Texas there is no state income tax, and the cost of living would be much lower. But again, I said no. I had given my word to USC.

So to USC I went, determined to get the center off the ground as quickly as possible. The time was right for it. The only problem was that USC had not hired me to start a telecom center; no part of my contract related to such an endeavor. Consequently, no resources were allotted to it. Nevertheless, Steele saw that this was important to me and did not want to stand in the way. I told Steele, "Okay, I know there is no money, but how about people?" He let me have Thomas Hauser, from the business communications department. Steele knew a center for the telecommunications industry would be right up Hauser's alley. So Hauser became my first colleague and his office became the center's first home.

While at Illinois, I did some work for Whirlpool, and Whirlpool published a weekly newsletter that gathered information about what was happening in the appliance industry. It went out to all the top officers of the company, and since I was an advisor, I received one too. I thought that was a great idea for us to create a newsletter. I asked Hauser to manage it, which he was happy to do.

But where would the content come from? I knew that the information in the Whirlpool newsletter came from a little research company in Chicago who agreed to provide research for us too, but it would cost us. This was before the Internet, so there was real work involved in finding and clipping hard copy articles from various newspapers and magazines. Since the center had no budget, I gave a personal loan of $40,000 to get the newsletter off the ground.

The newsletter gave me something tangible to offer, so I began to knock on the doors of potential sponsors. My original plan was to bring in all the telecommunications enterprise customers, particularly, the large business customers. I approached about 100 companies, offering each one of a membership in the center for $1,000 a year. I figured that the phone companies would urge their customers to become members because the game was now all about customers and competition, and the market was heating up. I thought the phone companies might even pay for their key customers' memberships, since these were the people who would be driving the industry. Out of the 100 approached, I was only able to recruit about 25 members, and even those few, seldom showed up at organized events. Why? They were consumed with crisis management. They were putting out fires. I had to admit that my idea was a flop and I had to change my game plan.

My new plan entailed going directly to the phone companies—the seven Baby Bells and AT&T, along with independents like MCI, GTE, and Continental Telephone (which would later merge with United Telephone and become Sprint). I also decided that if I was going to beg, I might as well beg big. I told them I wanted their most-senior person, their fastest-rising officer and a possible CEO successor to serve on my board. This person had to be their superstar.

I would have four mandatory board meetings—two in person and two by phone. "It will be just like your own board meeting," I offered. "This is *your* center. I will be a catalyst and a thought leader, and you will learn how to look at your industry from the customer's perspective." The price for founder-members was $100,000 per year for a three-year commitment.

The first "customer" was Richard McCormick from U.S. West. His boss was Jack McAllister, the maverick who became the first head of U.S. West. McCormick was the rising star. By the time I made my pitch, it was clear that McCormick would succeed McAllister. McCormick said the words I longed to hear: "Okay, I'm in." The second "customer" was Robert Barnett from Ameritech, where the first chairman, and change maker, was William Weiss. Weiss put his chief human resources officer on my board. At Bellsouth I approached John Clendenin, Chairman and CEO, and he nominated his chief of staff to serve on my board. Pretty soon, all of the Baby Bells, with the sole exception of Pacific Bell, were on board, and my center was up and running. The Board was comprised of twenty members, including USC's Dean of the Business School.

The Center for Telecommunications Management (CTM) was, in many respects, the center of my life during my years at USC. These were interesting times for the industry. The boundaries that defined customers, suppliers, and competitors had become blurry, so our purpose—to help these telecom companies survive the transition from a regulated to a competitive industry—was important. The center was successful and grew rapidly.

Of several functions, perhaps the most important was our annual roundtable retreat. Its key mission was to foster a clear understanding of this evolving industry, to help players inside the industry see it from a customer and competition viewpoint. In essence, the roundtable was a retreat for all of the board members and a varying number of invited guests. We convened twice a year, once on the West Coast and once on the East Coast. Each roundtable had a theme, chosen, in advance, by the board. Each board member invited one or two people (either customers or officers from their companies) for a limit of about 50 or 60 attendees. Often, an industry stakeholder, like an FCC commissioner, a senator or congressman, or a top technology guru was invited to participate in or moderate the roundtable discussion.

The round table was literally a discussion and it was always off the record. In fact, the round table was so uniquely organized that I began to call it a "square table." There was no podium, no designated speaker or presenter. Since the focus was to learn from each another, nothing more complicated than a flip chart could be used during discussions. Active participation, spontaneity, and genuine dialogue were encouraged.

Executives were not used to this format. As regulated monopolies, telephone companies *always* had everything planned and orchestrated such that there were no surprises. Our goals were different, as were the outcomes, so we started each roundtable with a provocative statement about the industry's future, about a particular company, or about a new technology. I specifically pushed participants to the edge of the outrageous until someone at the table responded. Fortunately, many participants were board members, people who understood what I was trying to do. Once the discussion was in full swing, the moderator was phased out.

Roundtable retreats occurred over a three day period (Thursday through Saturday afternoon). Participants were encouraged to bring their spouses and to stay through Sunday. The goal was for participants to relax, socialize, and create friendships. The hope was that they would return to work refreshed, with new ideas and new enthusiasm. More importantly, that they would look forward to coming back each year. From both professional and social standpoints, the round table was a world-class event.

A second major function of CTM was the creation of executive education programs focused on the telecom industry. We actually ran two of these—a two-week program for senior executives and a month-long program for middle managers. In addition to founder member companies, participants came from British Telecom, the Dutch company KPN, Korea Telephone, Bell Canada, and several independents and cable companies who were thinking about jumping into the telecom industry. The programs were designed specifically around management and leadership issues within the industry. We held the classes on or near the USC campus. Like the roundtable, the executive education programs were both popular and profitable.

A third important function was writing research reports, in most cases about the future of the industry. One of our documents, *Telecom Outlook Report*, became a key strategic planning tool for many of these companies. For the report, we polled 400 to 500 experts around the world—experts in technology, policy, globalization, customers, and competition—posing specific scenarios and asking about the likelihood of these scenarios being realized over the next five years, 10 years, and on out into the future. Then we tracked the questions and responses over time, from one year to the next. It was the best information available and people loved to get that report, which was co-authored by Massoud Saghafi, who is now at San Diego State University.

Also on the research side, CTM organized academic conferences. The objective for the conferences was to convince people in academia that telecom was relevant to the marketing discipline. We wanted to get the word out that the industry was rapidly changing and that marketing, especially branding and segmentation were going to be instrumental to the industry's ongoing evolution. We wanted faculty to become motivated to work in this industry, and we saw academic conferences as a great way to get faculty involved. Out of these conferences came a publication containing all the research papers which spread "the gospel" even further. I even tried to start a master's degree program—the MS in Telecom and Information Management. The rationale was that telephone companies had been sending their executives to MIT's Sloan School of Management, a nine-month program, whereas what was needed was something specifically targeted to the telecom industry. To start a degree program at *any* university is a very complicated process, and although the program ran once, it failed to gain internal traction. USC's CTM was really quite unique. Other universities had telecom centers in areas like engineering and policy research, but there was nothing like it in a business school. It grew so fast that it created a potential problem. There was not enough space in the business school for the CTM. However, USC had a College of Continuing Education, which had been funded by a food services entrepreneur named Devry Davidson. His money was used to create the Davidson Conference Center, but the college itself was not doing well. CTM, on the other hand, was booming, so I met with Davidson and his executive director, Phil Rapa, and they were more than happy to relocate the CTM to their facility. That gave me plenty of teaching space inside a beautiful new facility, so all CTM programs were taught there. It was on USC's campus, but not attached directly to the business school. Eventually, I also relocated my office to the Center.

By launching and managing the CTM, I learned a lot about the telecom industry, academic alignment, and how to organize an enterprise. The CTM grew to include a dozen or so full-time staff. We managed several programs and a number of faculty members were actively involved with programming. It was a challenge to pull all the working pieces together and get them to gel. Since there was no financial support from USC, one of the key requirements for CTM's success was fundraising. As a

result, I was on the road almost weekly, trying to convince telephone companies and their suppliers to buy into the program.
I had a very busy schedule.

Los Angeles Loses Its Appeal

My life at USC was engaging, productive, and rewarding. CTM
was a great success and, personally, deeply gratifying. So why
was I dissatisfied?

My biggest problem with being at USC was location. Los
Angeles was just too far away. Nearly 40 weeks out of the
year, I was flying somewhere, and virtually every trip, whether
to an academic conference, to do fundraising, or to accept an
invitation as a visiting scholar, made me realize that most of
the world was still east of the Mississippi and not west of the
Rockies. Most of the companies we worked with—AT&T, MCI,
Bell Atlantic, Southern Bell, Bell Canada, British Telecom, and
others—were on the East Coast. By being on the West Coast, I
thought that we would be more involved with Asian companies,
but in most cases they were not yet ready for the transition
from regulated to competitive industry. Consequently, I was
always flying from one side of the United States to the other;
often accumulating more than 2,000 miles each way. Long treks
and multiple meetings in different cities the same week meant
regularly building in layovers at the O'Hare Hilton in Chicago.
That kind of travel took its toll.

Another source of dissatisfaction was commuting. Like
Columbia in the 1960s, USC's urban location made it difficult to
live nearby. The suburban area Madhu and I had chosen to reside
was a popular suburb with USC faculty, but the commute was
time-consuming. There was a stark difference between campus
life in Illinois, sans traffic problems, and Los Angeles, the traffic
capital of the nation. Even when I was in town, I spent a lot of
time in my car. From home to the office, then from the office to
the airport and finally, from the airport back home was a chore.

Los Angeles traffic was both overwhelming and bizarre. It
was not uncommon to hear a radio alert about the freeway being

snarled because of a sofa in the middle of lane two. If I had to teach an executive education class at 8 o'clock in the morning, I would drive up the night before and stay in a hotel near the campus just to make sure I was on time. I never got used to Los Angels traffic.

The talent pool in Los Angeles was also a source of dissatisfaction. It was almost impossible to get really talented support staff with great work ethics like those in the Midwest. California's workforce was filled with people who were talented, but did not want to work for anyone. It seemed like we were always dealing with high turnover at CTM, a source of ongoing frustration.

Additionally, the CTM was never integrated into the university. After the departure of Jack Steele, we had two interim deans: Steve Kerr, a top scholar in management, and Doyle Williams, who had been dean of the School of Accountancy. Both had good intentions and both were very receptive to CTM. But because of the discipline-based departmental structure in the School of Business, CTM never became a true part of USC. My original intention was to house the center in the marketing department, but Steele recommended that it should be a management center rather than a marketing center, and therefore the CTM was housed at the "dean level." When that happens, when you become "the dean's program" rather than the department's program, you are essentially homeless. Despite best efforts to brand the CTM as a USC program, it was always perceived as Jag Sheth's center and driven by "what Jag wants to do." All these factors stood in the way of the real integration that the CTM needed.

Jack Borsting, who had been the provost at the Post Naval Academy in Monterrey and a dean at the University of Miami, was named dean of the School of Business. When he became dean, he brought about change—which is the role of the dean—and some of those changes were not well received by the faculty. We were in the 1990–1991 recession, and budget issues loomed. On the other hand, he was supportive of CTM and felt it was a valuable asset to the university. Ironically, after I left USC, Borsting became the director of the CTM.

Slowly, but surely, the incentive to leave Los Angeles began to outweigh the benefits of staying. BellSouth had become a significant supporter of CTM. The company routinely put high-ranking executives on the board; people likely to become CEO—like Duane Ackerman. It did not take Ackerman long to realize my dissatisfaction with Los Angeles. He felt that the CTM could do more and grow faster if it were located on the East Coast, and he believed the center would be great for Atlanta. Ackerman was aware of the strong drive in the state of Georgia, as there had been in Texas in the 1980s, to bring world-class faculty members to the institutions of higher learning: Georgia Tech, University of Georgia, Georgia State, and Emory University. Georgia's government had figured out that this was the key to encouraging corporations to move to Atlanta.

At the same time, Emory was looking to invest in its business school. It had earned its reputation with a first-class undergraduate liberal arts program and its medical school. Now Emory wanted to grow its graduate programs, especially its School of Public Health and its School of Business. The business school had already hired a leader from outside academia (which was unusual): John Robson, a Ph.D. in economics, who had worked for the Federal Reserve Board and then became Chairman and CEO of G.D. Searle, which he subsequently sold to Monsanto. Wanting to make a contribution on the academic side, he came to Emory in 1989 with the idea of ramping up the School of Business to become the "Harvard of the South." Emory had always aspired to be a "Southern Ivy," so Robson's plans fit into the grand design.

Robson quickly brought in two senior faculty: Bob Miles (Harvard) in management and strategy and George Benston (University of Rochester) in finance and accounting. Both were highly respected, so an exciting transformation was already underway.

I have always liked being at a place that is growing; one that is moving up in the world. I like to build rather than manage, so Emory had a lot of appeal. The president at the time was James Laney, who had been a professor at the Candler School of Theology. We were introduced by John Clendenin, who preceded Duane Ackerman as CEO of BellSouth, and who was a friend of mine from the BAMP program. Clendenin and Laney served on the board of Coca-Cola Enterprises, and he suggested to Laney that I would be a good fit for Emory. Laney was enthusiastic about the idea. He said to me, "You must come here. It's a good place." So already I had a dynamic leader at the university level personally encouraging me to relocate.

I was 52 at the time, and my perhaps overly optimistic view was that by age 55, I would be able to change my focus and begin giving back to society. Although I agreed to come to Emory, my passion was to be of service. I wanted to change my orientation to focus on social causes in just a few years, which is something I shared with Laney. Laney was smart. His response was:

> Look, we have the Carter Center here in Atlanta, which we are planning to integrate into the university. You can become a Carter Fellow and do all the social work you want to do in that capacity. We'll find a way for you to do what you want to do.

I had first visited Emory in the 1980s. I was a visiting scholar for a day and was impressed by the experience. It was a university carved out of a forest. The Midwest could only offer cornfields, but Emory offered a panoramic scene of trees, creeks, and hills. I liked the campus and its natural setting. Because of the presence of the Centers for Disease Control and Emory University Hospital, there were hundreds of doctors and scientists who lived nearby and there were good neighborhoods close to the university. Emory was a campus community, more like Illinois than USC. I missed the college town life and found Emory appealing.

I agreed with Ackerman that moving the CTM to Atlanta would be a tremendous advantage. Atlanta was a growing, vibrant city and a number of other corporations were relocating there. Also, Atlanta is a great convention city. One of the biggest conventions is SuperComm, where all the communications suppliers exhibit their latest gadgetry, and all the service providers check out all the new stuff. It is a huge event—50,000 to 60,000 attendees—and we thought that CTM could link with SuperComm.

That possibility seemed even more likely because of Robert Janowiak, who had become director of a National Engineering Consortium (NEC) in Chicago, which eventually became International Engineering Consortium (IEC). Janowiak had become a strategic member of my board, and our organizations had a great relationship. We envisioned putting together an integrated executive education program at SuperComm, which would greatly increase the CTM's awareness. It was all very exciting. Revenue could be increased, especially with BellSouth no longer having to spend so much money on travel to Los Angeles for its participants. We believed that if we moved the CTM to Atlanta, it would likely grow exponentially, especially with the additional presence of a great engineering school like Georgia Tech, with which we could link.

I was excited about the prospect of moving to Atlanta, but there were a number of challenges. The biggest obstacle was overcoming my wife's desire to remain in Los Angeles. Madhu loved living in Los Angeles, for several reasons. First, our house was spectacular. We were 1,300 feet above the sea level, overlooking the Pacific Ocean on one side where you could see the whole Los Angeles basin. On a clear day you could see the famous Hollywood sign 30 to 40 miles away. On the northeast side you could see the Palm Springs Mountains. At night it was nothing but twinkling lights. It was very tranquil up on our hillside, and we even had wildlife in our backyard. At night, we would walk to the top of the hill above our house, about a quarter of a mile. The view was absolutely breathtaking.

In addition, we had discovered lots of family friends and relatives from India living in Los Angeles. We had no idea they were even in America, and Madhu took great pleasure in getting all the news about family members and old friends still living in our native country. Finally, Madhu had become very active with the Jain Center in Los Angeles. That was her passion, and I knew she would hate to break ties with the Center. Even though both of our children were also in Los Angeles, they were young adults who could move where they liked, so this was not as much of a "family problem" as it had been when we moved away from Illinois.

Another obstacle had to do with compensation. I was on a 12-month salary at USC, with a lifetime contract. Emory could only offer me a nine-month contract. In effect, I would be sacrificing one-third of my salary. I also had two research assistants at USC and at Emory I would have none. Given the importance of my research work throughout my career, this was a significant loss. Finally, Emory had no Ph.D. program. This was a huge drawback because the most satisfying part of my job, wherever I was working, was mentoring doctoral students and being involved in their various research projects. I knew that I would miss that tremendously.

Why Move?

How to rationalize what was basically an irrational proposition? First, I told myself that CTM would grow much faster in Atlanta, especially by linking with BellSouth and SuperComm. Second, I told Madhu, who not only loved Los Angeles, but who hated the moist heat typical of the Southeast, that humidity was good for her complexion. That did not work. In fact, the three things Madhu still dislikes about living in Atlanta are the humidity, cockroaches, and snakes.

While my attempts were lame, what Emory did to bring Madhu around was phenomenal. The person who worked on my behalf was Brown Wittington, an Emory icon, who eventually became marketing department head. Wittington pulled out all the stops. He would fly all the way to Los Angeles just to meet with me at the airport for a couple of hours. We met in the airline's lounge (no security issues in those days), then he would turn around and fly back to Atlanta. One of his undergraduate students was the daughter of an Indian professor in Emory's School of Medicine, Dr Bhagirath Majmudar, who was very much a leader in the Indian community in Atlanta. Wittington got in touch with him and asked him and his wife to meet with Madhu and me. This delightful couple insisted upon hosting Madhu for an entire week's stay. I came for my interview and had to return to USC, but Madhu stayed for the whole week. They worked hard to convince her that Atlanta would be a good place, with an interesting, growing Indian community and lots of other things she could get involved in. I think that was a big factor in her eventually saying yes and, in fact, Madhu is now quite active in Atlanta's Jain Center and other volunteer activities (although even today she tells me she will never forgive me for taking her from Los Angeles).

As for the reduction in compensation, I convinced myself that housing would be more affordable in Atlanta (a mortgage payment half as big as ours in Los Angeles), and that since we would be able to live near the campus, we could save time and money. I also rationalized that traveling would be more convenient and less stressful. Atlanta is a major hub, and I am able to get anywhere in the eastern states in just an hour or two.

Another argument I mustered was that there is a great talent pool in Atlanta. The city was attracting smart young professionals from all over the country. In fact, young people could afford to live in Atlanta and appeared to take their work seriously. That was important in light of our anticipation that CTM would grow.

Finally, since I like to build rather than manage, Emory offered the opportunity to build. The business school was touted as "up-and-coming," with aspirations to become world class. It was another new slate, much like the opportunity that drew me to Illinois. And part of my mandate was to attract other top-notch young faculty scholars.

Those were my rationalizations, and they proved to be sufficient. The formal offer came in January 1991. I accepted within a month and relocated to Atlanta in the fall.

On the family front, Reshma had graduated from Illinois and had gone to IBM, but discovered that she was not an engineer and decided to return to school for an MBA. We encouraged her to attend USC with the added bonus that she could live at home. She entered USC's two-year MBA program and taught part-time, which is something she really enjoyed. While at USC, Reshma met the man who would become her husband, Hitesh. He was a New Yorker, working for BellCore, and when the company gave him a year off to complete his master's degree in electrical engineering, he came to USC. He and Reshma fell in love and set the wedding date for July 1989.

As a student leader, Reshma had organized a fundraising campaign which included a photo of the university's famous mascot, "the Trojan Horse," in the middle of the Coliseum, where the USC Trojans play football. So for her wedding—to satisfy the Indian tradition requiring that the bridegroom ride in on a horse—she was able to get the Trojan Horse, and, in fact, the Trojan marching band as well. The typical Indian wedding ceremony is full of fanfare, but nobody had ever seen anything like this. It took place in the huge parking lot of a hotel in Torrance—an area large enough for all of the festivities. It was really quite an event—and still talked about today in the Indian community in Los Angeles.

Our son Rajen, had gone to Illinois for his undergraduate degree in 1985. He joined AT&T and relocated to Los Angeles and became an account manager for Hughes Corporation, an AT&T customer. He also completed his MBA at USC in the evening program.

LIFE LESSON

If you are serious about starting a center at a university, work to institutionalize it from day one. The best way to do that is to integrate it into existing curriculum, like a minor at the undergraduate level or a degree program at the graduate level. That way, Ph.D. students can immediately do research based on what the center is doing. If the center is viewed from the beginning as peripheral, it will remain peripheral, rather than part of the core of what the university does. *In short, if you begin with the end in mind, you will reach your end.*

10

NEW CHALLENGES AND
A NEW CENTER

In many ways, my move to Emory University was like déjà vu. Leaving Los Angeles for Atlanta was a lot like my earlier move from New York to Illinois. In both cases I was moving from an urban environment to a college town, which was very much to my liking.

Different from Champaign-Urbana, Atlanta is no small town. It is a major airline hub, which gave me easy access to the rest of the world. Also, Atlanta is the capital of the state, which makes policy research convenient. There is access to the governor's office and to the economic development planners who are always looking to foster Atlanta's expansion. At the same time, Emory University has a college-town feel. I was able to live close to the university, even within walking distance, which meant that once again, as at Illinois, I was escaping from the nightmare of commuting.

In fact, minimizing my commute was an essential requirement as my wife and I went house hunting in Atlanta. I told Madhu that she could have a choice of any house within one mile of the campus. My only other requirement was that I must have a much larger home office. I had never had enough space at home for all my books, and I knew that my office on campus would not be nearly large enough. As it happened, by April we found a house in Victoria Estates, a long-established neighborhood near the campus with lots of older residents and very little turnover. We were maybe a decade younger than the average resident, and probably the only immigrant family. The broker who sold us the house also lived in the neighborhood and introduced us to all the neighbors, who welcomed us warmly.

Madhu, an avid gardener, quickly discovered not one but two garden clubs in the neighborhood. Both of us found Atlanta very friendly—even more so than Los Angeles for immigrants. It is the southern culture of smiles and personal warmth. In fact, before too long, both of our children joined us in Atlanta.

We did have one lingering issue: Difficulty selling the house back in Los Angeles. Because Madhu did not really want to let it go anyway, our solution was to rent it—which we reasoned would also make it possible to return to Los Angeles during the summers. But that did not happen. Quicker than expected, our lives became very Atlanta centric. We did end up renting out the Los Angeles house for 11 years, and probably lost $20,000 a year doing so since we were still paying mortgage and property taxes. Fortunately, by the time we finally sold it in 2002, the real estate market in Los Angeles had become so pricey that we were able to recover most of the money we put into the home.

Another aspect of the déjà vu I experienced was that, like the University of Illinois, Emory's organizational structure was basically flat. Illinois is a much larger campus, with 36,000 fulltime students compared to Emory's 11,000. Nevertheless, at both institutions you get the feeling that the president and provost are available to meet you anytime. USC, with its vast campus and several separate schools—medicine, engineering, etc.—is not easy to navigate. But more to the point, at USC it was very hard to reach senior administration. You have to make an appointment, outline your agenda, get on the schedule, etc. At Emory I felt like I could get together with pretty much anybody for an informal cup of coffee, which made me very comfortable.

Yet another parallel was that Emory's academic program, like Illinois', had a fine reputation. It is with good reason that

Emory boasts of being "the Ivy League school of the South." My view is that the greatness of any university is defined, not by its infrastructure or even by the reputation of its faculty, but rather by the quality of its students. The higher the admissions standards, I believe, the better the school as a whole, and both Emory and Illinois attracted great students.

An even more striking parallel to Illinois was that at the time of my arrival Emory was also looking for a new identity. You will recall that Illinois was in the middle of a major business school restructuring while the recession was driving huge numbers of students out of liberal arts and into the school's undergraduate program. Emory's overhaul was even more dramatic. The thrust of its long-term strategic plan was to make a major investment in graduate education in the 1990s. The historic mission, with its heavy emphasis on excellence in the undergraduate program, was viewed as no longer sustainable. Three professional schools—public health, business, and law—were to be ramped up, a strategy which would attract a wider range of students and at the same time counterbalance the prevailing emphasis on pre-med.

For me, this scenario was both attractive and unique because at most universities the business school is considered a cash cow, with its revenues subsidizing liberal arts programs. But now Emory was set to become one of the few schools in the nation actually investing in the business school. So here was another similarity: Both schools enjoyed a fine legacy but were facing a midlife crisis. The difference was that at Illinois, there was no real game plan at the university level for the College of Commerce, but at Emory, the business school was very much a part of the university's strategic plan.

Also at both schools, I was starting with something of a clean slate. Admittedly, at Illinois I had to do a lot of the housecleaning. I had to motivate faculty to leave—or retire them gracefully. I had to consolidate and restructure programs before the new journey could begin. In both cases, I was recruited as a senior faculty member to bring in new leadership and thinking about the business school, but at Emory, the restructuring had already begun. The university had a plan; many of the older faculty members had left or were about to.

The rebuilding at both institutions also had similarities. For example, there was the "geographical challenge." At Illinois I faced the problem of recruiting excellent young faculty members to the cornfields, when most of the desirable young candidates were on the East or West Coast. I had a similar issue at Emory except I had to figure out how to lure the best young minds to the South. Also, at both institutions I tied the future to the emerging field in marketing at the time. At Illinois it was consumer behavior; at Emory, it was relationship marketing. At Emory however, a small "boutique" school without vast resources, I was not going to have 20 or more faculty members as a resource, just 10 or 12.

In short, at Emory, like at Illinois, I was arriving at an exciting time. Change was afoot and challenges were waiting. The tradeoff for implementing my grand relocation strategy to Atlanta to be a part of Emory's change was relinquishing the CTM to USC. Borsting wanted to run it. Particularly in science and engineering, it is quite common for founders to take their centers with them when they change location. As it happened, my new dean at Emory, Ron Frank, encouraged me to create a new discipline-oriented center, rather than an industry-oriented center. BellSouth was disappointed, because the potential for CTM in Atlanta was indeed great, but I did not insist that the CTM move to Atlanta with me.

Talent Recruitment for Emory

Before I arrived, Emory's business school had initiated its new trajectory by recruiting Robson. Robson tasked Miles and Benston with transforming the school from undergraduate-focused and teaching-oriented, to graduate focused and research oriented. It was a two-dimensional shift that would enable the school to embrace both knowledge dissemination and knowledge creation.

However, Robson, a noted economist, left after only three years to become part of President George H.W. Bush's administration. Emory replaced him with Ron Frank. While a couple of good people who had been here before Robson's arrival were motivated to leave, one member of the old guard stayed on and served as the bridge between the old and the new. This was the man who played such an active part in my recruitment: Brown Wittington, an Emory legend. All of his executive MBA students remember him to this day. He was a brilliant teacher and a great human being.

That was the situation when I arrived and my job was to create new excitement and a new vision of what we could and should do in marketing. Just like Illinois, recruiting would be a key endeavor, but with a focus on relationship marketing rather than consumer behavior. Could I have similar success? Given our small size, we had to have faculty who could do all three important things right, who represented a "triple threat." They had to demonstrate potential as top scholars, be great teachers, and be able to forge strong links to industry.

I was recruiting from that viewpoint not realizing, by the way, that Emory hoped I would attract young people from other top private universities—Wharton, Harvard, Columbia and the like. I came from a different perspective. I was looking for excellence, and my view is that excellence can be found anywhere. Well-known universities can produce world-class scholars, but probably 80 percent of their graduates do not become world class. I recruited wherever I found the talent. And since the Illinois experience had been so positive, I thought I could do the same at Emory. I recruited Joe Cannon from University of North Carolina-Chapel Hill, with whom I would redesign the marketing curriculum. We were soon joined by Sundar Bharadwaj, a rising star from Texas A&M, and C.B. Bhattacharya from the Wharton School.

An especially key recruit early on was Atul Parvatiyar, who had been teaching in India at the Xavier Labor Relations Institute (XLRI), a Jesuit organization. We had been corresponding, even while I was still at USC, about how he could come to the United States. Finally, by the time I came to Emory in 1991, he was able to get his J1 Visa, permitting him to come as an exchange scholar. He was to become a crucial colleague in ramping up the Center for Relationship Marketing. At the same time, we worked together to write three academic papers in quick succession. All were frequently cited, a testimony to the fact that relationship marketing was clearly coming into its own.

It was exciting to recruit these bright young people, these "triple-threats," but our recruiting effort faced a very interesting challenge. As at Illinois, Emory's business school was in growth mode, and we needed to expand our faculty. The difference was that at Emory, a relatively small school, there were limits on how many new hires we could put on tenure track, so I had to figure out how to hire nontenure-track faculty

The standard model in such programs is to hire industry executives to teach evening courses. We call them adjunct faculty. They teach one course and go back to their day job. The problem is that these people rarely bond well with the academic community. The teaching is a peripheral activity for them, so they just come to teach. It occurred to me that these classes might be better taught by faculty members who were full-time but nontenure track. Who would fit that profile? I saw the potential candidate as a person with a doctorate who had been on tenure track, but for some reason or another had fallen off. Perhaps he or she had not been ambitious enough. Maybe more and more time was spent in other pursuits like teaching executive education or consulting, and the tenure clock had run out. Based on the policy of "up or out," such a person would now have to leave the university and would probably look for work in industry. But what if such a person did not really aspire to the corporate life? What if he or she still wanted to be part of an academic institution?

I believed that there were probably quite a few people who we could attract as nontenure-track faculty. It would work like this: Since tenure track means 50 percent research and 50 percent teaching (in terms of compensation), these faculty members would receive half the salary of a tenure-track faculty member of the same rank who is required to do research, too. They would be required to be on the campus three days a week: Two days for teaching plus Friday, when the entire faculty got together for other activities such as committee work, curriculum design, and collegiality. Also, they would participate in all decision-making except tenure decisions.

The other two days of the week belonged to them, to do their consulting work or whatever. We did impose the condition that while they could use their university affiliation in their consulting work, they could not use university facilities or resources. That meant they were required to have an off-campus office for such work. These people knew very well that in those two days off campus they could earn more than enough to make up for the half salary they were sacrificing. In other words, it was a win-win and a satisfying solution for everybody. I was able to hire a number of very good faculty members who taught a full load (four courses a year, not just one) and these new hires were happy to have a way to remain a part of the university community. It was a boon for our teaching needs.

Another key piece in our revitalization program was the creation of the Center for Relationship Marketing. Relationship marketing was an idea whose time had come. Marketing as we know it today came into being some 100 years ago when America was rapidly industrializing and consumers began to buy branded products rather than producing their own. It was "outsourcing comes home," as I like to put it. Back then, branding was at the center of marketing, and the primary goal was customer acquisition. Over time, as the economy matured, it was clear that new customers would come into the market at the rate of demographic change which, with the aging of the population, was slowing down. As a result, marketing needed to focus not on new customers but rather on existing customers. We needed to think about how to retain loyalty, and how to build trust. This was a huge paradigm shift that involved all aspects of marketing, including how to allocate resources.

Another big trend was thrusting relationship marketing into the limelight: the evolution from a manufacturing-based to a services-based economy. This was significant because in the services sector, the customer is involved in a relationship from the day he engages with the service provider (a doctor, dentist or financial advisor). Those are the kinds of services we typically think about, but utilities, too, are big services companies and their relationship to their customers is essential to their success. Think about it: When a household moves into a new town or neighborhood, they immediately sign up for electricity, water, telephone, cable and typically, will remain with each service provider indefinably—unless the service provider creates a problem in the customer's mind. Changing one's electricity provider is not as easy as changing one's brand of coffee. So, somewhat by default, customers tend to remain loyal. And service companies understand that if they fail, their customers will become loyal to their competitors. As service industries that included airlines and telecommunications were becoming deregulated, the relationship platform was becoming increasingly important,

In fact, the new paradigm was already very much alive on the Emory campus when I arrived, thanks to the work of Robson in putting together his board of advisors with all those CEOs. Ron Frank inherited that board and, as the new dean, had written all the members to introduce himself. One member, Ed Ardtz, Chairman and CEO of Procter & Gamble (P&G), responded by commenting that the way we had been teaching marketing, anchored to branding and consumer focus, was now obsolete. P&G had moved on, he said, and P&G was considered a world-class marketing organization. Ardtz had spent some time as a manager in Japan, where he learned what the Japanese figured out in the 1960s and 1970s—that retailers are valued customers, not merely channels. And as such, retailers have power.

For Ardtz, this lesson was reinforced by P&G's "relationship" with Walmart. Because P&G was organized around product categories—coffee, detergent, cosmetic, soaps, etc.—nobody at P&G had realized that Walmart was its biggest customer. P&G knew all about consumers at the micro level, but overlooked the macro level. Consequently, with its dozens of product lines, all acting independently, P&G's relationship with Walmart as a whole suffered. There was confusion, poor accounting, and a lack of coordination. Walmart wanted P&G's brands; it had become a world leader in supply chain technology, and dealing with the complexities and inefficiencies of P&G was frustrating. The situation deteriorated until Walmart founder, Sam Walton personally stepped in and told P&G to fix its systems or lose its biggest customer. Ardtz heard that wake-up call loud and clear. He began to see the fallacy of "brand management" marketing and began to think instead about Walmart as a customer and a market segment.

Ardtz came to meet Ron Frank, and they agreed that the next generation of Emory MBA students needed to learn a new marketing view. Brown Wittington worked with Ardtz and developed a wonderful program called Customer Business Development or CBD. P&G would recruit a selection of our MBA students during their first semester and if they qualified, they would be given internships during the summer to focus on one of P&G's big retailers as a customer—Walmart, K-mart or Kroger, for example. Students would have a great learning experience. When they returned to Emory, they enrolled in a terrific seminar taught by Wittington. It really was a unique class. Not only the MBA students, but faculty across all business disciplines attended the seminar, because the relationship between Walmart and P&G crossed functional boundaries. In addition, each MBA student was mentored by an executive who also came to the weekly Friday seminar.

The program was so successful that P&G changed the name of its "trade" organization to "CBD"—Customer Business Development. That is, what can P&G do and what insights can it provide that will grow Walmart's business? Because the more Walmart grows, the more P&G grows.

I realized, of course, that this was "relationship marketing," and it was related to my work at Whirlpool. There I had witnessed the longest relationship ever between a manufacturer and retailer—Whirlpool and Sears (with its Kenmore Brand). Big retailer Sears had taken a small, struggling manufacturer—Upton Machine Co.—and made it into a giant. The reverse had historically been the case, with large manufacturers wielding all the power over small, mom-and-pop retailers. With the arrival of the big box stores, the power began to shift.

152 *The Accidental Scholar*

Establishing the Center for Relationship Marketing

With the P&G program already established, Ron Frank, who had also come to see the power of relationship marketing, suggested that I start a new center in that area. The P&G program, which was originally part of the MBA curriculum, immediately came under the auspices of the new Center for Relationship Marketing, where it was a perfect fit—although the program did change and evolve to meet the Center's needs. For example, I discovered that the students who went into the internship had no academic knowledge of relationship marketing, so we designed a course for spring semester, Foundations of Relationship Marketing, which they took first. That way, when they went for summer internships, they had frameworks and formulas to understand and analyze the real world.

Another change involved the program's expansion to include more companies. I did not want to rely exclusively on P&G, and even P&G agreed we should add other companies. Students would have opportunities to learn about other industries, and just as important, the companies would be able to learn from each other. So, soon after the program came under the aegis of the Center, we had added five or six more companies. One was Chubb Insurance, which primarily sold insurance to businesses. Motorola, a company for which I had done some consulting, was another. Then there was Coca-Cola, of special interest to our work because its fountain business fosters relationships with the large fast food chains like McDonald's. As the number of companies grew, the pool of students became larger and more diversified.

As for the establishment of the Center itself, I had learned the hard way at USC that if you do not integrate the new paradigm into the curriculum and nurture your center as a part of the marketing discipline, it will always remain a peripheral activity. At Emory we started a center that was run by the faculty. We were fortunate to get great support from Ernst & Young, the auditors for Coca-Cola at the time, who were very interested in the customer relationship concept.

It probably helped, too, that I had a book coming out at that time, *Clients for Life*, which defined the relationship concept as becoming a trusted advisor for clients of professional services companies and Ernst & Young gave us a large grant to launch the center. Actually, they hoped for a CRM center—customer relationship management—with an IT focus. But our faculty wanted a customer relationship *marketing* center, with more focus on strategy than on IT, and we went ahead with our own concept.

In addition to adopting P&G's CBD program, the center launched a number of worthy initiatives. We organized a biannual academic conference, which quickly became *the* destination for scholars interested in relationship marketing. Parvatiyar put the first one together in 1994 and by 1996 the conference was attended by 150 to 160 academics, many of them young aspiring scholars. We put out a call for papers and had a strong group of scholars reviewing them. We published the proceedings, a key accomplishment because the intent of the Center was to create new knowledge in this emerging discipline, to examine it from different perspectives, and to encourage scholars to embrace this viewpoint. Indeed, relationship marketing became the new paradigm in the discipline, so the conference played an important role on the scholarship side.

We generated a large-scale research project. The study focused on understanding suppliers in the context of customer relationships; that is, it was what in marketing we call "B-to-B" (business-to-business), rather than business-to-consumer. Approximately 40 scholars from all over the country were involved in designing the questionnaire. The results formed a database that became valuable for continuing research—a great resource for our students as well as the faculty.

Another of the center's accomplishments was the creation of an award for the company that did the best job in relationship marketing—the one whose customers were not merely satisfied but "delighted." We devised our own formula, and our process was much like the renowned Malcolm Baldridge's Total Quality Management awards. A recent hire, Mike Cummings, was a key colleague in developing and judging the awards program.

Our award recognized companies motivated by a customer-driven approach to their business, rather than a manufacture-driven approach. Companies applied for the award by sending us the process they used to create relationship marketing, and how they achieved "customer delight." Eventually, we even brought in as our partner, The Conference Board from New York to put on a one-and-a-half-day seminar. They organized the conference and we provided the speakers and presented the awards. This became an annual affair and, unlike the academic conference, it targeted practitioners rather than professors. It also succeeded handsomely, with some 150 to 200 participants every year.

Although it was not directly a part of the Center, but related to it, the American Marketing Association, the large professional body to which virtually all marketing professors belong, was already considering the idea of creating sub-groups, so-called special interest groups, or SIGs. Other professional organizations had already initiated this practice, and our center began promoting the idea of a national-level subgroup of AMA devoted to relationship marketing. The relationship marketing SIG became one of the most popular.

To sum it up, the Center for Relationship Marketing provided a new area of exciting research, scholarly activity, and pedagogy. Creating and managing the Center has been a tremendously satisfying experience, especially as the thought leader in the marketing area.

Creating the Marketing Consulting Strategy Program

Outside the confines of the center, but very much a part of the new vitality sweeping through the business school, was another great initiative that helped raise the school's profile. It would come to be called the Marketing Strategy Consulting Program and Parvatiyar, using his experience at XLRI, took the lead in developing it.

Emory, like most of the top MBA programs in the country, required its entering students to have several years of work experience. This was a shift since my student days, when MBA students were all recent college grads. Emory had embraced the new trend, and our faculty could now teach students who had seen some of these industries from the inside. The MBA courses use one of three types of pedagogy. First are case studies, a concept pioneered by the Harvard Business School (HBS). Business cases are written by Harvard faculty and other schools who want to teach these case histories pay HBS for the privilege. Second is simulation, which had arrived in the 1970s, thanks to computerization. You design a game, in marketing or other strategy and have student teams compete in this virtual world. Third is lecture and discussion.

It occurred to me that as the world moved rapidly into the 1990s—with the collapse of communism and with globalization and world trade agreements—the old Harvard cases were becoming obsolete. Some dated from the 1970s and though they still teach interesting lessons, the stories themselves were simply too ancient. Certainly we could write new ones, but it takes a lot of time to write a case and even more time to disseminate it for use. So Parvatiyar and I came up with another idea: live consulting. It would be experiential, with accountability. This would not be the "fun and games" of simulation, but rather the real world. We figured that since our students came to us with four or five years of experience, they could consult just as effectively as the new MBA graduates recruited by McKinsey and other strategy consulting companies.

I had done something like this at Whirlpool. The company had a good market research division, and we identified problems that needed fresh thinking. For example, with the aging of the population and a growing segment of infirm or disabled people, how could appliances be redesigned to target this growing market?

Our idea at Whirlpool was to come up with live projects where a new business opportunity or business challenge was presented, write the problem, and then give it to managers in

Whirlpool's in-house training programs to solve. Managers in the program were divided into teams and each team was assigned a problem to work on for its own "corporate client."

At Emory, Parvatiyar or I went to various companies and incentivized them to participate in the program. The win-win was good for the company as well as our students. If a company signed on, one of the teams was assigned to the company just as though they had been hired as consultants. The team would diagnose problems and make strategy recommendations. There is no end to the fascinating problems these teams might be called upon to solve.

The results were judged by non-Emory faculty and executives from other companies, and as many as 60 to 100 judges were involved. It was a huge deal. The idea of getting judges from companies not involved in the competition was great, because those companies might very well become the next year's client group—especially after seeing how relevant and useful the whole project was. After all, they would be getting very affordable consulting. As for the academic judges, they had to come from outside because our own marketing professors were advisors to the teams, based on their own interests. The model was perfected eventually, where the second-year MBA students mentored the first-year students and became team leaders.

We hosted a huge banquet after the competition. There was a team and a representative from the client company at every table. Winner names were kept a secret, and the excitement grew throughout the evening. And no wonder! We awarded $5,000 to the winning team, $3,000 to the second place winner, and $2,000 for third place. It was really a wonderful celebration.

Our Marketing Strategy Consulting Program became so successful that it is now included in many business schools all over the world. Thanks to Parvatiyar, the basic idea came from India. We should not look at America as the only place where people innovate especially in education and healthcare. Emerging economies have their own ways of innovating and some of those models may be transferrable to the United States.

Of course, that message is becoming increasingly main stream in the twenty-first century.

Naturally, the program has evolved over time. For one thing, while it started out as what might be called a student club—that is, an extracurricular activity—it eventually became an elective course because the program became so popular that faculty members from other disciplines complained that students were spending too much time on this non-credit work and not enough time on their credit assignments. Also, faculty members involved in the project began wondering why they were doing it for free. As a course, it would become part of their teaching load and they would be compensated accordingly. We charged $10,000 per client for the project, so in its original design, we always generated a surplus for the school. Faculty time was volunteered and the student work was pro bono. The only real costs were the prizes, the banquet, and travel and accommodations for the judges.

Eventually, Parvatiyar wanted to move on, so the program needed a new manager. Parvatiyar's replacement was my daughter, Reshma (now a Shah), who joined the Emory faculty in 1996. Reshma increased the visibility of the Marketing Strategy Consulting Program by enabling students at top business schools all over the world to participate. The judging was done on the Internet, so that a professor or executive sitting in Malaysia, for example, would judge the work of a team from London.

It was exciting to watch the program grow to such heights, but ultimately the logistics became unwieldy. For example, foreign students were required to come to Atlanta at the beginning of the project, where they spent two or three days studying the client's needs and formulating a game plan; then they would return to their own countries to do their work remotely. It was difficult and expensive to arrange all that travel. The "virtual" judging began to pose problems, too, because it required the coordination of time zones all over the world. There was also the ongoing feeling that the program sucked up too much energy, at the expense of other programs and other curricula. In support of the School of Business' branding efforts and the central purpose of the program, it was renamed to Goizueta Marketing Strategy Competition (GMSC) and then Goizueta Marketing Strategy Consultancy.

Amidst all the logistical problems, Reshma opted to revert back to the original program format, which catered to only Emory students. Also, while we originally had 10 or 12 projects in the program each year, the school wanted Reshma to cap the number at 5 or 6. On the other hand, except for nonprofit companies, which we have always tried to include in the program, Reshma increased the fee to $40,000 per client. Many students are in fact interested in the nonprofit segment of the program, and we ended up working with many social organizations in Atlanta.

In short, good things were happening at Emory. The CBD Program and the internships with P&G and other companies were a huge success, and the Marketing Strategy Consulting Program really put us on the map. Approximately 70 percent of business students who enrolled at Emory came primarily for this unique experience and participated in one of these programs. Today, Emory now competes, not just coexists, with other top business schools.

Meanwhile, the marketing department continued its revitalization with some additional new hires. In addition to Joe Cannon, Sundar Bharadwaj and C.B. Bhattacharya, we were able to attract Tom Gruen, Anil Menon, and Terry Clark. We gave the whole discipline a new focus—relationship marketing—and at the same time, recruited young people who could contribute their own perspectives. For example, Bhattacharya was an expert in modeling, data mining, and mathematics. Clark was just a great thinker at the macro-level, a big-picture scholar. Bharadwaj was in marketing strategy. Cannon brought a specific interest and expertise in relationship marketing which proved to be immensely helpful.

In fact, Cannon helped me in the immediate and urgent task of redesigning the marketing curriculum so it reflected the new relationship marketing paradigm. For example, all MBAs have to take a core course in marketing management, but the old textbook still emphasizes customer acquisition marketing. Since that course is a basic requirement, we had to make sure it included customer retention marketing. It needed to emphasize relationship-building, loyalty programs, and a broader knowledge of the services economy. At the same time, Cannon and I revised electives such as market research, customer behavior and brand management so they incorporated a relationship perspective. Also, as mentioned, we created the new course, Foundations of Relationship Marketing, which anybody could take as an elective, but marketing majors were required to take. It was exciting and innovative and Cannon and I went on to write a paper about our new curriculum. It was named "best paper" in one of the marketing education journals.

My early days at Emory was something of a macro view of what was to come, some of the challenges I faced, and some of the work I undertook to raise the profile of its business school in general and its marketing department in particular. I believe that creating the Center for Relationship Marketing and the Marketing Strategy Consulting Program continued the upward trajectory initiated under the leadership of John Robson and Ron Frank. In the next chapter, I will share a more micro look at my day-to-day work—both as an administrator under Ron Frank's leadership and in my academic and professional life.

LIFE LESSON

As a successful professional, giving back to society is something to do not after retiring, but while you are active in your career. *Giving back will enhance your reputation and relationships, and will provide opportunities and ideas that will propel you forward.*

11

EMORY: ADMINISTRATION AND ACADEMICS

Emory's business school was "up and coming" and had great aspirations. The university was committing a significant amount of resources to its success. After Robson's hasty departure, Ron Frank was brought in as the new dean, but the mandate remained the same: Continue the urgent work of the business school's transformation into a world-class institution.

Frank was perfect for the job. He had vast experience as vice dean at the Wharton School, where he had served for many years. He had been dean at Purdue, had taught at Stanford and was a University of Chicago graduate. These were all top private universities, and since Emory, too, was private, the idea was that he could bring in the best practices from these other institutions at a level we aspired to reach.

A dean whose job is to transform his school cannot act the part of a swashbuckling corporate CEO. He cannot simply say, "I'm the new boss. Here is my vision. Now go out and execute it." Rather, the dean's approach has to be participatory. He must have the faculty on board and, to this end, Frank engaged his senior faculty in a number of important initiatives.

Committees Introduced Important Changes

Frank tackled governance first by organizing an Executive Committee comprised of the leaders of all five disciplines in the business school, the dean, and his staff. We met every Monday morning and pretty much put everything on the table: What was happening in the school daily, and where the school needed to head tomorrow. For example, our committee's work to envision the future resulted in a new emphasis on information sciences. By the early 1990s, the computer was ubiquitous, impacting everything, and information sciences was emerging as an important discipline. Other schools had begun to elevate its importance, and we, too, needed to bring information sciences to bear on the traditional study of production and operations management. Of course, that meant recruiting new faculty.

Then there was the Nondegree and External Affairs Committee, which I was asked to chair for several years. "Nondegree" included our executive education programs, an area we really wanted to bring to the forefront. Wharton has a world-class executive education program, and so does Stanford, so Ron brought with him some great experience in that area. "External affairs" meant, essentially, how to present ourselves to our external stakeholders—not just internal stakeholders like students and faculty, but to businesses, the community and policy makers. Obviously, how those stakeholders saw us would reflect directly upon fundraising, which was critical to our continued growth.

This committee's work included creating new research-oriented centers (such as the Center for Relationship Marketing), which we saw as a way to raise the profile of the business school. We already had Jeffrey Sonnenfeld's Center for Leadership, a CEO College Sonnenfeld had created with Bob Miles. It did provide outreach, since by its nature it connected with many CEOs, but it lacked strong internal and research components. So we established guidelines to cover both the creation of new centers as well as the review, every three years, of existing centers like Sonnenfeld's. In this way, the centers could be made to embrace both research and outreach missions, with the desired outcome of getting more faculty members involved.

Another of our guidelines was that center directors should be tenured professors. Centers could hire associate directors from industry or from the ranks of nontenured faculty to help run day-to-day operations, but tenured leadership is needed to make sure such centers remain research centric and encourage faculty involvement. We wanted them to be part of the business school's mission and identity, not peripheral activities. The nondegree and external affairs committee became important in terms of shaping strategies for the business school's future.

I also served on the MBA Curriculum Committee—a key assignment since the curriculum needed a complete overhaul. (To clarify, this was a different task from the work Joe Cannon and I did on the marketing curriculum specifically.) Because most curricula require an immense multi-year effort to get established and accredited, they tend to remain in place. Change requires intervention. So we began to take a close look at Emory's 25-year-old program and to question whether it was still viable. The result was a huge transformation, one that went even as far as the basic structure of class-hour contacts.

Some of the material we were teaching in our regular semester-long classes came out of what I would call the "soft sciences"—the "touchy-feely" subjects that seemed to pervade curricula across disciplines in those days. I am referring to things like leadership, communication skills, and personal development. In marketing, we even had classes on creating commercials, and we began to realize that this was closer to vocational technical than to anything truly academic. It was not that such courses lacked relevance, but they lacked academic rigor and we decided we would no longer sacrifice academic rigor for relevance. We did not want to ignore these topics completely, but we did not want to devote entire courses to them either.

Our solution was to reduce the number of classroom contact hours from 14 weeks to 12, which created a two-week period just before the start of the semester during which all these practitioner-oriented subjects and issues could be addressed with intensity. This worked particularly well, because once we removed these topics from the academic curriculum, we found we could bring in specialists who could deliver everything our students needed in just a couple of days. For instance, "creativity" was popular and relevant, especially when tweaked to include group creativity in the workplace, but it was not necessary to devote a full course to it. Two or three days on such a subject, though, might be time well spent.

Moreover, we also took the opportunity afforded by these two weeks plus the winter break, to add an intensive study abroad program. The world was globalizing in the 1990s. Markets were liberalizing. Communism had collapsed and the WTO was gaining ascendency. Our students needed international experience and exposure, so we organized "immersion" programs to places like China, India, Russia, Eastern Europe, and Latin America, all the countries and regions that were emerging as the new growth engines for the world economy. Alternatively, an immersion experience might be in a particular industry with worldwide operations. The work of the curriculum committee really helped get the MBA program ready for the new century.

I especially enjoyed serving on committees that provided new knowledge and experience for me, and a good example was the Point System Committee. This group addressed the problem of how to evaluate and compensate teaching in our nondegree executive education programs. The standard model is for faculty members to take on teaching in addition to their regular load and to receive extra compensation. But unlike regular classes, those in executive education were not subject to any review or evaluation process. That was a problem because, after all, the programs were part of the business school, so our reputation was at stake. The solution was to figure out how to make executive education part of what the faculty does fundamentally. Again, this was supposed to be part of our larger "triple threat" strategy: Recruiting faculty who can do outreach to industry via executive education in addition to scholarly research and teaching degree programs. It was supposed to be integral to the mission.

We came up with a point system whereby one could quantify the number of contact hours faculty spent in executive education programs, factoring in that such hours are unusually intense (in a one-week or three-day course, for example) and determining their equivalency to regular teaching hours. I suggested that we go one step further. As I saw it, as an "add-on," this work could become too seductive: If you do well, senior executives give you immediate praise and gratification. And the money is nice, too. The danger is that you are tempted to put your research on the back burner. Unfortunately, business school research is not driven by funding from outside agencies, which would impose a deadline for the delivery of research findings. Without such a deadline, research is easy to postpone, even though the professor's tenure clock might be ticking. The core work of tenure-track faculty is to do research and generate new knowledge, whereas executive education is knowledge dissemination. The fear was that work in executive education could become a seductive distraction.

Our recommendation was to create a system where 25 percent of a faculty member's teaching time (one course out of four per year) would be in executive education, and it would be evaluated formally, just like any other course. We still needed the point system to evaluate the "worth" of teaching an intensive course in executive education, and to figure out how to "bank" that worth. After all, executive education is feast or famine. In good times, it gets accelerated to meet the demand from all the companies wanting custom programs. It is just the opposite in bad times.

Such reforms were timely because of our popular new evening MBA program—a major initiative under Ron Frank. Emory did not have an evening program, but Atlanta was growing, and many companies were relocating their headquarters to Atlanta, and that meant plenty of managers, and people who wanted an MBA but did not want to give up their jobs to go back to school. Under Frank's leadership, we also expanded the executive MBA program (the so-called weekend program) already in place. Lacking sufficient facilities on campus, we moved the program to rented and retrofitted space in Lenox Mall in Buckhead. Our executive MBA programs quickly became nationally recognized and an increasingly prominent part of the business school's profile. Clearly, the questions our committee was addressing were important ones. Ultimately, our recommendations were approved but never fully implemented because of a change in leadership that was soon to come. Nevertheless, it was fascinating to be on a committee dealing with such issues and a real learning experience for me.

The Conflict of Interest Committee was another that I was asked to chair. Conflict of interest had to do with the work professors engaged in outside the university—and how they were compensated for this work. The issue had come to the forefront in the late 1970s, after the first energy crisis, when many universities were under budgetary pressure. State governments funding state universities (particularly in California) began to look at the kinds of nonuniversity related work their faculties were taking on. In Silicon Valley, for example, university-based scientists were creating lucrative personal ventures on the side. Consequently, state universities began to demand accountability. Faculty had to report the number of days spent on outside projects, and the guideline eventually established was that one day a week was allowable—or 39 days over a nine-month contract. Faculty on a nine-month contract was free to spend summers at their own discretion. At the end of the year, faculty members had to report their time spent outside the classroom on a standardized form, which would be turned over to the university.

This trend among public universities eventually made its way to private campuses. It was not surprising since schools like Stanford and MIT, with their world-class engineering schools, were producing some very wealthy faculty members. Then, too, there was the related issue of intellectual property. If a university gets a contract to conduct research and the faculty researcher on the project ends up with a patent, who owns the property? Who gets the royalties?

Our Conflict of Interest Committee was established to address these issues and create guidelines. What are the boundaries?

Should a faculty member be allowed to use university resources for their own gain? What is the disclosure policy? We produced solid guidelines, at the center of which was a requirement to file an annual report—still in place today. Business school faculty have to report, for example, whether they taught executive education programs at other universities and how much time they spent doing it. Or whether they served as board members of companies or corporations—how many companies and, again, how many days? All such activities had to be disclosed. And our committee ultimately adopted the "one day per week" guideline endorsed by state universities.

One more interesting and eye-opening assignment was the Post-tenure Review Committee. As you can imagine, this was a very sensitive issue. Again, the idea came out of state governments who worried about what their faculty members were up to outside the classroom. The original post-tenure review was established by Ronald Reagan, who, as governor of California, got fed up with his state's professors spending so much time in political activism. Colorado's university system followed suit. As chair of our committee, I looked back at what had happened elsewhere, and why, hoping to be able to bring the best practices to Emory.

Our motives were no doubt less ideological than Governor Reagan's. Our problem, and the general one at most institutions, is that many faculty members, once tenured, begin to plateau. The standard expectation is that after a faculty member is tenured, which often comes with promotion to associate professor, he or she has roughly seven to 10 years to achieve the rank of full professor. Of course, that means writing books or publishing research papers, but at the same time, having tenure can vitiate the desire for further achievement and advancement. So many faculty members plateau, creating a bulge of associate professors. We needed some kind of review, some kind of guideline, to make sure faculty members continued to be productive after tenure.

In Emory's case, there was tremendous debate over whether we would be a "review" committee or a "development" committee. "Review" implied judgment—and possibly censure.

"Development" implied a means of enabling the professor to go forward to the next level. Our decision was to make our committee a faculty development tool, whereby faculty members would be encouraged, through a formal process, to think about their futures. What do you want to do over the next five or 10 years? And given your goals and aspirations, what commitment can the university make to help you get there? We wanted a sort of social contract. The process might lead to the conclusion that the faculty member is right on track for full professorship; on the other hand, the conclusion might be that it is time to retire or go in another direction. In any case, there would be clarity on both sides. On the part of the faculty member, there would be self-awareness. Along with that, we offered communication between the faculty and the administration.

Globalization Task Force was something I found hugely interesting given my own longtime interest in international trends and events. Emory was unique in this regard: While most business schools failed to include international business as a part of the core curriculum, Emory, under Robson's regime, required two courses on global issues for every MBA student—one micro, one macro. Moreover, in each of the five disciplines there had to be a special course on the relevant international aspect, like international finance, international marketing or international accounting. I saw this as a very positive thing because, to me, understanding global issues is fundamental, not discretionary. Our debate centered on the contention that international business itself is not a discipline. It does not have its own unique paradigms; it is an extension of a discipline, more like a domain than a discipline in its own right. Then, too, if we wanted to elevate international business to a discipline, we had to concede that we didn't have top experts in these areas. The goal of the Globalization Task Force was to figure out where to go with our international program.

Our recommendation was to create the opportunity for a double major (or double specialization) in the business school. If students took the two core courses in international business already required, plus one special course in their individual area, along with two or three international electives, then they would earn a "specialization" in international business in addition to their original area of specialization. It was a great idea, especially since more and more corporations were recruiting students who were knowledgeable in international business. In the mid-to-late 1990s, American companies were flocking overseas. It was clear that Emory needed to get some global content into the curriculum.

As was the case with the Point System Committee, the recommendations of the various committees were not always fully implemented, and for the same reason—the impending change in leadership. Nevertheless, they were all a part of my own journey, my continuing education, and I enjoyed the assignments tremendously.

Leadership Changes Lead to New Emphasis

Ron Frank decided to accept the opportunity to become the president of the newly created Singapore Management University (SMU). This school, Singapore's third major university, was created in partnership with the Wharton School, world-renowned for its undergraduate business program. Because of his long experience at Wharton prior to coming to Emory, Frank had already been appointed to the new university's board of trustees. SMU had initially named a Wharton professor as president, who remained on Wharton's faculty as well. When this president decided that she did not want to commute between Singapore and Wharton, she stepped down.

I was on the Search Committee for Frank's replacement. It was an interesting process. A couple of decades earlier, the search for a new dean would have been managed by "the good old boy network." A committee member would call up friends and ask, "Who do you know who would be right for this job?" But as the dean's job description has evolved from internal governance to external fundraising, the search process has become more formalized and placed in the hands of an outside search firm. Essentially, the firm returns to the committee with a report that says, "Here are the candidates who said they were not interested and here are the candidates who are interested along with detailed information about them."

Using the search firm's report, the school narrowed candidates to our top three choices, with the President selecting Tom Kinnear from the University of Michigan. Michigan had a stellar dean who trained several world-class associate deans before moving up to provost. All of them were constantly pursued by other schools. Kinnear was one of them and had already moved into university-level administration as a fundraising leader. We hired him away—or thought we had. He negotiated an incredible commitment from the university, which included investing in new facilities and expanded faculty. He realized the school was running out of capacity and did not want that to happen on his watch. Despite an unprecedented negotiation, Kinnear walked away.

In the second round, we discovered Tom Robertson, an exciting candidate from the London Business School, a renowned private university with great global presence. Robertson had remarkable experience at Wharton as department head and leader of the executive education program, and at the London Business School, he had also been a candidate for deanship. When that job went to someone else, Robertson became available.

Robertson's job was to take the business school to the next level, and he brought great energy to the task. Many of the initiatives from Frank's tenure were put on hold while Robertson studied the business school and its needs from his perspective. He then went to work with his own initiatives.

Robertson took from his experience at Wharton and the London Business School with the firm conviction that to be among the top 10 business schools, you had to be strong in two functional disciplines: finance and marketing. At Emory, he immediately began to promote that message. He quickly obtained funding to recruit and hire two very senior faculty members in marketing—chaired professors, no less.

One was Ajay Kohli, a well-known scholar from the University of Texas-Austin. Ironically, I had also tried to recruit Kohli back in 1991 when I was new at Emory. In fact, he was the first person

I called, a rising star in the discipline, with a new paradigm called "market orientation" that was getting great traction. His research was on what the role of the company should be—should it be customer driven or product driven?—and had come out with a paper on the subject that really made waves. I could see that his work fit very well with relationship marketing, which was also customer centric. I saw in Kohli the triple threat that we wanted at Emory and thought he just might be the future of Emory's marketing department. My job was to bring in the next generation of great scholars, so I made Kohli an offer. But he declined. He had a young family and was happy in Austin. Every six months, I would call him up and ask him if he was ready yet. It took 10 years, but we were finally able to add him to our faculty.

The second senior marketing faculty member was also a top-rated scholar from UT-Austin, Rajendra Srivastava. He was more senior than Kohli and brought a depth of experience in executive MBA programs, which was another dimension we wanted to expand. In fact, Robertson's motive in these hires was not just to build the strength of the marketing department. He saw that these two individuals could also help revitalize the executive education program and achieve a major goal of the business school—the creation of a doctoral program.

Creating Emory's Doctoral Program

Virtually all world class business schools have a doctoral program. Out of the top 20, I believe the only two exceptions are Dartmouth and Southern Methodist University. Emory had long debated whether to create one, but the problem was that in business schools, doctoral programs are generally a cost center. In schools of engineering and medicine, doctoral programs can be funded by research contracts from outside agencies, like the NSF, NIH, or the Department of Defense. Business schools do not generate that type of funding. On the other hand, our doctoral students would be able support our academic scholars in their research, and thus help enhance our reputation for new knowledge generation. Also, if our newly minted Ph.D.s were to go on to other universities and succeed, Emory's reputation would be further enhanced. The circle is completed when a growing reputation enables a school to attract better faculty—and better students. A doctoral program became the mandate.

The related mandate (and this is where Srivastava comes in) was that since the doctoral program would be a cost center, we would need to fund it by expanding our nondegree, executive education programs. Our revenues from those programs stood at about $2.5 to $3 million annually, and we figured we needed to increase it to about $10 million. We would use the 25 percent surplus to fund the doctoral program.

So while Srivastava brought his experience to the executive education programs, Kohli was tasked with starting the new doctoral program. Actually, Emory does not have a "business school doctoral program." Emory has a graduate school, and all University doctoral programs come under the auspices of the Graduate School. So Kohli's first job was to petition the Graduate School to inaugurate this program, and then his second job was to recruit doctoral students. He succeeded, and the doctoral program for the business school has done very well.

Overall, Robertson enjoyed a great five-year run as dean. He got the university to commit to a major expansion of the school's facilities, and then did a good job fundraising and ended up doubling the size of the Goizueta Business School (GBS) building that had just come to fruition during Frank's tenure. The expansion provided badly needed space to house the executive education and doctoral programs.

Robertson also went on to recruit more senior faculty in other departments—notably in finance and in management, where he again found funding for new chaired professorships. Unlike Frank's approach, which had been to hire young faculty and nurture them, Robertson succeeded in recruiting world-class senior level faculty, which gave us a larger base of leadership and enabled our growth curve to continue upward. Robertson did an outstanding job and enjoyed tremendous respect among his fellow deans and colleagues. Ultimately, Wharton called, and he returned to assume the deanship there, where he remains today.

Though my work on the administrative side was extensive, I did find time to pursue my professional work and my day job as teacher and scholar. As for the teaching, as a chaired professor, my class load was held to two courses a year (much like my contract at USC). In the absence of a doctoral program, I taught one course in the regular MBA program and one weekend executive MBA (WEMBA) course. Since we had grown the executive MBA program enormously, from 25 to 70 or so senior executives enrolled, we wanted the courses to be taught by senior faculty. I had the experience from both USC and Illinois, so I was comfortable with the assignment. I usually taught the introductory core class in marketing management.

In the daytime MBA program, I started a new course called "Marketing Seminar." When I came to Emory in 1991, my idea was to add to the new curriculum we had created on relationship marketing. But over time, as new colleagues joined us, we gradually shifted our focus to strategy—a broader approach encompassing what a given company should be doing in total. The curriculum was evolving, too, in response to this broader focus, so in the seminar my job has been to try to capture the newest emerging trends and concepts—especially about changing demographics, globalization of competition and growth of emerging markets.

Looking at the nature of competition in this seminar, I introduced my new framework called "The Rule of Three," and I could talk about the competitive threat (or opportunities) posed by the world's emerging economies. Over time I began to shift toward a new perspective in marketing based on the question: How do you create value for customers? I built this inquiry around yet another framework called "The Four A's of Marketing—Acceptability, Affordability, Accessibility and Awareness," with a focus on customer-centric marketing rather than product-centric marketing. I began to teach that new framework as well. The course continues to evolve. It is especially valuable because it is taught in the fall semester of the second year, at which time the students are being recruited by prospective employers, who expect them to solve problems.

These frameworks give them a way to approach problems that they might not otherwise have. As a result, their job prospects increase.

Creating our doctoral program brought a change in my teaching assignments, however, such that every second year I target a doctoral seminar on marketing theory along with my MBA seminar.

The chapter that follows will cover my return to writing books for the professional audience, but at this point I should mention that the decade of the 1990s was quite productive in terms of my academic writing. While we were expanding the new relationship marketing paradigm, I published several articles in top academic journals, including an article in the *Journal of the Academy of Marketing Science (JAMS)*, which took off. Another article, co-written with Parvatiyar and covering the evolution and history of relationship marketing, appeared in one of the European journals, and it was also widely cited. Eventually I ended up editing (with Parvatiyar) a *Handbook of Relationship Marketing*, a collection of the best essays on relationship marketing written by leading scholars and published by SAGE Publications. It has become a valuable textbook for graduate seminars.

LIFE LESSON

Your professional life outside the academic life can be as rewarding. Find a way to balance the two. *No matter where you go in life, you will return to your passion.*

12

MY PROFESSIONAL LIFE

At Emory I resumed a journey that had begun—out of sheer economic necessity—at Illinois. Those early beginnings of my professional life had resulted in a number of books written for a professional audience: *Winning Back Your Market*, *Bringing Innovation to Market*, and *The Customer Is Key*. I found that I really enjoyed writing for the wider audience of professional managers, and those books were enjoyed and appreciated both by managers and by my academic colleagues.

I wanted to continue that work, but at USC I reverted back to the academic audience in order to complete my book on marketing theory. At Emory, the time was right to return to my professional audience. First, I was determined to finish my book *The Rule of Three*, which articulated a powerful framework I had been working on all through the 1980s in my work with various companies. I discovered a wonderful young colleague, a fine academic and brilliant writer named Raj Sisodia, and persuaded him to write with me. We completed that book and have continued to work together for more than 20 years now.

One of our most enjoyable endeavors has been contributing op-ed pieces to the *Wall Street Journal* (*WSJ*). Thanks to the success of *The Rule of Three*, the *WSJ* editor began contacting us for our perspective on major business developments, like Chrysler being bought out by Daimler-Benz, for example.

My demographic work resulted in another *Wall Street Journal* piece by Sisodia and me titled, "Outsourcing Comes Home." It was an interesting take on the outsourcing phenomenon.

Sisodia has also helped me develop the "Four A's" framework over the past several years, and, based on that theory, we wrote a *Wall Street Journal* article explaining why Iridium failed and cell phones succeeded. The theory is that products must meet customers' needs in four ways—the "Four A's" of affordability, accessibility, acceptability, and awareness—and we demonstrated how Iridium, with its poor technology, failed on the grounds of affordability and acceptability. The article also analyzed the failure of the Concorde from the same perspective. Recently, Sisodia and I also published the book, *The 4 A's of Marketing: Creating Value for Customer, Company and Society.*

Establishing IN-CORE

A key development in my professional life took place because of USC's refusal to let go of the CTM. I moved to Atlanta largely at the behest of BellSouth, and they wanted me to provide in-house vision and thought leadership on the continuing transformation in the telecommunications industry. As a result, I created a separate company here in Atlanta for telecommunications training and education. It is called IN-CORE, or Institute for Communications, Research, and Education. It actually serves the entire industry—not just BellSouth, though BellSouth was our first major customer.

We designed a program called "Our Competitive Marketplace," based on "the rule of three," that addressed the basic questions: Who are your competitors and what is their strategy to compete with you? I figured we would be presenting it to the company's top 250 senior executives, but they liked the framework so much that they wanted everybody at director level and above (about 1,000 people) to go through the program. It became a perennial program. We have done 60 to 65 separate sessions over time. And it has had measurable impact, based on testing after six months to see if managers were actually using the concepts.

IN-CORE evolved naturally from the work I had begun much earlier. It was in response to Ameritech's offer to become their strategic planner. Although I declined their offer on two separate occasions, I was inspired to design a program on customer perspectives called MASTERS, a completely customized program focused on customer centric perspective. That is where I really got educated on how to design a large scale program specific to a company's needs as it moved into the future. We did many such transformational sessions at Ameritech, and typically I ended up writing a white paper about what the future looked like. Again, the requirement was that the top leadership of the company had to truly participate and become educators in the program.

As IN-CORE grew, we recruited several talented people. Two key people were Lokesh Sehgal, who had just landed from India and who BellSouth had asked me to help find a job, and Mark Hutcheson, who had moved to Atlanta from Birmingham, Alabama. Mark was exceptionally good at doing everything to support me and Lokesh. We gave them knowledge of the industry and they continued to learn by example. Soon we had Sprint as another major customer and tailored programs to their specific needs in marketing and strategy. We employed the most contemporary frameworks, like "The Four A's of Marketing" to the contrast of the Four P's of Marketing. We showed managers how these frameworks and audits could be used to solve very real marketing problems. The programs proved popular and effective.

Coincidentally, our son Rajen, who started with AT&T, moved to Atlanta and when he found no comparable position with the company's Atlanta office, he quit AT&T and joined IN-CORE. He quickly became one of our best trainers. He had the domain knowledge, could speak the industry language, and was familiar with the newer frameworks. It delighted me to see him become one of our really popular instructors. Our staff grew to include faculty and other professionals. Our daughter Reshma also began to teach in some of the programs in addition to her professorship at Emory University.

In addition to its educational programs, and equally important, IN-CORE also generated some world-class research studies. For example, we looked at the future of the emerging wireless industry, asking where it is going and where it will end up. With Raj Sisodia as my research colleague, we looked at the industry based on six external drivers of change: regulation, competition, technology, investors, customers, and globalization.

For each of the six external drivers, we identified two dimensions. The first dimension was generally well known to the experts (for example, analog to digital in technology). The second dimension was often nonintuitive, bringing in variables or conditions the industry had not thought about. That meant we really had to do our research. We ended up producing some significant monographs: for the wireless industry, for long distance, for cable, for electric utilities, etc. The papers were widely read and the work was gratifying.

More Publishing for the Professional Market

At the same time, I renewed my interest in writing professional books, and my years in Atlanta proved to be a prolific period for me in that regard. After finishing *The Rule of Three*, I began working with Andrew Sobel, who had made a name for himself at Gemini Consulting. When Sobel left that company, he and I had an idea for a niche consulting company. We got in touch with all the CEOs I had worked with over the years and arranged to conduct in-depth interviews with them. Sobel conducted the interviews, either in person or by telephone, which were designed to discover what these CEOs were looking for in terms of transformational leadership. Sobel and I teamed up to advise companies on leadership issues and strategies for the future.

Sobel and I then shifted our focus to customer relationships and co-authored the book that became quite popular—*Clients for Life*. I had always been fascinated by the idea of the "trusted advisor," those historic counselors to world leaders, monarchs, presidents. Many great rulers trusted everything to their advisors—their empires as well as their personal lives. Why? I wanted to know. So Sobel and I started a research project, again interviewing all of the top CEOs, asking what they looked for in a trusted advisor. We also interviewed several world-class leadership and management thought leaders such as Ram Charan, Warren Bennis, Noel Tichy, and David Ulrich.

My theory was that the consultants are experts for hire and paid on a project by project basis and that most of us will eventually be marginalized by the internet. In other words, the pattern of the industrial age would be essentially repeated. After all, we could already see it happening. The steno pool we all depended on just a few years earlier was gone, and the trend was continuing to the full range of front-line, clerical, white collar people. I saw no reason why it would not automate growing numbers of white-collar professional occupations (as opposed to clerical staff). So much of a lawyer's work, for example, is just boilerplate, and much of it is already being done online. Who will survive? Our answer was "trusted advisors." The book was a success. Sobel actually created an entire practice using the book as a platform: How to become a trusted advisor. Professional services companies love it—investment banks and law, accounting and consultancy firms—because they all depend on relationships. In a way, the relationship marketing center that we started became transmogrified into this work on the professional side—with Sobel taking the leadership role.

My range of interests has evolved over the years from the micro (individual customers) to the macro (institutions, governments, religions, businesses) and from behavioral (psychology) to policy disciplines. In Atlanta, I found myself increasingly interested in geopolitics. My time in Singapore as an External Examiner whetted this appetite. During the 1980s and 1990s, I began paying attention to an interesting phenomenon: In terms of trade and investment patterns, the world was reorganizing its geography after the collapse of communism. The impact of the Industrial Revolution had been from East to West. Trade and investment had expanded along those lines, both above and below the equator. Now, however, we were seeing a North to South integration taking place, and the reorganization was forming new trade and economic blocs. Moreover, as advanced nations began to age and to age rapidly, their domestic markets plateaued, and trade became the new growth engine of the world economy.

The shift was becoming increasingly apparent. I had seen Singapore become the center point for the surging north to south trade between Australia and New Zealand on the south and the ASEAN countries and mainland China on the north. NAFTA was the same, a new trading bloc from Canada to Mexico. And then there was the new European Union—an integration of northern Europe with southern.

I became so interested in this phenomenon that I began to give speeches and write papers on the topic. I then discovered a local, world-class writer, John Yow, with whom I set out on a remarkable journey. I had seen samples of his work, mostly corporate histories, and I liked his informal and approachable style. I asked him if he would be willing to write this book with me, and once we were underway, I got the most pleasant surprise of all. Yow is also a phenomenal researcher. A great writer and a great researcher—the classic skill set of the academic. What is more, Yow is also a quick learner. With things that are outside his domain, he takes initiative and says, "Okay, I will learn the language and get it done."

I also invited Sisodia into this project because we were writing so much together, and he helped finish the book. It was published under the title *Tectonic Shift*, and it has been widely appreciated for its rigor and prescience. Given the speculative nature of the project (and unlike *The Rule of Three* and *Clients for Life*, which have sold well in multiple translations), we did not receive a substantial advance for *Tectonic Shift*, but it was a wonderful learning experience and allowed me to expand my horizons and grow intellectually.

My next project grew out of my work at BellSouth, where I was asked the most insightful question I have ever been asked by a CEO: Why do good companies fail? I had never thought about that. My assumption was that companies never fail. After all, we teach the success of great companies. They are always there. But something had happened, after the first energy crisis there had been a huge restructuring of corporate America. Conglomerates were breaking apart. Foreign investors were buying the pieces of iconic American companies. Corporations were coming and going. Duane Ackerman, Chairman and CEO of Bellsouth, had read *In Search of Excellence*, which had been a great hit in the 1980s, and he pointed out to me that several of the companies praised in that book were now in trouble. These included IBM, Xerox, Kodak, and Sears.

I told him that I did not know the answer to his question, "why good companies fail," but that I would look into it, on my own rather than as an advisor to BellSouth. As I began to do the research, I realized that while we had always talked about two paradigms in management strategy—first, that competition can destroy you; and, second, that the company with the resource advantage will win the race—there was another angle on the question. I became increasingly convinced that, in reality, the incumbents destroy themselves. I began giving presentations and speeches about what I came to call "the seven bad habits of good companies." Of course, I had read Stephen Covey's hugely successful *The Seven Habits of Highly Effective People* which outlines *good* habits and had been struck by the power of its message.

But what I saw on the macro level of institutions persuaded me that something needed to be said about the "bad habits." I again teamed up with Yow, and we began to do research on dozens of companies that had failed or come close to it in recent years. The seven bad habits I postulated turned out to be a perfect framework within which to tell their stories. The book went to the publisher, Wharton School Publishing, and, unfortunately, their intellectual property lawyer advised them that we needed to change the title. "Seven habits" was off limits. Ultimately, the book was published as *The Self-Destructive Habits of Good Companies and How to Break Them*. It has been translated into more than a dozen languages and has become something of a "platform" book. That is, I have been asked to follow up with a book on the self-destructive habits of good Indian companies, for example, or good Japanese companies, and so forth. I have even been encouraged to write a book about the self-destructive habits of great nations and great universities.

In the meantime, Sisodia and I began thinking about our next project—another step in the journey that began long ago with the notion of market share, which is the basis for *The Rule of Three*. The evolution from there was to relationship marketing, with the shift from market share of a given product to share of the customer's wallet. But then I began to see that relationship marketing, as it became more data mining and IT centric, would basically be taken over by the IT people. Marketing would be in search of a new paradigm, and we came up with the idea that it was winning share of the hearts of your customers. Our research took the form of the question: How do you bond with customers not just financially but emotionally? We saw that as the basis of a new paradigm, as well as a book concept.

At first our idea was to provide insight on how to create this emotional bond, how to win "share of hearts" of customers; consequently, our original title was *Share of Heart*. But as our research continued, we were convinced that we should talk about broader issues—in other words, not just the marketing side of the company, but the leadership of the corporation. So we began to think in terms of "share of heart" of all five important stakeholders: customers, employees, suppliers, investors, and the community in which the company operates.

We continued our research on how companies proved exceptional in winning share of heart in any or all of these five areas, eventually looking at more than 200 companies nominated by students and colleagues. We winnowed the field to 60 and eventually researched 30 companies in-depth.

It was a fascinating project. We studied companies we would have never thought of, and we often found a reality that was at odds with a company's public image. The take-away message was what gave the book its punch: these companies, while they delivered exceptional financial performance, were also very good to their employees, their communities (by investing back), their suppliers, and their customers. In other words, we shattered the old theory that in order to make money for your investors, you have to exploit your other stakeholders. We proved that it is not a zero sum game and great companies know how to create a win-win among all of its stakeholders.

Out of the 30 companies, only 18 were publicly traded, and a couple of interesting generalizations came to the surface. First, quite a few of our "Firms of Endearment" (which became the title of the book) were headquartered in small towns rather than in big cities. Second, many were privately owned and family run and therefore not driven by Wall Street analysts and earnings reports. Still, the financial results were incredible.

Our analysis was based on investing one dollar in 1995 and cashing out 10 years later, which meant that we covered both the boom of the late 1990s and the bust of the early 2000s. We found that over the years, our companies *increasingly* outperformed the S&P 500. By the end of the study period, our firms were producing returns *four times* higher than the S&P average. We also compared our firms to the companies Jim Collins had analyzed in *Good to Great*. He had used exceptional financial performance as his starting point and then tried to figure out what caused such success, but our average annual return was twice as high as Collins' companies.

Who were our firms? UPS, back when it was held by its employees, was one. Patagonia was another, along with New Balance, Whole Foods and Costco. And the point was: They all had some purpose in life beyond profit which drove them, but they managed to be very profitable at the same time. The book's thesis was that you do not have to make those trade-offs. With these surprising revelations, *Firms of Endearment* became one of the most successful leadership books of 2007. Now it is becoming main stream, and Sisodia, who took the lead on the book, has joined with John Mackey of Whole Foods to start a movement they call "conscious capitalism."

It has become their cause—trying to elevate the culture of corporations from the traditional view that shareholder value is the only thing that matters. Most recently, we have revised the book and added a larger number of companies, which are stakeholder driven. The results are even more impressive over a 15-year time period.

Geoeconomics

With my next project, I returned to geoeconomics. I also continued to work with Yow—this time examining what I considered to be the most important global phenomenon of our time: The inevitable rise of China and possibly India into world economic superpowers. Not only did I feel that the rise of China and India was certain to happen, but more controversially, that it would prove to be an economic boon for the whole world. Just as America's rise had lifted the world with it, so would China's and India's. I knew that my view was somewhat provocative. After all, China is a Communist nation with a questionable record on human rights. Would these factors militate against its economic rise? Similarly, India's political and economic systems are highly volatile and evolving. There's no national agenda, no effective infrastructure; there is enormous poverty, and chaos seems to prevail. But I saw something else, and there was plenty of evidence that the journey had already begun.

With the reforms instituted by Deng Xioping beginning in 1978, China had transformed itself from an ideology-driven system to an increasingly market-driven economy. India had thrown off the shackles of colonialism in 1947, but its "second independence" came in 1991, when the government was finally forced to institute broad economic reforms and free up its markets. Private capital began to flow into India, and its own industries began to flourish with the final end of the "license raj." Both nations had started their ascent.

The most provocative part of this thinking, however, was not that the two nations would rise, but that, rather than becoming colossal competitors, they would learn to cooperate with one another during the journey. That notion led to the book's title,

Chindia Rising. The phrase was coined by the economic advisor to the ruling Congress Party in India, Jairam Ramesh, who had strongly advocated that the two countries must partner with each other through open borders, trade, and investment. He recalled that 500 years earlier China and India were the world's two largest trading economies and argued, in effect, for a kind of reestablishment of the ancient Silk Road.

The book acknowledged the tremendous obstacles to the rise of "Chindia." We noted that the emergence of a vast middle class in China and India, with the rise in consumption that such numbers would entail, would place an unprecedented strain on world resources—especially the natural resources to meet rapidly growing energy needs. My conclusion was that the one great potential show-stopper would be neither capital nor technology, but rather the environment. For the rise of Chindia to have a positive global effect, leaders there and in the West would need to commit to a program of "nurturing nature." Moreover, such a policy would lead to a tremendous wave of innovation: "scarcity-driven innovation" to replace vanishing resources; "affordability-driven innovation" to bring more goods and services to more people; and "conservation-driven innovation" to create the green technologies of the future.

We also noted that the rise of China and India economically and politically would produce another interesting phenomenon, which I like to call the "easternization" of the world; it is in direct conflict with Kipling's famous phrase, "East is East and West is West, and never the twain shall meet." But as I tell audiences today, Kipling was dead wrong. He is not only dead, but he will be proven wrong. The East is coming to the West, and the West will have to come to grips with its arrival. We see it everywhere; in spirituality with the rising popularity of eastern spiritual practices such as yoga and meditation; in cuisine; and in literature, film, and other cultural markers. And we also see innovation and technology originating in the East and migrating to the West. This is referred to as reverse innovation.

The book was published by Tata McGraw-Hill in India, because it so directly reflects the concerns of that nation, and it has done quite well. Just as important, out of my work on that project came the creation of a nonprofit research entity called the India China America Institute (ICA Institute), the mission of which is to disseminate new knowledge—through workshops, conferences, webinars and newsletters—on the increasingly important relationships among these three powers. The Institute's premise is that those relationships will define the global economy going forward, and that a peaceful balance of interests among them is crucial for world stability. (As an aside, our first inclination was to call it the China India America Institute, but we quickly realized that the acronym CIA Institute would hardly be appropriate.)

Business Book Review Breakthrough

I should mention that back in 1983, while I was still at Illinois I started a publication called *Business Book Review* (BBR). It grew out of my experience teaching executives in the Bell system. At the end of these courses, the executives would routinely ask, "What is a good book to read?" I would say, "Don't you know?" In fact, they did not know, which surprised me, but then I figured out why. Back then, publishers were more interested in selling to bookstores and managers had no time to go to the bookstore and browse the aisle except maybe at an airport. Also, business books got little notice from the big book retailers, and readers had to browse rather painstakingly to find titles of interest. That scenario was at the point of changing with the publication of *In Search of Excellence* but, in the meantime, I saw a need.

I started a company for the purpose of selecting and summarizing the 50 best business books each year. Out of thousands of business books published in a given year, we provided in-depth abstracts, 4,000–5,000 words, so that managers and executives would really be able to have a grasp of what these books were about. I also discovered a company in Champaign-Urbana, Illinois, that would produce the finished publication for me—take the manuscript, and provide all the editorial, layout, and design work—and that company's founder became my partner.

When I went to USC in 1984, we continued to run the business from Illinois, but it was difficult. We had not done a great job marketing the publication, and fulfillment costs were rising. But then I found a great writer at USC, Lydia Johnson, who had been hired to edit the business school's new journal, a journal that would presumably compete with the *Harvard Business Review* and the *Sloan Management Review*. USC abandoned the journal however, and suddenly Johnson was available. I asked her to be editor-in-chief of my publication and with her on board, we shifted the business to USC.

I kept Johnson in charge after I moved to Atlanta, and the business continued to provide value, but did not exactly prosper. I had so many other preoccupations that I could not give it sufficient attention, and, frankly, I was losing money on it. In 2001, I decided that it needed some focus, so I recruited John Fayad, who had worked as a consultant to Bellsouth, to team up with Johnson. Our first move was to go completely digital—including digitizing all of our archives—and move to digital-only subscriptions. We also shifted from individual subscribers to corporate subscribers (who would make the content available to their employees). It was a big investment on my part—to digitize, create a website, and do all the online fulfillment—but we needed to bring the business into the new millennium. We also shifted to B to B marketing by targeting the chief learning officer (CLO) of large enterprises. Finally in 2007, I decided to sell BBR to EBSCO, a leading online content distribution company.

My Role as Corporate Board Member

My professional life includes one final arc of my long, interesting, and varied career: my experiences as a board member for a diverse range of corporations. Like everything else in my professional life, this development was accidental. Surprisingly, it began not in Atlanta, where I was living, nor in California,

Illinois, or New York, where I had lived and worked, but rather in Minneapolis.

In 1994, Norstan was one of the nation's largest independent systems integration companies. It installed the PBX, a piece of hardware that created a telephone exchange system on a university or corporate campus, so that employees would not need to depend on more expensive Centrex telephone lines every time they wanted to make a call within the company. It was a good business, and Norstan was doing well—about $500 million a year. It bought the hardware from Rolm, the number three maker of this equipment, which was the first to come out with a digital switch.

Rolm was sold to IBM, which later sold the company to Siemens, but Norstan survived the changes Rolm was going through and continued to install its equipment. Consequently, Norstan had representatives at telephone industry conferences where I was invited to speak, and that's how I got to know them. The company was founded by two partners, and one of them asked me one day if I would be interested in serving on their board. I said I would be delighted—adding that my main strength was strategic thinking, about today and, especially, about tomorrow.

The company's ambition was to grow, and it was quite successful and profitable. They had a great corporate culture, featuring the process Ken Blanchard had created in *The 60-Minute Manager*. Blanchard, one of the great humanistic management consultants, formulated the idea that if you are too small to be in the "Fortune 500," you can nevertheless aspire to belong to the "Fortunate 500." That is, you can be employee centric and you can be customer centric. You do not need to be exclusively investor- or owner centric. It is a great concept, and I really did love this company, its founders, and its culture. When I came on, the original board members were retiring, and it was time to bring in leadership for the next generation.

It was a fascinating experience, especially when the company chairman, Paul Baszucki, asked me to be on the compensation committee, which I would eventually chair. We had to decide on salaries of everybody, including the founder. Obviously, such a situation could be awkward, but that is exactly the kind of thing an independent, nonexecutive board member must learn to deal with.

The entire experience was new, exciting, and challenging— and I had much to learn from it. How should I behave in such an environment, particularly as the only foreign-born American? (There was one woman on the board, but otherwise, as you would expect, it consisted of white men.) I learned quickly that the chemistry among the board members is critical, and I hoped to inject the right ingredient into the mix. Eventually, I did become the thought leader of the board, and the experience was very enriching.

My own learning increased enormously. In some sense, rather than looking through the eyes of a functional expert in marketing, I had to look at the world from a corporate viewpoint, across all functions. Suddenly I became much more interested in leadership issues, succession planning, and conflict management among functional area heads. As a result, I began to see myself as what you might call a "deep generalist." In another sense, I realized that I was circling back to my earliest roots, back to the family business, where out of necessity, we worked across functions. Now, however, that breadth of knowledge— practical, experiential, tactical—was more professional, more process driven.

Ultimately to realize the company's ambition to ramp up to $1 billion in revenues, we diversified into software services, clearly a competency we needed, and we made a major acquisition. However, as sometimes happens in these cases, the diversification did not work out as intended. Because we were moving into IT, our founder decided to step down, and our succession plan was to bring in a new CEO from the IT industry. Since IBM had been the original acquirer of Rolm and there was a relationship there, we recruited a very senior executive from "Big Blue." The idea was sound, but the new leadership failed to make the transition. We ended up selling Norstan to a big telecom installation company, Black Box. At that point I retired from that board. The growth, the transition, even the selling of the company was a great experience for me.

It is fitting to mention my work for PacWest Telecom, in Stockton, California here. PacWest was an independent, entrepreneur-driven telephone company in competition with Pacific Bell, one of the Baby Bells. As such, it was looking to expand from northern California into all the territory west of the Rockies. It was trying to sign up all the ISP companies, such as AOL, whose traffic would go through their switch. The company was backed by a huge venture capital company, Safeguard Scientific, which wanted PacWest to do an IPO. Bear Stearns would do the underwriting. I was invited to join the board about the time the company headed out on its "road show," an intense selling campaign—often hitting two cities a day—to line up potential investors in advance of the IPO. The idea is that you get the IPO done and then, with all the new capital, you begin to manage your new growth strategy. It was exciting to go through that whole process, and in addition to being a strategic advisor, I also got to sit on the compensation and audit committees. I remained on that board until 2007, but ultimately wearied of all that travel to Stockton and back, I retired from the board.

Now, back to Minneapolis, where a company specializing in learning systems had spun off from Control Data Corp, which had created a learning platform called PLATO. Ironically, this initiative originated at the University of Illinois, where an ex-IBM scientist developed a system based on the premise that even very young children can learn through touching, even before they learn the alphabet. The system used touch-screen technology, then in its infancy, but showed great potential. The PLATO platform was eventually sold by Illinois to Control Data, which was beginning to realize that it could not continue to compete as a mainframe computer manufacturer against the monopoly power of IBM. Like Honeywell and Burroughs, it needed to find a specialty niche, and for Control Data that niche was education. The acquisition made sense, but Control Data eventually collapsed anyway, and one of the company's executives acquired the rights to the PLATO technology.

Dr Rajiv Tandon, an Indian who had been a customer when the technology was still owned by Control Data, became a founding partner in a start-up that bought the rights to PLATO. No doubt because of Dr Tandon's Indian origin, an Indian company became one of his biggest investors. It was that investment company that put me on Dr Tandon's board, as a way to make sure its interests were represented. Dr Tandon and his co-founder sold that company to a much bigger company, Digital Think, a player in the Learning Management Systems arena, at which point my services were no longer needed. But after the sale, the founders started another company, called Adayana, and asked me to serve on that board. (This time the invitation was not from the investment company, which had by now cashed out, but rather from the founders themselves.)

Adayana was and still is a private company, and the strategy was to grow through acquisitions into different segments. Its original purpose had been to train and certify people in the agricultural sector, in handling chemicals properly. So the job was creating online content for this certification program. Adayana was developing computer-based learning (CBL); in other words, creating a platform to convert paper-based content into digital. It's quite a challenge actually, because in-person one can train a student for eight hours, but on computers one must modularize the content into small units—maybe eight to ten minutes each. From agriculture, we diversified into the automotive and defense sectors, and then we bought a company the same size as ours which specialized in market research in the agriculture sector. Adayana has grown rapidly and at the same time is getting all kinds of awards for customer satisfaction. I retired from the board in 2007 but I am still active as an investor. Minneapolis was where all my board appointments originated. As of this writing, Adayana has sought chapter eleven protection due to lack of agreement among its key investors.

Soon, though, my corporate board experience went another route. Since 1985, I had been an advisor for the Indian company Wipro, which, in its early days, had been a small soaps and vegetable shortening maker. But it had diversified into IT big-time, and eventually the Chairman, the renowned Indian icon, Azim Premji asked me if I would like to be on the board. I joined in 1999 and still serve on that board today.

At Wipro, we convene for two days, four times a year, in Bangalore, India, and I have a dual role. I do not serve on any of the standing committees, so I am able to spend my first day with management, advising on strategic initiatives in each of the different divisions; then I spend the second day in the actual board meetings. Wipro is now a huge company. The IT division alone does more than $8 billion in revenues, and we have diversified into a range of branded consumer products as well as into infrastructure. Recently, we demerged the non IT part of the company into a separate entity in order to focus on the IT services identity. Wipro is now the world's largest engineering services company, and has more than 130,000 employees worldwide. The company has evolved from an ethnocentric domestic entity to a globally integrated enterprise, and it has been a real joy to witness this transformation. Growth was accomplished through acquisitions all over the world (global expansion) with human resource and finance processes that are world class. Watching this kind of growth and evolution is the kind of thing academics professors dream about.

Wipro is one of the few Indian companies that have produced more than 100 entrepreneurs. The leadership loves to see young people start out in the company, spend several years, then go out and successfully start his or her own company—especially in the IT field. To have this kind of positive impact on society is one of the company's missions. Azim Premji himself has a real knack for identifying great talent, and the very motto of the company is "to make ordinary people, extraordinary." The company has an exemplary board, on which every member learns from the others. Each brings a unique perspective from his or her own experiences, and the discussions are always energizing. Everyone contributes and everyone learns.

This "Asian trajectory" continued with my work for another Indian company. The son of a member of my brother's boarding school's board of trustees started a pharmaceutical company,

Shasun Chemicals and Drugs, Ltd, that manufactured so-called "bulk drugs" like ibuprofen. Two of his brothers also joined the business, which had grown into a midsize, publicly traded company, and they asked me to join their board. Since I was coming to India four times a year anyway, I agreed.

At the time, the company was at the $250–300 million level, but comparatively speaking, that would be like a $1 billion company here in the United States. It was still family owned and family run, and the plan was to expand further. We made a major acquisition by purchasing one of the biggest pharmaceutical manufacturing plants in the United Kingdom and created a separate subsidiary, Shasun Pharma Solutions. I was asked to serve on that board also and eventually became its Chairman for a short time. This was another tremendously exciting learning experience, considering all the due diligence involved in an acquisition.

Still in India, I got involved with the Manipal Group, the largest nongovernment (private) medical college. At the time of independence, the Indian government pushed two areas of education—engineering and medicine—and funded its own national institutes for both. The private sector was not granted access. But Manipal's founder went to Prime Minister Jawaharlal Nehru and pleaded for permission to start a private university, arguing that because of the government's policy of "reservation"—a form of affirmative action—many deserving students from the upper Brahmin classes were denied entry. Nehru relented, and the Manipal Group has become a world-class provider of medical education, with campuses in more than eight countries, including Malaysia, Nepal and Bhutan. Some 25 percent of Malaysian medical students are trained by the group, and Manipal has educated more than 30,000 medical doctors worldwide. More than 3,000 practice in the United States today, often in positions of great prestige.

I was asked to be on their board to help envision creating a world-class university in fields other than medicine. Manipal has extended its interests into management and engineering, and its vision was to create a great campus like a major U.S.

university. Eventually the CEO decided to leave Manipal and start a clinical trials company, Manipal Acunova, and I agreed to step down from the Manipal board in order to serve on the board of the new company. Acunova quickly acquired one of the clinical trials companies in Germany and has continued to grow through acquisitions and strategic alliances.

The last thread of this Indian tapestry leads back to the family. My sister's husband started a luggage company, Safari Industries, which I invested in early on and which subsequently became the third-largest luggage company in India. After growing the company and taking it public, the company prospered and the Safari brand became popular in India. However, the company began to plateau. My nephew wanted new investors and board members to reenergize the company, and to that end, they invited me to join the board. Recently, we sold the company to an experienced entrepreneur from the luggage industry who has ramped up growth of the brand and the company.

By this point my corporate board work encompassed the fields of telecom, IT, pharmaceuticals, education, and manufacturing. On a journey that took me to Minneapolis, California and India, my next stop was Tampa, Florida.

At Norstan, we decided to bring in an outside CEO, and one of the candidates was a woman from AT&T. It turned out that she was not interested in the CEO position but did want to serve on the board. Because we needed her telecom experience, we invited her to join. She eventually became the chairwoman of another company, called Cryocell International, based in Tampa. Cryocell was started in the 1990s by an early pioneer in stem cell storage, whose idea was to harvest and preserve, through freezing, stem cells from the umbilical cord, cells that would be otherwise disposed of. My female colleague on the Norstan board had become one of his advisors and then one of his board members, and because we worked so well together at Norstan, she invited me to join the board at Cryocell. I agreed—and was rewarded with a whole new range of experiences.

The goal was to grow. Cryocell granted a license for its technology to an entrepreneur in Mexico, and he was already producing huge numbers. This is how it works: if the soon-to-be mother and her family agree, the stem cells are harvested from the umbilical cord, a service for which the family pays a fee. Then the cells are stored against future need, for which the family continues to pay, like an insurance premium, creating annuity revenue for the company. The striking success in Mexico gave me the idea that we could grow this business in India. I arranged a licensing agreement with an Indian entrepreneur, and it has been very successful in India also. (By the way, I find it remarkable that a technology designed for advanced nations often finds its greatest success in emerging markets.)

So now I can add health care (stem cell technologies, no less) to my inventory of experiences. Also, my experiences have ranged from small domestic to large global corporations. They are simply a measure of how fortunate I have been. Who would not relish such a rich treasure of experience?

My final destination was San Jose, in the Silicon Valley, and an organization called The Indus Entrepreneurs (or TiE). It started when an Indian entrepreneur sold his company, made a lot of money, and decided to help his fellow Indian entrepreneurs succeed. TiE, the organization he founded, has become the largest entrepreneurship organization in the world, a nonprofit with more than 50,000 members, and has created more than $100 billion of wealth in less than 30 years. In 1999, I was invited to San Jose to be the keynote speaker at their second annual conference. The conference usually features two speakers, one Indian and one American, and my counterpart that year was the CEO of Yahoo! My speech went well, and because of that exposure, I suddenly found myself on the boards of at least a half-dozen start-ups—primarily to offer guidance and strategic thinking. Working with venture capitalists took my experience to a new level, and serving on the board of a start-up is unique in itself. The meetings are monthly rather than quarterly, but that is just part of it. As a board member, you are likely to get a call anytime, day or night, because a crisis is always breaking out somewhere.

A year later Atlanta started its own TiE chapter, and I became active in that organization. As a result, witnessing the incubation of start-up companies has become a whole new aspect of my ongoing education. I have worked with some fascinating people, like Jay Chaudhry. He is a successful serial entrepreneur who specializes in building up new companies and then selling them to larger companies just before the inevitable IPO. One needs outside board members for these exit options, and I had the privilege of working with him on a couple of his companies. That gave me the chance to develop a whole new skill set—developing exit strategies: how and when to exit, how to get fair value for everyone, and how to create a win-win for all stakeholders.

I have also had the opportunity to think about what makes entrepreneurs succeed or fail. My experience at Whirlpool is where I first began to realize that successful start-ups are made with one key customer. In the case of Whirlpool, it was Sears, but the realization led me to study dozens of companies, including very large ones like HP, Microsoft, Intel, and Daimler-Benz. All were created by one customer. That became the entrepreneurial touchstone: one key customer will make all the difference.

I also learned that, interestingly, inventors generally are not good entrepreneurs. Inventors are too possessive of their inventions, and they tend to become ideologists rather than pragmatists. Conversely, start-up businesses are constantly evolving, and the entrepreneur must be extremely practical and flexible. You cannot say, "It's my way or the highway." So most inventors fail on the business end, and it is usually someone else, an entrepreneur, who seizes the opportunity that the inventor created. At the same time, entrepreneurs are usually not good managers. Their strength is deal-making. They know how to access resources, to get the government to enable them to create markets, but they do not know how to manage professionally. And my final observation along these lines is: If entrepreneurs are usually not good managers, the worst managers of all are consultants like me. We can advise, but please do not ask us to manage daily operations.

I should also mention that in several cases I have found myself on a company's advisory board, rather than on its board of directors. The traditional board of directors will often include the venture capitalists that are looking after their investment, while the advisory board's responsibility is simply to provide strategic advice. Over time I have found myself on several such boards, across a variety of industries, but mostly relating to new technologies like mobility platforms and IT services.

One thing that has surprised me is how much is the same across all boards, and even across all industries. The scene changes and each company has its own unique ecosystem, but the processes are the same, the concerns are the same, the responsibilities are the same. Once you have sat on one board, you are pretty well prepared to sit on any other board.

At the same time, what you might call the personalities of the boards themselves can vary tremendously. At one extreme are boards whose mission seems to be to provide rubber-stamp approval of whatever the executives decide to do. At the other extreme are boards that are fully engaged and fully committed to do whatever is necessary for the good of the company—even to the point of reminding the founding entrepreneur of the fiduciary responsibility to protect minority investors. In the middle are boards that take on the role of nurturing management and providing wisdom and guidance.

My greatest lesson, though, and one I have learned again and again, is that you have to be independent to make a meaningful contribution. Even though the founder or the CEO recruits you, once you become a board member, you are no longer working for him or her; you are working for the company. Moreover, if the founder is the majority shareholder and the minority shareholders are the institutional investors, your greater responsibility lies with the minority shareholders. Fortunately, after the debacles at Enron and WorldCom, the Sarbanes-Oxley Act has in effect legislated that boards become more independent and more responsible to investors and shareholders. In the end, only an independent-minded board member can truly serve the long-term interests of the company—which of necessity includes the interests of all stakeholders.

Remaining Active

What does the future hold for me? At age 75, perhaps I should content myself with looking back, and with offering a heartfelt thanks to all the great academic institutions and individuals that enabled me to fulfill my potential, to be productive, and to enjoy a long career of teaching and learning. But while looking back might be satisfying, I do not find it quite as exciting as looking ahead.

I have three endeavors that should keep me active going forward. One is the ICA Institute, which I believe is very strategic for policy research. I am convinced that a trilateral harmonious relationship between India, China, and America is truly the key to tomorrow's global economic stability. These three nations, whose combined resource demands far outweigh those of the rest of the world, must coordinate their talents and technologies to protect the earth from environmental collapse. Where they lead, other nations will follow. These three nations are the largest sourcing destinations as well as largest markets and China is emerging as a major economic and military power. Then, too, purely in terms of economic restructuring going forward, China is already the largest holder of currency reserves, opening the possibility of Chinese or Asian currency coexisting, if not, replacing the dollar as the world currency. There are many monumental issues and challenges facing these three great powers that I plan to devote more time and energy to the ICA Institute for the foreseeable future.

A second endeavor will keep me active is on the academic side. At the wonderful party held by Emory University to celebrate my 70th birthday, an idea emerged: to collect my academic publications into a number of volumes, edited by either a former student or a colleague who had worked with me. The idea was warmly embraced, and, in fact, the volumes have been published by SAGE Publications—providing a legacy for future scholars, especially in emerging markets, by providing access in one place. So often it happens that the new generation reads only the most recent articles in highly specialized journals and is not aware of earlier research and publications.

The idea is to offer the same kind of "complete works" opportunity to other lifelong scholars. Most of legendary scholar's
contributions consist of four to five decades of publications, and
I realized that we need to archive them, republish them, and
digitize them, and thereby create something like an Encyclopedia
of the work of these living legends. Consequently, I have agreed
to be the Series Editor for what is called "Legends in Marketing,"
and SAGE Publications has agreed to be the Publisher. I am
contributing my time and effort to get the series off the ground.

Already, the effort is immensely gratifying. All the legends we
have invited to participate absolutely loved the idea. The process
requires each to classify all of his or her writings and organize
them into the various volumes. Then we enlist an editor for each
volume, along with three well-known scholars to comment on
the writings in that particular volume. The three world-class
scholars are those who were influenced by the Legend's writings.
And finally, a unique touch: The volume editor asks seven to
eight questions to the legend, seeking his or her current views
on the subjects or topics covered in the volume. This seems
a wonderful way to get even more insight out of these living
legends, and what a boon for readers!

To date, 10 legends have signed on. These include Philip
Kotler, Kent Monroe, Shelby Hunt, V. Kumar, Naresh Malhotra,
Christian Grönroos, and Yoram (Jerry) Wind. The goal is to sign
up other legends in specialized areas such as consumer behavior,
marketing strategy, and research methods. We will digitize their
work, get all the permissions for reprint rights, and move forward.
This will be an ongoing project; an endless journey that will be a
tremendous contribution to the marketing discipline.

Finally, my third endeavor will be to continue to write,
both academically and professionally. In fact, there is so much
I want to write I scarcely know where to begin. For example,
one of the things I really must do, at some point, is go back
to some of my earlier publications in the professional area—
Winning Back Your Market, *Bringing Innovation to Market*,
The Customer Is Key, *Clients for Life*—and update them with
new data and examples.

At the same time, I am pulled to write new professional books. *Chindia Rising* has led me to think deeply about the problem of sustaining economic prosperity without destroying the environment, and the radically new kinds of innovation that will arise to meet this challenge. I already have a working title, *Nurturing Nature: Back to the Past*, and I know there is a book there. And there are other possibilities—books that could be spun out of *Self-Destructive Habits of Good Companies*.

LIFE LESSON

When it comes to deciding what to do first or, even next, and doing what will ensure continual growth and success, you will be pulled in many directions. *Be practical and do what you are most passionate about. It will energize you.*

13

SAYING THANKS BY GIVING BACK

Any account of my work in Atlanta and at Emory would not be complete without covering an aspect of my life and career that becomes increasingly important to me as the years pass. That area is philanthropic work.

Coming to this great and vibrant city has proven to be a wonderful development for me and my family. Both Emory and Atlanta were just "up and coming" when I arrived, and now Atlanta has emerged as a global hub city. It has great infrastructure, friendly people, and good ethnic diversity. My family has found it easy to make a home here because, after all, many residents are immigrants—whether from Florida, New York, or a foreign nation. Atlanta is also full of bright, young professional people. It is my permanent home and the idea of moving from Atlanta is unlikely. Emory University, too, has been a great institution for me.

It was from the vantage point of our final destination that Madhu and I began to think about what we might do in the philanthropic arena—how we might begin to pay our debt of gratitude for the wonderful help we have received along our long journey. I was still too busy to contribute a great deal of time to an effort, but Madhu and I realized that we could start by creating a foundation—the Madhuri and Jagdish Sheth Foundation at the University of Illinois. When I left Illinois, the financial office encouraged me not to cash out my state retirement. I was advised to wait until I was 55—another eight years or so—at which time I would be able to begin drawing a retirement pension. I followed that advice, and when the time came (after we had arrived in Atlanta), I not only began receiving retirement check, but the university bestowed me the professor emeritus designation. It was an honor and a pleasant surprise. It was the perfect final touch to my Illinois experience.

The Sheth Foundation

Madhu and I decided that the mission of the Sheth Foundation would be to support the two academic institutions that were instrumental in helping me fulfill my potential: The University of Pittsburgh, where I had been a student, and the University of Illinois, where I had served the longest as a faculty member before coming to Emory. At the same time, I wanted to contribute to the marketing discipline, which led to supporting four academic organizations including the American Marketing Association (AMA), the Academy of Marketing Science (AMS), the Association for Consumer Research (ACR), and the Academy of International Business (AIB). The Sheth Foundation has done well over the years and has become something of a role model for other marketing scholars who want to give back to the discipline. Colleagues have realized that if I could step up, they can too.

The Foundation's activities are primarily focused on doctoral students, the future scholars of the discipline, but it funds several activities. Specifically, it has provided the endowment to the University of Pittsburgh to host a "winter camp," where the doctoral students in marketing, along with the faculty, invite three or four top scholars to join them at a ski resort near Pittsburgh for a two-day retreat. In the morning the scholars present papers on their areas of scholarship and the afternoons are given to more informal activities, socializing, one-on-one conversation, and, of course, skiing.

The primary beneficiaries of the Sheth Foundation are the academic professional associations. For example, the American Marketing Association hosts an annual doctoral consortium, probably the best event of its kind in the world. As more than 100 universities around the world are now invited to nominate a top doctoral student to attend, and these young scholars have an opportunity to come together for the first time. Roughly the same number of renowned scholars is also invited, so the result is a three-day get-together, hosted by a university, of the world's top students and scholars. The Sheth Foundation makes a contribution, through AMA, to help support this activity.

The Association of Consumer Research (ACR), an organization of which I was a founding member, is another beneficiary. At ACR's highly regarded annual conference, the Sheth Foundation supports the Best Paper Award and also provides fellowships and stipends for three doctoral dissertations. Recently, the Sheth Foundation began to support the Best Long-Term Impact Award to a paper published in the *Journal of Consumer Research*.

Because of my long interest in the international scene, we also support the annual conference of the Academy of International Business (AIB), by helping cover the travel costs and other expenses of the Sheth Fellows who attend. For another organization, the Academy of Marketing Science (AMS), our support goes to the journal, *JAMS*, where we provide funding for the Best Paper Award as well as for editorial support. Similarly, the Sheth Foundation helps fund the Long-Term Impact Paper Award from the *Journal of Marketing*, the top journal of the discipline, under the auspices of the American Marketing Association. To earn this prestigious annual award, a paper must have been published at least five years earlier, and be deemed by a panel of scholar judges to still exercise important influence in the marketing discipline.

One of our most interesting activities has been the creation of a Living Legends Series, which honors exceptionally distinguished achievement among those who have retired from their academic careers. Selected by committee, the honorees sit for an extensive video interview, during which they share insights on how they began their careers, what and who influenced them, and the areas they excelled in. The videos are then archived by the Foundation. Overall, for a small foundation, we have accomplished quite a lot and had considerable impact.

Additionally, Madhu and I have been involved in other philanthropic activities both at Illinois and at Emory. At Emory, for example, we have endowed the annual Sheth Lecture on Indian Studies. It seemed to us that, in some ways, Emory University was insulated from its own local community, so we had the idea of a Sunday-afternoon lecture, an opportunity for the Indian community to come to the campus and meet with the academic community, both faculty and students. The lecture lasts one hour, followed by a reception for the speaker, and the whole thing has been a great success. The Indian speakers represent the pinnacle of their respective professions (anthropology, culture, history, arts, politics, etc.). We have had the renowned novelists Salman Rushdie and Abhitab Ghosh, filmmakers Mira Nair and Deepa Mehta, and Medha Patkhar, a top social activist in India. It is okay if they are controversial, they just have to be world-class. It has been a fabulous line-up of people and something Madhu and I have been very proud of.

At Illinois, we have supported a different sort of program, but one that also honors the achievements of international talents. That university has long been known for the size and success of its international programs. It is truly a national leader and a model institution in that regard, going back to its long history of excellence in engineering and agriculture. The problem was that we had a world-class university with 5,000 international students, but once these foreign students complete their studies at Illinois and return to their native country, nobody knows them anymore, despite the fact that many become luminaries in their chosen fields. The Office of International Programs wanted to figure out a way to honor these distinguished alumni, on behalf of the university, and they asked me if we would help support it financially. It meant establishing some very strong evaluative criteria, but it sounded like a wonderful thing for

Illinois. My notion of philanthropy has always been to give in such a way that the receiving institution can benefit beyond the dollar amount of the donation.

Each academic unit (agriculture, business, law, architecture, etc.) keeps record of its foreign alumni, which is easy with today's technology. Possible candidates are identified by a number of measures, including by asking emeriti professors whom they would like to recommend—which is a great way to keep emeriti engaged. An annual evaluation ensures that one candidate is selected from the pool of candidates. The chosen candidate comes to campus for two days and gives a public speech, as well as one in his or her discipline. The event is hosted by the Office of International Programs, but the entire university is engaged in it. All recipients are world class scholars with doctorate degrees from Illinois in diverse fields like economic development, education, rice genetics, food sciences, and agricultural economics. Some are Heads of States, Heads of Universities, and Heads of Corporates.

Supporting Eminent Scholars

The most satisfying part of the Distinguished International Alumni Award is the gratitude of the recipients. The institution unlocked their potential, and now they are being honored by that institution for the fulfillment of that potential. At the gala dinner, attended by the chancellor and the provost, we also present the Distinguished International Faculty Award, recognizing a top faculty member from any discipline who has done outstanding work in the international aspect of his or her discipline. Given my own passion for the international arena, it is one of the best philanthropic activities in which I have ever been involved. In fact, it has been such a successful program that we duplicated the effort at Emory University and, most recently, at Kennesaw State University (located in metro Atlanta). At the University of Pittsburgh, we support a program that recognizes outstanding young international alumni who have graduated in the last 10 years. Recent recipients have been extraordinary young women from India and Kenya.

Also at Emory, we endowed the Sheth Distinguished Lecture on "Creativity in Later Life." Emory is part of a great community, with a livable campus where many faculty members continue to work and serve Emory, Atlanta, and beyond—even after they retire. However, it was not until 2001 that a retired Emory faculty member, Eugene Bianchi, got the ball rolling, and co-founded the Emory University Emeritus College with another retired faculty member, John Bugge. I have always thought it important for retired professors to continue to contribute, especially considering all they have to offer, so I really wanted to support Bianchi's effort. To that end, we launched the Lecture, which is an annual event that brings emeriti faculty and their spouses back to the campus. Our first speaker was former Emory president, James Laney. Subsequent speakers include Presidential Medal of Freedom recipient, Dr William Foege; former U.S. President, Jimmy Carter; Pulitzer Prize–winning poet, Natasha Trethewey; Maestro Robert Spano; and Atlanta Journal-Constitution editorial cartoonist, Mike Luckovich. The Lecture is a popular event that caters to nearly 100 guests.

In 2007, we began to endow fellowships for successful Emory doctoral students—across all the business disciplines. Doctoral students typically spend two years getting through their coursework and their qualifying exams then begin to write their dissertations. That is when the Sheth Fellow Award kicks in. In any given year, as many as 15 students, who have passed their qualifying exams and are approaching that final hurdle, are awarded $1,000. They can use the money at their discretion, for travel or research or other scholarly needs, and the recipients are also given a plaque designating them as Sheth Fellows.

Eventually our efforts to give back began to reach out beyond the confines of the university. Since Atlanta is now our "hometown," with our children and grandchildren settled here, I wanted to contribute to its larger community. This contribution has taken two forms. The first addresses the fact that Atlanta has a large and fast-growing Indian community, with some 85,000 Indian residents. We have supported a number of Indian causes, both cultural and social—such as helping new immigrants get settled and helping teens with alienation problems. Madhu has volunteered tirelessly to raise funds to establish a Jain Community Center and the Jain temple to serve more than 500 Jain families.

Second has been the creation of the Sheth Family Foundation, through which we have been able to engage our children in the effort to give back. Our commitment to this work stems from our religion, Jainism, the chief principles of which include *ahimsa*, or nonviolence; *anekanta*, or tolerance for the diversity of viewpoints; and (most relevant here) *anegraha*, or rejecting the accumulation of material possessions. The more you accumulate, the more you must give back. It is the latter principle, in which I believe strongly. Our ideal is that whatever wealth comes to the family should produce even more wealth for the community, so we contribute generously to organizations like CARE, the American Red Cross, the American Diabetes Association, the Salvation Army, Habitat for Humanity, Ashoka for Social Entrepreneurship, as well as others that directly address the needs of Atlanta citizens, including its minority and/or immigrant communities. Having Reshma and Rajen involved, and seeing them embrace the idea of a purpose in life beyond one's personal career and success, has been especially gratifying.

Like my other endeavors, the philanthropic work will continue. It is the least I can do. In order to make impact locally, I have also agreed to join the Board of the Community Foundation of Greater Atlanta, which focuses on assisting hundreds of charities in the metropolitan area as well as surrounding counties.

LIFE LESSON

Similar to how pursuing your passion energizes you, giving back while you are alive is more fulfilling and enjoyable than after you are dead. *Joy and satisfaction comes with seeing the results of your giving.*

14

MADHU IS MY BACKBONE

When Madhu came to America, I felt a tremendous sense of responsibility, as well as extreme delight. Although she could read and write English at the time, she could not speak English as well. Television became her greatest teacher. We watched a lot of television together and that is how she became fluent in English. Our favorite television shows were situational comedies—"My Three Sons," "I Love Lucy," and "Father Knows Best." We also regularly went to the movies—on average, once per week. The funny thing was, back in India, the further back you sit in a theater, the higher your ticket prices were. So in essence, you paid more for the better seats. Madhu and I were amazed that every ticket cost the same in America.

Over the years, I have watched my wife make choices and sacrifices to support my career. She gave up her teaching career. Our vegetarian diets proved to be another obstacle that she did not let drive her back to India. When we lived in New York, initially, we associated the red pizza sauce with the blood of animals. For about a month, our upstairs neighbor tried to convince us that it was safe to eat pizza to no avail. Finally, he took us to watch how pizza was made and we have been fans ever since—so much so that Madhu befriended our Italian neighbors and soon learned how to make the best marinara sauce for pasta. She is one of the most resilient individuals I know.

Madhu's Resolve

Madhu has made sacrifice after sacrifice in order to support me. I would not be who I am today without the hand of fate coupled with Madhu's love, flexibility, and partnership.

From the time our children were born, we moved around quite a bit. At one point, we moved *twice* in one-and-a-half years yet Madhu singlehandedly packed all of our belongings and made each move as smooth as possible for the family. Despite the physical and emotional toll that frequent moves took on her, Madhu has been the bedrock for the family. Not only has she provided unconditional support to me in my endless pursuits, she has maintained and continues to maintain relationships with our family members and friends in India and the United States.

Madhu has boundless energy. Her passion for life and her social skills are legendary. She brings light and life to every event (our 50th wedding anniversary is an example) such that friends and family look forward to interacting with her, especially during social and community gatherings. Madhu is the glue that binds all of us. When she is absent, people feel a sense of emptiness. She is extraordinary in everything that she does.

LIFE LESSON

Family love and support is as essential as breathing air. Madhu, Reshma, and Rajen are my safety net as well as my support system. *There is nothing more fulfilling than for your family to respect and love you.*

EPILOGUE

My long and unpredictable journey has often seemed guided by a benevolent fate. Equally important have been the kindness and generosity of the people and institutions that reached out to help me along the way. I have been blessed. I have had a fantastic "voyage" thus far and can attest to the fact that no matter what the destination, there is nothing more meaningful than a purpose-driven journey of life. Living a purpose-driven life gives you the passion and the energy to reach your full potential.

If you take a grain of wheat and make a loaf of bread, the value add is about three times. If a diamond cutter takes a rough diamond and polishes it, the value add is probably 15 to 20 times. However, if you take a human being and educate and mentor him/her, the value add is infinite. Making ordinary people extraordinary is probably the greatest purpose of life. Without education and mentorship, I would not have reached my full potential and, neither would have those whose lives that I have had the privilege to touch. Life is as much about the journey as the destination, and also the people impacted along the way....

APPENDIX—PUBLICATIONS

Books

The Business School in the Twenty-First Century (with Howard Thomas and Peter Lorange), Cambridge University Press, 2013, 292 pages.

4 A's of Marketing: Creating Value for Customers, Companies and Society (with Rajendra Sisodia), Routledge, 2012, 209 pages.

Chindia Rising: How China and India Will Benefit Your Business, Tata McGraw-Hill, India, 2008 and 2011 (updated Edition).

Legends in Marketing (Seven Volumes), SAGE Publications, 2011.

Deregulation and Competition: Lessons from the Airline Industry (with Fred C. Allvine, Can Uslay and Ashutosh Dixit), SAGE Publications, 2007, 344 pages.

The Self-Destructive Habits of Good Companies and How to Break Them, The Wharton Publishing Group, 2007, 270 pages.

Firms of Endearment: The Pursuit of Purpose and Profit (with Rajendra Sisodia and David Wolfe), The Wharton Publishing Group, Fall 2006, 284 pages.

Does Marketing Need Reform? (with Rajendra Sisodia) (editors), M.E. Sharpe, 2006, 352 pages.

Tectonic Shift: The Geoeconomic Realignment of Globalizing Markets (with Rajendra Sisodia), SAGE India, 2006, 350 pages.

Customer Relationship Management: A Strategic Perspective (with G. Shainesh), McMillian India Ltd. 2006, 198 pages.

Customer Behavior: A Managerial Perspective (with Banwari Mittal), Thomson/Southwestern Publishing, 2004, 2nd edition, 487 pages.

Customer Behavior: Consumer Behavior and Beyond (with Robert Widing and others), Thomson (Pacific Rim Edition), 2003, 560 pages.

The Rule of Three: Surviving and Thriving in Competitive Markets (with Rajendra Sisodia), Free Press, 2002, 277 pages (translated into several languages including German, French, Japanese, and Chinese).

Customer Relationship Management (Editor with G. Shainesh and Atul Parvatiyar), Tata McGraw-Hill India, 2001, 554 pages.

ValueSpace: Winning the Battle for Market Leadership (with Banwari Mittal), McGraw-Hill, 2001, 265 pages.

Internet Marketing (with Abdolreza Eshghi and Balaji Krishnan), Dryden Press, 2000.

Clients for Life (with Andrew Sobel), Simon & Schuster, 2000.

Handbook of Relationship Marketing (with Atul Parvatiyar), SAGE Publications, 2000, 660 pages.

Telecom Outlook Report (with Massoud Saghafi and Robert Janowiak), IEC, 1999, 300 pages.

Customer Behavior: Consumer Behavior and Beyond (with Banwari Mittal and Bruce Newman), Dryden Press, 1998, 800 pages.

Contemporary Knowledge of Relationship Marketing (with Anil Menon), 1998 Research Conference Proceedings, Center for Relationship Marketing, Emory University, 1998.

Research in Marketing (with Atul Parvatiyar), Volume 14, JAI Press, 1998.

Telecom Outlook Report (with Massoud Saghafi and Robert Janowiak), IEC, 1997.

A Strategic Vision of the Wireless Industry: Communications Unbound (with Rajendra Sisodia), IEC, 1997.

Research in Marketing (Series Editor with Atul Parvatiyar), Volume 13, JAI Press, 1997.

The Consolidation of the Information Industry (with Rajendra Sisodia), IEC, 1996.

Contemporary Knowledge of Relationship Marketing (with Atul Parvatiyar), Third Research Conference, Center for Relationship Marketing, Emory University, 1996.

Telecom Outlook Report (with Massoud Saghafi and Robert Janowiak), IEC, 1996.

Research in Marketing (Series Editor with Atul Parvatiyar), Volume 12, JAI Press, 1995.

Telecom Outlook Report (with Massoud Saghafi and Robert Janowiak), IEC, 1995.

Research in Marketing (Supplemental 6). Explanations in the History of Marketing (Series Editor), JAI Press, 1994.

Advances in Telecommunications Management (Volume 4). Strategic Perspective on the Marketing of Information Technologies (Series Editor), JAI Press, 1994.

Relationship Marketing: Theory Methods and Applications, Second Research Conference Proceedings (with Atul Parvatiyar), Center for Relationship Marketing, Emory University, 1994.

Telecom Outlook Report (with Massaid Saghafi and Robert Janowiak), Center for Telecommunications Management, USC, 1994.

Advances in Telecommunications Management, Volume 4 (with Gary Frazier), JAI Press, 1994.

Research in Marketing (editor), Volume 11, JAI Press, 1992.

Consumption Values and Market Choices: Theory and Applications, Southwestern Publishing Co., 1991, 218 pages (with Bruce Newman and Barbara Gross).

Advances in Telecommunications Management, Volume 3 (with Gary Frazier), JAI Press, 1990.

Advances in Telecommunications Management, Volume 2 (with Gary Frazier), JAI Press, 1990.

Advances in Telecommunications Management, Volume 1 (with Gary Frazier), JAI Press, 1990.

Global Macroeconomic Perspectives, Southwestern Publishing Co., 1990, 201 pages (with Abdolreza Eshghi).

Global Microeconomic Perspectives, Southwestern Publishing Co., 1990, 169 pages (with Abdolreza Eshghi).

Global Organizational Theory Perspectives, Southwestern Publishing Co., 1990, 216 pages (with Golpira Eshghi).

Research in Marketing, Volume 10, JAI Press, 1990.

Marketing Theory: Evolution & Evaluation (with David Gardner and Dennis Garrett), John Wiley and Sons, 1988, 231 pages.

Global Marketing Perspectives (with Abdolreza Eshghi), Southwestern Publishing Co., 1988, 186 pages.

Global Strategic Management Perspectives (with Golpira Eshghi), Southwestern Publishing Co., 1988, 174 pages.

Global Financial Perspectives (with Abdolreza Eshghi), Southwestern Publishing Co., 1988, 171 pages.

Global Operations Perspectives (with Golpira Eshghi), Southwestern Publishing Co., 1988, 147 pages.

Global Accounting Perspectives (with Abdolreza Eshghi), Southwestern Publishing Co., 1988, 174 pages.

Global Human Resource Perspectives (with Golpira Eshghi), Southwestern Publishing Co., 1988, 173 pages.

Bringing Innovation to Market (with S. Ram), John Wiley and Sons, November 1987, 225 pages.

Contemporary Views on Marketing Practice (with Gary Frazier), Lexington Books, 1987, 282 pages.

The Customer Is Key (with Milind Lele), John Wiley and Sons, November 1987, 225 pages.

Research in Consumer Behavior (with Elizabeth Hirschmann), Volume 2, JAI Press, 1987.

Research in Marketing, Volume 9, JAI Press, 1987.

Marketing Management: A Comprehensive Reader (with Dennis Garrett), Southwestern Publishing Company, 1986, 1026 pages.

Marketing Theory: Classic and Contemporary Readings (with Dennis Garrett), Southwestern Publishing Company, 872 pages.

Political Marketing: Readings and Annotated Bibliography, American Marketing Association (with Bruce Newman), 1986.

A Theory of Political Choice Behavior (with Bruce Newman), Prager Books, 1986, 190 pages.

Research in Marketing, Volume 8, JAI Press, 1986.

Historical Perspective in Consumer Research: ACR Proceedings (with Chin Tiong Tan), National University of Singapore, July 1985.

Research in Marketing (with Elizabeth Hirschmann), Volume 7, JAI Press (June 1985), 288 pages.

Research in Consumer Behavior, Volume 1, JAI Press (April 1985), 321 pages.

Winning Back Your Market, John Wiley and Sons, November 1984, 228 pages.

Research in Marketing, Volume 6, JAI Press, January 1983, 282 pages.

Research in Marketing, Volume 5, JAI Press, January 1982, 282 pages.

Research in Marketing, Volume 4, JAI Press, January 1981, 264 pages.

Research in Marketing, Volume 3, JAI Press, January 1980, 303 pages.

Export Marketing: Lessons from Europe (with H. M. Schoenfeld), BEBR, University of Illinois, March 1981, 350 pages.

Research in Marketing, Volume 2, JAI Press, June 1979, 357 pages.

Research in Marketing, Volume 1, JAI Press, 1978.

Consumer and Industrial Buying Behavior (with Arch Woodside and Peter Bennett), American Elsevier, 1977, 523 pages.

Multivariate Methods for Market and Survey Research, American Marketing Association, 1977, 388 pages.

Models of Buyer Behavior: Conceptual, Quantitative and Empirical, Harper and Row, 1974, 441 pages.

Marketing Analysis for Societal Problems (with Peter Wright), BEBR, University of Illinois, 1972, 270 pages.

Multinational Business Operations: Advanced Readings (with S. P. Sethi), Goodyear Publishing Company, 1973:

Volume 1: *Environmental Aspects of Operating Abroad*

Volume 2: *Long Range Planning, Organization and Management*

Volume 3: *Marketing Management*

Volume 4: *Financial Management*

The Theory of Buyer Behavior (with J.A. Howard), John Wiley and Sons, 1969.

Articles/Parts of Books (Chapters)

"Extending the Extended Self in the Digital World" (with Michael Solomon), *Journal of Marketing Theory & Practice*, Volume 22 (Number 2), Spring 2014, pp. 123–132.

"The Conceptual Foundations of Relationship Marketing: Review and Synthesis" (with Atul Parvatiyar and Mona Sinha), *Economic Sociology, the European electronic newsletter*, Volume 13 (Number 3), July 2012, pp. 4–26 (translated to Russian by *Russian Management Journal*, Volume 11, Issue 1).

"The Resurgence of India: Triumphs of Institutions over Infrastructure" (with Gopal Krishnan Iyer and Arun Sharma), *Journal of Macromarketing*, Volume 32 (Number 3), September 2012, pp. 309–318.

"The Double Helix of Marketing: The Complimentary Relationship Between Marketing History and Marketing Theory," *Marketing Theory*, Volume 11, December 2011, pp. 503–505.

"Impact of Emerging Markets on Marketing: Rethinking Existing Perspectives and Practices," *Journal of Marketing*, Volume 75, July 2011, pp. 166–182.

"Mindful Consumption: A Customer Centric Approach to Sustainability," *Journal of the Academy of Marketing Science*, Volume 39, pp. 21–39.

"Reflections on Vargo and Lusch's Systems Perspective" (with Nirmal Sethia and Shanthi Srinivas), *Industrial Marketing Management*, Volume 40 (Number 2), 2011, pp. 197–198.

"India's Comparative Advantages and Challenges," Emerging India Summit, Emory University, March 2011.

"Innovate or Adapt?" *Harvard Business Review*, 2011.

"Entrepreneurship? The Real Competitive Advantage of a Nation" in Corporate Dossier, *Economic Times*, 2011.

"A Framework of Technology Mediation in Consumer Selling: Implications for Firms and Sales Management" (with Arun Sharma), *Journal of Personal Selling and Sales Management*, Volume 30 (Number 2), Spring 2010, pp. 121–129.

"Peter Drucker on Marketing: An Exploration of Five Tenets" (with Uslay, Can and Robert E. Morgan), *Journal of Academy of Marketing Science*, Volume 37 (Number 1), 2009, pp. 47–60.

"Why Integrating Purchasing with Marketing is Both Inevitable and Beneficial" (with Arun Sharma and Gopal Krishnan Iyer), *Industrial Marketing Management*, Volume 33 (Number 8), 2009, pp. 865–871.

"The Call Center Couple: India's New Middle Class", Corporate Dossier, *Economic Times*, January 2009.

"A Critical Review of Meta-Analysis in Marketing" (with Arne Floh), submitted to *International Journal of Research in Marketing*.

"Unlocking India's Potential," *India Today*, October 2008.

"The Impact of Transitioning from Products to Services in Business and Industrial Markets on the Evolution of the Sales Organization" (with Arun Sharma), *Industrial Management*, Volume 37, 2008, pp. 260–269.

"Exploring the Relationship Between Market Orientation, Entrepreneurial Orientation and Learning Orientation" (with Can Uslay), *UIC Research Symposium on Marketing and Entrepreneurship*, Stockholm, 2008.

"Globalization of Markets and the Rule of Three" (with Can Uslay and Rajendra Sisodia), in Phil Kitchen (ed.), *Marketing: Metaphors and Metamorphosis*, London, UK: Palgrave-Macmillian, 2008, pp. 26–41.

"Relationship Management" (with Arun Sharma), in John T. Mentzer, Matthew B. Meyers and Theodore P. Stank (eds), *Handbook of Global Supply Chain Management*, SAGE Publications, 2007, pp. 361–370.

"Evolution of the Sales Force in a Global Economy" (with Arun Sharma), in Olaf Plotner and Robert E. Spekman (eds), *Bringing Technology to Market*, John Wiley and Sons, 2007, pp. 77–86.

"Emerging Research Opportunities for Doctoral Students in B-to-B Marketing," *Journal of Business to Business Marketing*, Volume 14 (Number 1), 2007, pp. 13–22.

"Implications of the Revised Definition of Marketing: From Exchange to Value Creation" (with Can Uslay), *Journal of Public Policy and Marketing*, Volume 22 (Number 2), 2007, pp. 302–307.

"E-Services—A Framework for Growth" (Arun Sharma), *Journal of Value Chain Management*, Volume 1 (Number ½), 2007, pp. 7–12.

"Marketing's Final Frontier: The Automation of Consumption" (with Rajendra Sisodia) in Sheth and Sisodia (eds.), *Does Marketing Need Reform?* M.E. Sharpe, 2006, pp. 180–190.

"How to Reform Marketing" (with Rajendra Sisodia) in Sheth and Sisodia (eds.) *Does Marketing Need Reform?* M.E. Sharpe, 2006, pp. 324–334.

"The Image of Marketing" (with Rajendra Sisodia and Adina Barbulescu) in Sheth and Sisodia (eds.), *Does Marketing Need Reform?* M.E. Sharpe, 2006, pp. 26–36.

"A Dangerous Divergence: Marketing and Society" (with Rajendra Sisodia), *Journal of Public Policy and Marketing*, Volume 24 (Number 1), May 2005, pp. 160–162.

"Does Marketing Need Reform?" (with Rajendra Sisodia), *Journal of Marketing*, Volume 69 (Number 4), October 2005, pp. 10–12.

"How Competition Will Shape Indian Markets" (with Rajendra Sisodia and G. Shainesh), *Journal of Marketing and Communication*, Volume 1 (Number 1), 2005, pp. 1–17.

"Why Good Companies Fail" (with Rajendra Sisodia), *European Business Forum*, Number 22, Autumn 2005, pp. 25–30.

"Customer Relationship Management: The Strategic Imperatives" (with G. Shainesh) in *Revue Francais du Marketing* (in French), Volume 215 (Number 202), May 2005, pp. 85–97.

"International e-Marketing: Opportunities and Issues" (with Arun Sharma), *International Marketing Review*, Volume 22 (Number 6), 2005, pp. 611–622.

"Tectonic Shift: The Realignment of Nations and the Rise of Regional Super States," *FSO Magazine*, Volume 1 (Number 3), 2004.

"Making India Globally Competitive," *Vikalpa*, Volume 29 (Number 4), October–December 2004, pp. 1–9.

"Web-based Marketing: The Coming Revolution in Marketing Thought and Strategy" (with Arun Sharma), *Journal of Business Research*, Volume 57, 2004, pp. 696–702.

"Behavioral Approaches to Industrial Marketing: Extant and Emerging Research" (with Arun Sharma), in Klaus Backhaus and Klaus Backaus (eds), *Handbook of Industrial Marketing*, Gabler Verlag, pp. 147–174.

"Till Death Do Us Part ... But Not Always: Six Antecedents to a Customer's Relational Preference in Buyer-Seller Exchanges" (with Reshma Shah),

Industrial Marketing Management, Volume 32 (Number 8), November 2003, pp. 627–631.

"The Future of Marketing" (with Rajendra Sisodia) in Philip Kitchen (ed.), *The Future of Marketing: Critical 21st Century Perspectives*, Palgrave McMillian, 2003, pp. 140–162.

"A Generic Concept of Customer Behavior," *Journal of Customer Behavior*, Volume 1, 2002, pp. 7–18.

"The Future of Relationship Marketing", *Journal of Services Marketing*, Volume 16 (Number 7), 2002, pp. 590–592.

"The Seismic Impact of Technology" (with Rajendra Sisodia), *Optimize*, February 2002, pp. 1–5.

"The Rule of Three in Europe" (with Rajendra Sisodia), *European Business Forum*, Number 10, Summer 2002, pp. 53–58.

"Competitive Markets and the Rule of Three" (with Rajendra Sisodia), *Ivey Business Journal*, September/October 2002.

"Marketing Productivity: Issues and Analysis" (with Rajendra Sisodia), *Journal of Business Research*, Volume 55, 2002, pp. 349–362.

"Customer Relationship Management: Emerging Practice, Process and Discipline" (with Atul Parvatiyar), *Journal of Economic and Social Research*, Volume 3 (Number 2), 2001, pp. 1–34.

"Evolving Relationship Marketing into a Discipline" (with Atul Parvatiyar), *Journal of Relationship Marketing*, Volume 1 (Number 1), 2001.

"From International to Integrated Marketing" (with Atul Parvatiyar), *International Marketing Review*, Volume 18 (Number 1), 2001, pp. 16–29.

"The Soul of the Great Professional" (with Andrew Sobel), *Consulting Management*, Volume 11 (Number 2), 2000, pp. 9–15.

"Marketing's Final Frontier: The Automation of Consumption" (with Rajendra Sisodia), *Defying the Limits*, Montgomery Research, Inc., 2000, pp. 63–69.

"Future Perfect: Assisted Living for All?" (with Rajendra Sisodia), *Defying the Limits*, Montgomery Research, Inc., 2000, pp. 63–69.

"The Antecedents and Consequences of Customer Centric Marketing" (with Rajendra Sisodia and Arun Sharma), *Journal of the Academy of Marketing Science*, Volume 28 (Number 1), 2000, pp. 55–66.

"The Domain and Conceptual Foundations of Relationship Marketing" (with Atul Parvatiyar) in Sheth and Parvatiyar (eds), *Handbook of Relationship Marketing* (SAGE Publications, 2000), pp. 3–38.

"Relationship Marketing: A Paradigm Shift or Shaft?" in Sheth and Parvatiyar (eds), *Handbook of Relationship Marketing* (SAGE Publications, 2000), pp. 609–620.

"Consumer Behavior" in *Marketing: Best Practices*, Dryden Press, 2000, pp. 136–175.

"Outsourcing Comes Home" (with Rajendra Sisodia), *Wall Street Journal*, June 28, 1999.

"Iridium's 66 Pies in the Sky" (with Rajendra Sisodia), 9 pages (abridged published in WSJ in August 1999).

"Revisiting Marketing's Lawlike Generalizations" (with Rajendra Sisodia), *Journal of the Academy of Marketing Science*, Volume 27 (Winter), 1999, pp. 71–87.

"Is Your IT Architecture Upside Down?" (with Rajendra Sisodia), *CIO Magazine*, November 15, 1999, pp. 84–88.

"High Performance Marketing in the 21st Century" (with Rajendra Sisodia), *Brand Equity Economic Times*, 1999 (three-part series).

"The Future of Wireless Industry" in 1999 *Annual Review of Communications*, IEC (Chicago), pp. 165–170.

"The Future of Retailing" (with Rajendra S. Sisodia), *Financial Times*, Series of Managing Marketing, October 19, 1998.

"Consumer Behavior in the Future" (with Rajendra Sisodia) in Robert Peterson (ed.), *Electronic Marketing and the Consumer*, SAGE Publications, 1997, pp. 17–37.

"The Health of the Health Care Industry: A Report Card from American Consumers" (with Banwari Mittal), *Health Care Marketing*, AMA-Winter 1997, pp. 29–35.

"Communications Outlook: Competition, Growth and Consolidation" (with Robert Janowiak and Massoud Saghafi), *Annual Review of Communications*, IEC, 1997, pp. 219–227.

"Paradigm Shift in Interfirm Marketing Relationships: Emerging Research Issues" (with Atul Parvatiyar), *Research in Marketing*, Volume 13, JAI Press, 1997, pp. 233–250.

"Supplier Relationships: Emerging Issues and Challenges" (with Arun Sharma), *Industrial Marketing Management*, Volume 26, 1997, pp. 91–100.

"Relationship Marketing: An Agenda for Research" (with Arun Sharma), *Industrial Marketing Management*, Volume 26, 1997, pp. 87–90.

"The Relationship Orientation of Firms: A Framework for Analysis" (with Arun Sharma), paper presented at the AMA Relationship Marketing Conference, Dublin, Ireland, 1997.

"Does Relationship Marketing Pay? An Empirical Investigation of Relationship Marketing Practices in Hospitals" (with G.M. Naidu, Atul Parvatiyar, and Lori Westgate) (*Journal of Business Research*, 1998).

"Instilling Social Responsibility Through Marketing Research Field Projects" (with C. Bhattacharya), *Marketing Education Review*, Volume 6 (Summer), 1996, pp. 23–31.

"Securing Customer Loyalty" (with Banwari Mittal), *GAMA News Journal*, May–June 1996, pp. 4–7.

"Becoming a World Class Customer," *Strategic Purchasing: Sourcing for the Bottomline*, Conference Board, 1996, pp. 11–13.

"A Framework for Managing Customer Expectations" (with Banwari Mittal), *Journal of Market Focused Management*, Volume 1, 1996, pp. 137–158.

"Organizational Buying Behavior: Past Performance and Future Expectations," *Journal of Business and Industrial Marketing*, Volume 2, 1996, pp. 7–24.

"The Evolution of Relationship Marketing" (with Atul Parvatiyar), *International Business Review*, Volume 4, 1995, pp. 397–418.

"An Experimental Approach to Investigating Satisfaction and Continuity in Marketing Alliances" (with Prem Shamdasani), *European Journal of Marketing*, Volume 29, 1995, pp. 6–23.

"Relationship Marketing in Consumer Markets: Antecedents and Consequences" (with Atul Parvatiyar), *Journal of the Academy of Marketing Science*, Volume 23 (Number 4), 1995, pp. 255–271.

"Feeling the Heat" (with Rajendra Sisodia), *Marketing Management*, Volume 4 (Number 2), 1995, pp. 9–23.

"Feeling the Heat: Part 2" (with Rajendra Sisodia), *Marketing Management*, Volume 4 (Number 3), 1995, pp. 19–33.

"Growth, Productivity and the Visible Hand: An Interview with Jagdish N. Sheth," *Journal of Asia-Pacific Business*, Volume 1, 1995, pp. 1–11.

"Ecological Imperatives and the Role of Marketing" (with Atul Parvatiyar), in Michael J. Polonsky and Alma T. Mintu Wimsatt (eds), *Environmental Marketing*. New York: The Haworth Press, 1995, pp. 3–20.

"The Reincarnation of International Marketing," *International Business: An Emerging Vision*, USC Press, 1995, pp. 41–47.

"Improving Marketing Productivity" (with Rajendra Sisodia), in Jeffrey Heilbrunn (ed.), *Marketing Encyclopedia*, NTC Books, 1995, pp. 217–237.

"Cellular Communications: The First Decade" (with Rajendra Sisodia), *Annual Review of Communications*, 1995, IEC, pp. 795–801.

"Cellular Communications: What's Ahead" (with Rajendra Sisodia), *Annual Review of Communications*, 1995, IEC, pp. 802–810.

"Paradigm Shift in Marketing Theory and Approach: The Emergence of Relationship Marketing" (with Atul Parvatiyar), in *Relationship Marketing: Theory, Methods and Applications*, Center for Relationship Marketing, 1994 (two-page abstract).

"Toward a Theory of Alliance Governance" (with Atul Parvatiyar), in *Relationship Marketing: Theory Methods and Applications*, Center for Relationship Marketing, 1994 (two-page abstract).

"Convergence: Driving the Information Industry Evolution" (with Bill Wallace), *Transformation*, Spring 1994, pp. 2–9.

"A Normative Model of Retaining Customer Satisfaction," in J. Sudharshan and Kent Monroe (eds) *P.D. Converse Awards Symposium in Marketing*, American Marketing Association, 1994.

"An Empirical Study of the Scientific Styles of Marketing Academics" (with Siew Meng Leong and Chin Tiong Tan), *European Journal of Marketing*, Volume 28, 1994, pp. 12–26.

"Developing a Curriculum to Enhance Teaching and Research of Relationship Marketing" (with Joseph P. Cannon), *Journal of Marketing Education*, June 1994, pp. 3–14.

"How to Retain Satisfied Customers," *GAMA News Journal*, July–August 1994, pp. 4–7.

"Strategic Importance of Information Technology," in Ruby Roy Dholakia (ed.), *Advances in Telecommunications Management*, JAI Press, 1994, pp. 3–16.

"Technology and New Service Creation" (with Rajendra Sisodia), in R. Johnson and N.D.C. Slack (eds), *Service Operations*, 1993, Operations Management Association, U.K., pp. 473–478.

"The Information Mall" (with Rajendra S. Sisodia), *Telecommunications Policy*, July 1993, pp. 376–389.

"Overcoming the Barriers to Global Economic Development and the International Flows of People, Products, and Resources: Strategic Recommendations" (with Michael Erony), *Telematics and Informatics*, Volume 10, 1993, pp. 41–49.

"User-Oriented Marketing for Non-Profit Organizations," in Dennis R. Young and David C. Hammack (eds), *Non-Profit Organizations in a Market Economy*, Jossey Bass, 1993, pp. 378–397.

"The New Information Industry of the 21st Century," *Infovision*, National Engineering Consortium, 1993, pp. 20–25.

"The Future of Advertising in the Information Age," *Infovision*, National Engineering Consortium, 1993, pp. 159–164.

"Toward a Theory of Macromarketing," *Canadian Journal of Administrative Sciences*, Volume 9 (Number 2), 1992, pp. 154–161.

"Acrimony in the Ivory Tower: A Retrospective on Consumer Research," *Journal of the Academy of Marketing Science*, Volume 20 (Number 4), 1992, pp. 345–353.

"Emerging Marketing Strategies in a Changing Macroeconomic Environment: A Commentary," *International Marketing Review*, Volume 9 (Number 1), 1992, pp. 57–63.

"Toward a Theory of Business Alliance Formation" (with Atul Parvatiyar), *Scandinavian International Business Review*, Volume 1 (Number 3), 1992, pp. 71–87.

"Why We Buy What We Buy: A Theory of Consumption Values" (with Bruce Newman and Barbara Gross), *Journal of Business Research*, Volume 22, 1991, pp. 159–170.

"R&D—Marketing Integration" (with Massoud M. Saghafi), *R&D Strategist*, Volume 1 (Winter), 1991, pp. 15–20.

"The R&D/Marketing Interface in the Telecommunications Industry: Actors Perspective" (with Massoud Saghafi and Ashok Gupta), in *Advances in Telecom Management*, Volume 1, pp. 163–176.

"Hurdling the Barriers to Technological Innovations" (with S. Ram), *R&D Strategist*, Fall 1990, pp. 4–14.

"Segmenting the Health Care Market," in Seymour Fine (ed.), *Social Marketing*, Allyn & Bacon, 1990, pp. 132–139.

"Time Oriented Advertising: A Content Analysis of United States Magazine Advertising 1890-1980" (with Barbara Gross), *Journal of Marketing*, Volume 53, October 1989, pp. 76–83.

"Consumer Resistance to Innovation: The Marketing Problem and Solution" (with S. Ram), *Journal of Consumer Marketing*, Volume 6 (Number 2), 1989, pp. 5–14.

"Breaking Barriers to Technological Innovations" (with S. Ram), in Raymond Smilor (ed.), *Customer Driven Markets. Lessons from Entrepreneurial Technological Companies* (Lexington Books), 1989, pp. 57–77.

"Marketing Barriers to New Product Ventures: The Case of the Entrepreneur" (with S. Ram), in Gerald Hills (ed.), *AMA Symposium on Research Activities in Marketing Entrepreneurship*, 1988, pp. 403–409.

"Changing Demographics and the Future of Graduate Management Education, *Selections*, Spring 1988, pp. 22–27.

"Search for Tomorrow," *Public Relations Journal*, Volume 43, December 1987, pp. 22–31, and 51.

"Parallel Development of Marketing and Consumer Behavior: A Historical Perspective" (with Barbara Gross), April 1987, The Stan Hollander, Festschrift.

"A Normative Theory of Marketing Practice," in Frazier and Sheth (eds), *Contemporary Views on Marketing Practice* (Lexington Books, 1987), pp. 19–32.

"A Review of Political Marketing" (with Bruce Newman), Volume 9, *Research in Marketing*, JAI Press, 1987, pp. 237–266.

"A Model of Primary Voter Behavior" (with Bruce Newman), *Journal of Consumer Research*, Volume 12, September 1985, pp. 178–187.

"History of Consumer Behavior: A Marketing Perspective," in C.T. Tan and J.N. Sheth (eds), *Historical Perspectives in Consumer Behavior: ACR Singapore Conference*, July 1985, pp. 5–7.

"An Attitude-Behavior Framework for Distribution Channel Management" (with Gary Frazier), *Journal of Marketing*, Volume 49, Summer 1985, pp. 38–48.

"Segmenting the Health Care Market," *Group Practice Journal*, March/April 1985.

"The Strategic Determinacy Approach to Brand Management" (with M. Shaikh and B. Hansotia), *Business Marketing*, February 1985, pp. 68–69ff.

"New Determinants of Competitive Structures in Industrial Markets," in R.E. Spekman and D.T. Wilson (eds), *A Strategic Approach to Business Marketing*, 1985, American Marketing Association, pp. 1–8.

"Are Cross-National Differences in Consumption Patterns Diminishing?" (with Abdolreza Eshghi), Academy of International Business National Meeting in Cleveland, October 1984.

"Group Mission" (with John Pollard), *Group Practice Journal*, July/August 1984, pp. 12–22.

"The 'Gender Gap' in Voter Attitudes and Behavior: Some Advertising Implications," *Journal of Advertising*, Volume 13, 1984, pp. 4–16.

"Winning Again in the Market Place: Nine Strategies for Revitalizing Mature Products" (with Glenn Morrison), *Journal of Consumer Marketing*, Volume 1, 1984, pp. 17–28.

"Broadening the Horizons of ACR and Consumer Behavior," in E. Hirschman and M. Holbrook (eds), *Advances in Consumer Research*, Volume 11, 1984, ACR Proceedings.

"El Comportamiento del Consumidor," in V. Ortega (ed.), *Enciclopedia de dirección y. administration de la Empresa* (with Dennis Garrett), Ediciones Orbis Barcelona, Spain, 1984, pp. 161–180.

"Managerial Relevance of Consumer Behavior," in L.R. Bittel and J.E. Ramsey (eds), *Encyclopedia of Professional Management*, Second Edition, McGraw-Hill Book Company (with Dennis Garrett), 1984, pp. 168–180.

"Government and Business Purchasing: How Similar Are They?" (with R.F. Williams and R.M. Hill), *Journal of Purchasing and Materials Management*, Volume 19, Winter 1983, pp. 7–13.

"Cross-Cultural Influences on the Buyer-Seller Interaction/Negotiation Process," *Asia Pacific Journal of Management*, Volume 1, September 1983, pp. 46–55.

"Emerging Trends in Retail Industry," *Journal of Retailing*, Volume 59, Fall 1983, pp. 6–18.

"Marketing Megatrends," *Journal of Consumer Marketing*, Volume 1, Summer 1983, pp. 5–13.

"A Margin-Return Model for Strategic Market Planning" (with Gary Frazier), *Journal of Marketing*, Volume 47, Spring 1983, pp. 100–109.

"A Behavioral Model for Strategies of Planned Social Change," *Academic Psychology Bulletin*, Volume 5, March 1983, pp. 92–114.

"Cross-Cultural Influences on Buyer-Seller Interaction Process," *WWG Information*, Volume 90, December 1982, pp. 130–135.

"Reply," *Journal of the Academy of Marketing Science*, Volume 10, Winter 1982, pp. 10–15.

"Cross-Cultural Influences on Buyer-Seller Interaction/Negotiation Process," in P.H. Reingen and A.G. Woodside (eds), *Buyer-Seller Interactions: Empirical Research and Normative Issues*, American Marketing Association (1982).

"Consumer Behavior: Surpluses and Shortages," in A. Mitchell (ed.), *Advances in Consumer Research*, Volume 9, 1982, ACR Proceedings, pp. 13–16.

"Determinants of Intention-Behavior Discrepancy in the 1980 Elections," in R. Lutz (ed.), Proceedings of the Division 23 Program, 89th APA Annual Convention, Los Angeles, 1982, pp. 21–22.

"Discussion," in A. Mitchell (ed.), *Advances in Consumer Research*, Volume 9, 1982, ACR Proceedings, pp. 313–314.

"History of Marketing Thought: An Update," in R. Bush and S. Hunt (eds), *Marketing Theory: Philosophy of Science Perspective*, American Marketing Association (with David Gardner), 1982, pp. 52–58.

"An Integrative Theory of Patronage Preference and Behavior," in W. Darden and R. Lusch (eds), *Patronage Behavior and Retail Management*. North Holland: Elsevier, 1982, pp. 9–28.

"Some Comments on the Triandis Models of Choice Behavior in Marketing," in L. McAlister (ed.), *Choice Models for Buyer Behavior*, JAI Press, 1982, pp. 163–168.

"Alternatives to Canonical Correlation Analysis in Consumer Research: A Structural Equation Approach," in G.T. Gorn and M.E. Goldberg (eds), Proceedings of the Division 23 Program, 88th APA Annual Convention, Montreal (with Richard Bagozzi and Johnny Johansson), 1981, pp. 59–65.

"A Theory of Merchandise Buying Behavior," in R.W. Stampfl and E.E. Hirschman (eds), *Theory in Retailing: Traditional and Nontraditional Sources*, American Marketing Association, 1981, pp. 180–189.

"Psychology of Innovation Resistance: The Less Developed Concept (LDC) in Diffusion Research," in J.N. Sheth (ed.), *Research in Marketing*, Greenwich, CT: JAI Press, 1981, pp. 273–282.

"Impact on Asking Race Information in Mail Surveys," *Journal of Marketing*, Volume 44, Winter 1980, pp. 67–70.

"Identification of Opinion Leaders Across Cultures: An Assessment for Use in the Diffusion of Innovations and Ideas" (with Stephen Cosmas), *Journal of International Business Studies*, Volume 11, Spring/Summer 1980, pp. 66–73.

"Research in Industrial Buying Behavior: Today's Needs, Tomorrow's Seeds," *Marketing News*' April 1980, pp. 10–11, 15.

"Emerging Importance of Export Marketing for U.S. Products," in J.N. Sheth and H.M. Schoenfeld (eds), *Export Marketing: Lessons from Europe*, BEBR (Urbana, Ill.), 1980, pp. 3–13.

"How to Succeed in Export Marketing: Some Guidelines" (with H.M. Schoenfeld), in J.N. Sheth and H.M. Schoenfeld (eds), *Export Marketing: Lessons from Europe*, BEBR (Urbana, L), 1980 pp. 185–204.

"Discussion," in K.B. Monroe (ed.), *Advances in Consumer Research*, Volume 8, ACR (Ann Arbor, Michigan), 1980, pp. 355–356.

"The Future of Market Research Products and Markets," in *The Challenge of the Eighties*, 32nd ESOMAR Congress, September 1979, pp. 7–20.

"Surpluses and Shortages in Consumer Behavior Theory and Research," *Journal of the Academy of Marketing Science*, Volume 7, Fall 1979, pp. 414–427.

"How Consumers Use Information," *European Research*, Volume 7, July 1979, pp. 167–173.

"Attitudinal Theories of Consumer Choice Behavior: A Comparative Analysis" (with R.S. Bhagat and P.S. Raju), *European Research*, Volume 7, March 1979, pp. 51–62.

"A Model of User Behavior for Scientific and Technical Information," in W.R. King and G. Zaltman (eds), *Marketing Scientific and Technical Information*. Boulder, Colorado: Westview Press, 1979, pp. 49–66.

"Should Multi-Country Advertising Research be Universal or Unique?" in *It Won't Work Here* (AMA) ESOMAR Conference, 1979, pp. 1–12.

"Strategies of Advertising Transferability in Multinational Marketing," in James Leigh and Claude R. Martin, Jr. (eds), *Current Issues and Research in Advertising*, 1978 (Division of Research, Graduate School of Business, University of Michigan, April 1978), pp. 131–141.

"Analysis of Intended Bus Usage" (with K.S. Krishnan and G.C. Nicolaidis), *Transportation Planning and Technology*, Volume 4, Spring 1978, pp. 219–226.

"Carpooling to Work: A Psychosocial Analysis," in Jerry C. Olson (ed.), Proceedings of the Division 23 Program, American Psychological Association, 84th Annual Convention (with Gary Anderson), p. 23.

"Comparative Analysis of a Complex Data Set," in Jerry C. Olson (ed.), Proceedings of the Division 23 Program, American Psychological Association, 84th Annual Convention (with Gary Anderson), p. 23.

"A Conceptual Model of Buyer-Seller Interaction Process," in Howard C. Schneider (ed.), *AIDS Proceedings*, Atlanta, GA, pp. 420–422.

"Demographics in Consumer Behavior," *Journal of Business Research*, Volume 5, June 1977, pp. 129–238.

"A Market-Oriented Strategy of Long-Range Planning for Multinational Corporations," *European Research*, Volume 5, January 1977, pp. 3–12.

"Making the Data Useful to Management" (with A.M. Roscoe), in *Marketing Management Information Systems* (ESOMAR, Amsterdam), 1977, pp. 169–186.

"Canonical Correlation and Marketing Research" (with Johnny Johansson), in J.N. Sheth (ed.), *Multivariate Methods for Market and Survey Research* (American Marketing Association, 1977), pp. 111–132.

"Cluster Analysis and Its Applications in Marketing Research," in J.N. Sheth (ed.), *Multivariate Methods for Marketing and Survey Research* (American Marketing Association, 1977), pp. 193–208.

"Factor Analysis in Marketing" (with D.T. Tigert) in J.N. Sheth (ed.), *Multivariate Methods for Marketing and Survey Research* (American Marketing Association, 1977), pp. 135–156.

"Ridesharing to Work: An Attitudinal Analysis" (with A. Horowitz), *Predicting Carpool Demand*, Special Report, Transportation Research Record 637, 1977, pp. 1–7.

"Recent Developments in Organizational Buying Behavior," in Arch Woodside, J.N. Sheth and Peter Bennett (eds), *Consumer and Industrial Buying Behavior* (American Elsevier, 1977), pp. 17–34.

"Seven Commandments for Users of Multivariate Methods," in J.N. Sheth (ed.), *Multivariate Methods for Marketing and Survey Research* (American Marketing Association, 1977), pp. 333–338.

"Strategies of Increasing Carpooling Behavior Among Urban Commuters," in *Seminar on Social Research* (ESOMAR, Amsterdam, 1977), pp. 183–198.

"A Theory of Cross-Cultural Buyer Behavior" (with S.P. Sethi), in Arch Woodside, J.N. Sheth and Peter Bennett (eds), *Consumer and Industrial Buying Behavior* (American Elsevier, 1977), pp. 369–386.

"Presentation d'un Modele du Component des Aceteurs Industriets," *Encyclopedie du Marketing*, Volume 4, 1976 (1-72A), pp. 1–8.

"Theorie du Component de L-acheteur " (with John A. Howard), *Encyclopedie du Marketing*, Volume 4, 1976 (1-71C), pp. 1–15.

"Why Consumer Protection Efforts Are Likely to Fail," *Zeitschnift FUR Market-Meinungs-Und Zukenfgsforschung*, Heft 3 and 4, January 19, 1976, pp. 4191–4206.

"How to Get the Most Out of Multivariate Methods," *European Research*, Volume 4, January 1976, pp. 229–235.

"The Future of Marketing Models," in *Marketing for Today and Tomorrow*, ESOMAR, Amsterdam, 1976.

"Howard's Contributions to Marketing: Some Thoughts," in *Public Policy and Marketing Thought* by Andreasen and Sudman, American Marketing Association, Chicago, IL, 1976.

"A Psychological Model of Travel Mode Selection," in Beverly Anderson (ed.), *Advances in Consumer Research*, Volume 3 (Association for Consumer Research, 1976), pp. 425–430.

"Buyer-Seller Interaction: A Conceptual Framework," in Beverly Anderson (ed.), *Advances in Consumer Research*, Volume 3 (Association for Consumer Research, 1976, pp. 382–386.

"Impact of Prior Familiarity and Cognitive Complexity on Information Processing Rules" (with C.W. Park), *Communications Research*, Volume 2 (July 1975), pp. 260–266.

"Toward a Model of Individual Choice Behavior," in *Marketing Modeling*, Part 2, ESOMAR, Amsterdam, June 1975, pp. 17–26.

"Follow-up Methods, Questionnaire Length and Market Differences in Mail Surveys" (with A.M. Roscoe and D. Lang), *Journal of Marketing*, Volume 39 (April 1975), pp. 20–27.

"Impact of Questionnaire Length, Follow-up Methods and Geographical Location on Response Rate to a Mail Survey" (with A.M. Roscoe), *Journal of Applied Psychology*, Volume 50, April 1975, pp. 252–254.

"Mechanisms of Choice and Information Processing Models in Consumer Behavior" (with P.S. Raju), *Markeds Kommunikasion*, Volume 12 (Number 1), 1975, pp. 10–22.

"Predictive Validation and Cross-Validation of the Fishbein, Rosenberg and Sheth Models of Attitudes" (with P.S. Raju and R.A. Bhagat), in M.J. Schlinger (ed.), *Advances in Consumer Research*, Volume 2 (Association for Consumer Research), pp. 405–426.

"Prediction of Attitude Models, A Comparative Study of the Rosenberg, Fishbein and Sheth Models" (with P.S. Raju and R.A. Bhagat), in M.S. Schlinger (ed.), *Advances in Consumer Research*, Volume 2 (Association for Consumer Research), pp. 405–426.

"Recent Failures in Consumer Protection" (with N.J. Mammana), *California Management Review*, Volume 16, Spring 1974, pp. 64–72.

"Measurement of Advertising Effectiveness: Some Theoretical Considerations," *Journal of Advertising*, Volume 3 (Number 1), January 1974, pp. 6–11.

"Nonlinear, Noncompensatory Relationship in Attitude Research" (with P.S. Raju), in R.C. Curhan (ed.), 1974 Combined Proceedings (American Marketing Association), pp. 80–83.

"Intertechnique Cross-Validation in Cluster Analysis" (with A.M. Roscoe and W. Howell), in R.C. Curham (ed.), 1974 Combined Proceedings (American Marketing Association), pp. 145–150.

"Factor Analysis in Marketing Research" (with W.D. Wells), in R. Ferber (ed.) *Handbook of Marketing Research* (McGraw-Hill, 1974), pp. 2-458 to 2-471.

"A Market Oriented Strategy of Long-Range Planning for Multinational Corporations," in R. Holton and S.P. Sethi (eds), *Management of the Multinationals* (Free Press, 1974), pp. 206–218.

"The Next Decade of Buyer Behavior Theory," in J.N. Sheth (ed.), *Models of Buyer Behavior* (Harper and Row, 1974), pp. 206–218.

"A Field Study of Attitude Structure and the Attitude-Behavior Relationship" (with S. Sudman), in J.N. Sheth and P.L. Wright (eds), *Marketing Analysis for Societal Problems* (University of Illinois, BEBR, 1974), pp. 148–171.

"Advertising's Image—U.S. and Yugoslavia" (with M. Smiljanich), *Journal of the Academy of Marketing Science*, Volume 1 (Number 2), Fall 1973, pp. 167–179.

"A Model of Industrial Buyer Behavior," *Journal of Marketing*, Volume 37, October 1973, pp. 50–56.

"Brand Profiles from Beliefs and Importances," *Journal of Advertising Research*, February 1973, pp. 37–42.

"A Theory of Multidimensional Brand Loyalty" (with C. Whan Park), in Proceedings of 1973 Conference of ACR, Boston.

"Sequential and Cyclical Nature of Information Processing in Repetitive Choice Behavior" (with P.S. Raju), in Proceedings of 1973 Conference of ACR, Boston.

"Canonical Correlation Analysis of Competitive Market Structure" (with Johnny Johansson), in H.W. Hopfe (ed.), *Advancing, Applying and Teaching, the Decision Sciences*, Proceedings of the Fifth Annual Meeting, AIDS, Atlanta, Georgia, 1973, pp. 324–327.

"Perceived Attribute Importance in Public and Private Transportation" (with T.F. Golob and R.M. Dobson), in H.W. Hopfe (ed.), *Advancing, Applying and Teaching the Decision Sciences*, Proceedings of the Fifth Annual Meeting, AIDS, Atlanta, Georgia, 1973, pp. 7–10.

"Equivalence of Fishbein and Rosenberg Models of Attitude Structure" (with C.W. Park), in APA Proceedings of 1973 Conference, Montreal.

"A Multivariate Model of International Business Expansion," in S.P. Sethi and J.N. Sheth (eds), *Multinational Business Operations: Long-Range Planning, Organization and Management*, Goodyear Publishing Company, Volume 2 (with R.J. Lutz), 1973, pp. 84–92.

"Reply to Comments on the Nature and Uses of Expectancy-Value Models in Consumer Attitude Research," *Journal of Marketing Research*, Volume 9, November 1972, pp. 562–575.

"Demographic Segmentation of Long Distance Behavior: Data Analysis and Inductive Model Building" (with A. Marvin Roscoe, Jr.), Proceedings of the Third Annual Conference, ACR November 1972, pp. 258–278.

"The Future of Buyer Behavior Theory," Proceedings of the Third Annual Conference, ACR, November 1972, pp. 562–575.

"Relevance of Segmentation for Market Planning," in *Segmentation and Typology* (ESOMAR Seminar, 1972), pp. 1–18.

"Heavy Users and Early Adoption of Innovations," *Markeds Kommunikasion*, Volume 2, June 1972, pp. 65–72.

"Projective Attitudes Toward Instant Coffee in Late Sixties," *Markeds Kommunikasion*, Volume 3, June 1972, pp. 73–79.

"Perceived Instrumentality and Value Importance as Determinants of Attitudes" (with Wayne Talarzyk), *Journal of Marketing Research*, Volume 9, February 1972, pp. 6–9.

"A Conceptual Model of Long-Range Multinational Marketing Planning," *Management International Review*, Volume 5 (Number 4/5), 1972, pp. 3–10.

"Role of Motivation Research in Consumer Psychology," in *Consumer Psychology and Motivation Research*, ESOMAR, 1972.

"Dissonance Reduction or Artifact? A Reply," *Journal of Marketing Research*, November 1971, pp. 516–517.

"Generalized Brand Preference of Durable Appliances," *Markeds Kommunikasion*, Volume 2, June 1971, pp. 57–64.

"Multivariate Revolution in Marketing Research," *Journal of Marketing*, Volume 35, January 1971, pp. 13–19.

"Reply to Comments on 'Beliefs, Affect, Intention and Behavior,'" in Paul Pellemans (ed.), *Insights in Consumer and Market Research* (Namur University Press), 1971, pp. 13–19.

"Affect, Behavioral Intention and Buying Behavior as a Function of Evaluative Beliefs," in Paul Pellemans (ed.), *Insights in Consumer Market Research* (Namur University Press), 1971, pp. 98–122.

"Reply to Comments on A Theory of Family Buying Decisions," in Paul Pellemans (ed.), *Insights in Consumer and Market Research* (Namur University Press), 1971, pp. 52–55.

"A Theory of Family Buying Decisions," in Paul Pellemans (ed.), *Insights in Consumer and Market Research* (Namur University Press), 1971, pp. 32–48.

"Measurement of Multidimensional Brand Loyalty of a Consumer," *Journal of Marketing Research*, Volume 7, August 1970, pp. 348–354.

"Are There Differences in Post-Decision Dissonance Reduction Between Housewives and Students?" *Journal of Marketing Research*, Volume 7, May 1970, pp. 243–245.

"Multivariate Analysis of Marketing Data," *Journal of Advertising Research*, Volume 10, February 1970, pp. 29–39.

"Factor Analysis in Marketing Data: A Critical Evaluation," in P.R. McDonald (ed.), *Marketing Involvement in Society and the Economy* (American Marketing Association), 1970.

"Using Factor Analysis to Estimate Parameters," *Journal of the American Statistical Association*, Volume 64, September 1969, pp. 808–822.

"A Factor Analytical Model of Brand Loyalty," *Journal of Marketing Research*, Volume 5, November 1968, pp. 395–404.

"How Adults Learn Brand Preference," *Journal of Advertising Research*, Volume 8, September 1968, pp. 25–38.

"Risk Reduction Processes in Repetitive Consumer Behavior" (with M. Venkatesan), *Journal of Marketing Research*, Volume 5, August 1968, pp. 307–311.

"Influence of Brand Preference on Post-Decision Dissonance," *Journal of the Academy of Applied Psychology*, Volume 5, 1968, pp. 73–77.

"A Theory of Buyer Behavior" (with John Howard), *Revista Internazionale di Scienze Economiche e Commerciali*, Volume 16, 1969, pp. 589–618.

"Cognitive Dissonance and Consumer Behavior," *Stream* (Indian Institute of Management, Calcutta), Volume 3, 1968, pp. 1–3.

"Applications of Multivariate Methods in Marketing," in R.L. King (ed.), *Marketing and the New Science of Planning* (American Marketing Association), 1968, pp. 259–265.

"An Experimental Study in Risk Reduction" (with M. Venkatesan), in R.L. King (ed.), *Marketing and the New Science of Planning* (American Marketing Association), 1968, pp. 213–214.

"Cognitive Dissonance, Brand Preference and Product Familiarity," in Johan Arndt (ed.), *Insights into Consumer Behavior* (Allyn and Bacon), 1968, pp. 41–54.

"Perceived Risk and Diffusion of Innovations," in Johan Arndt (ed.), *Insights into Consumer Behavior* (Allyn and Bacon), 1968, pp. 173–188.

"Review of Buyer Behavior," *Management Science*, Series B, Volume 13, August 1967, pp. B718–B756.

Book Reviews

"Review of Eric Von Hippel: Sources of Innovation," in *Journal of Marketing*, 1989.

"Review of Stanley A. Mulaik: The Foundations of Factor Analysis," in *Journal of the American Statistical Association*, Volume 70, March 1975, pp. 250–251.

"Review of F.M. Andrews and R.C. Messinger, Multivariate Nominal Analysis and J.N. Morgan and R.C. Messinger Thaid, A Sequential Analysis Program for the Analysis of Nominal Scale Dependent Variable," in *Journal of Marketing Research*, Volume 11, May 1974.

"Review of Flemming Hansen Consumer Behavior: A Cognitive Approach," *Swedish Journal of Economics*, Volume 75 (Number 2), June 1973, pp. 214–217.

"Review of Limits to Growth," by D.H. Meadows et al., *ACM/Computing Reviews*, April 1973, Volume 4 (Number 4), pp. 166–167.

"Review of Massy, Montgomery and Morrison, Stochastic Model of Buying Behavior," *Journal of Marketing Research*, Volume 9, November 1972, pp. 472–473.

"Review of Massy, Frank and Lodahl, Purchasing Behavior and Personal Attributes," *Journal of Marketing Research*, Volume 7, August 1970, pp. 403–404.

"Review of John Myers, Consumer Image and Attitude," *Journal of Marketing Research*, Volume 7, February 1970, pp. 29–39.

INDEX

ABOUT THE AUTHORS

Jagdish N. Sheth, Ph.D., is the Charles H. Kellstadt Professor of Marketing at Emory University Goizueta Business School. He is known nationally and internationally for his scholarly contributions in consumer behavior, relationship marketing, competitive strategy, and geopolitical analysis. When he joined Emory's faculty in 1991, Professor Sheth had nearly 30 years of combined experience in marketing from the University of Southern California, the University of Illinois, Columbia University, and Massachusetts Institute of Technology.

Throughout his career, Professor Sheth has offered more than a thousand presentations in at least 20 countries. He has also provided consulting for numerous companies in the United States, Europe, and Asia. His client list includes AT&T, BellSouth, Cox Communications, Delta, Ernst & Young, Ford, GE, Lucent Technologies, Motorola, Nortel, Pillsbury, Sprint, Square D, 3M, Whirlpool, and others. Currently, Professor Sheth sits on the Board of Directors of several public companies including Norstan, Cryo Cell International, and Wipro Limited.

Professor Sheth's accolades include "Outstanding Marketing Educator," an award presented by the Academy of Marketing Science, the "Outstanding Educator" award twice-presented by Sales and Marketing Executives International, and the P.D. Converse Award for his outstanding contributions to theory in marketing, presented by the American Marketing Association. Professor Sheth is the recipient of the two highest awards given by the American Marketing Association: the Richard D. Irwin Distinguished Marketing Educator Award and the Charles Coolidge Parlin Award.

In 1996, Professor Sheth was selected as the Distinguished Fellow of the Academy of Marketing Science. The following year, he was awarded the Distinguished Fellow award from the International Engineering Consortium. Professor Sheth is also a Fellow of the American Psychological Association (known as APA). In 2014, he was awarded the William Wilkie Award, Marketing for a Better World by the American Marketing Association.

Professor Sheth has authored or coauthored hundreds of articles and books. In 2000, he and Andrew Sobel published the best seller, *Clients for Life*. In 2001, *Value Space*, which he coauthored with Banwari Mittal, was published. Professor Sheth's most popular book, *The Rule of Three*, was coauthored with Dr Rajendra Sisodia and published in 2002. He has since written notable publications: *Tectonic Shift*, *Firms of Endearment*, and *The 4 A's of Marketing*.

John Yow has been Professor Sheth's researcher and writer for several of his books, including *Tectonic Shift*, *Self Destructive Habits of Good Companies*, and *Chindia Rising*.

For the last few years, John has been writing books about birds including *The Armchair Birder* and *The Armchair Birder Goes Coastal*. He is currently working on a book about endangered birds.

He and his wife Dede live in Paulding County, Georgia, USA.